An Alternative Take on Twelve Turbulent Years at West Ham

Kirk Blows
Foreword by Julian Dicks

Pitch Publishing
A2 Yeoman Gate
Yeoman Way
Durrington
BN13 3QZ
www.pitchpublishing.co.uk

A CIP catalogue record is available for this book from the
British Library

ISBN 978-1-90917-883-0

Typesetting and origination by Pitch Publishing.
Printed and bound by
CPI Group (UK) Ltd, Croydon, CR0 4YY

CONTENTS

ACKNOWLEDGEMENTS

The author would like to thank: Patricia Laker, David, Jennifer, Helen, John and Rachel Laker, Karen, Jessica and Lewis Blows, Valerie Blows, Karen Glaseby, Julian Dicks, Jo Davies, Trevor Davies, John Smith, Lee Power, Dave Powter, Colin Munford, Gary Hawkins, Ben Sharratt, Tony McDonald, Steve Blowers, Tony Hogg, Rob Newell, Greg Demetriou, Paul Stringer, Rob Pritchard, Laura Burkin, Colin Benson, Joe Sach, John Raven, Gerry Levey, Brad Ashton, Justin Allen, John Matthews, Steven Ball, Elsie and Graham Rowe, Lee Dallimer, John Diamond, Colin Walton, Sai Gajan Mahendran, Steve Carroll, Conor Parkinson, Brendan O'Brien, Tim De Klerk, Jerry Phillips and Andrew Henderson. Special thanks to Steve Bacon for photographic material.

FOREWORD BY JULIAN DICKS

FOOTBALL is unpredictable in general nowadays but that's certainly been the case over the past 12 seasons at West Ham – the club I love, the one that gave me the best ten years of my life as a player.

I want the team to play well and win every game but we all know that's impossible because it never happens, especially at a club that has been relegated and promoted twice amid a number of unexpected highs and lows since I retired in 1999.

I have followed events closely since that time and love going back to Upton Park, which I have done frequently in recent seasons as a radio pundit. And what really makes it so enjoyable for me is not so much the football but the supporters, who I had such a great rapport with and are great to see again.

People ask me if I miss playing football and I do, but the only thing I really miss is playing at Upton Park. I don't miss the players, I don't miss the banter, I just miss playing for the fans.

The club has a wonderful tradition and has had some fantastic players over the years – the likes of Bobby Moore, Geoff Hurst, Billy Bonds, Trevor Brooking and Alan Devonshire, for example – but ultimately it's the fans that set it apart.

They are fantastic supporters who stick with the team through thick and thin. They know that West Ham are never going to win the Premier League but can hopefully enjoy a good cup run and get to a final now and then. They are knowledgeable supporters but all they expect from players is that they give 100 per cent every game. If you try, they're the best fans in the world but if you don't, then they can be the worst.

I was brought to West Ham in 1988 by John Lyall, who was only the club's fifth ever manager and nearing the end of his lengthy time at Upton Park. I also played under Lou Macari, Billy Bonds and Harry Redknapp before the turnover of bosses increased following the appointment of Glenn Roeder in 2001.

I look at managers from the point of view of having been a player. Would I like to play for Glenn Roeder? No, I wouldn't. Would I like to play for Sam Allardyce? Yes, I would because he has something about him.

I thought Alan Pardew did a decent job as the manager of West Ham, taking the team up to the Premier League and to an FA Cup Final, but I got the impression that he thought he was better than he was.

I knew Alan Curbishley from my early days at Birmingham but, to be honest, I didn't like his style of football when he took charge at Upton Park. It was a bit boring for me but, at the end of the day, football is about results. If you get results the fans will stick by you but it's when things start going wrong that the fans will make their voices heard.

I liked Gianfranco Zola because his teams play football the right way and when you've got a manager who the players really, really respect, that goes a long, long way. Things didn't go so well in his second season in charge but for me he wasn't given enough time.

I think he was harshly treated when sacked and I think he would have done well if he had stayed at the club – certainly much better than Avram Grant did when he came in.

I occasionally used to go and watch the team training at that time and I thought the manager was lifeless. When we used to have five-a-sides under Harry Redknapp there was lots of banter going on but when I watched those boys there was nothing there. No wonder they got relegated.

I think Sam Allardyce has done a good job. If you would have said West Ham were going to win promotion and then finish tenth in the Premier League, 99.99 per cent of people would have taken that.

I thought some of the football we played in the Championship was difficult to watch, but last season was a big improvement – although I still think it could be a lot better. But you need proper players to play football and you can't ask them to pass the ball if they can't do it.

So now it's a case of looking forward, with West Ham trying to consolidate their place in the Premier League ahead of their expected move to the Olympic Stadium in 2016.

After playing at Upton Park for ten seasons I obviously love the place, but my hope for the move to Stratford is that it makes football affordable to everybody, so families can attend games.

As I write, the club have recently made a big investment in Andy Carroll who I like as a striker and think brings another dimension to West Ham. But for the money that he's reportedly costing the club he has got to prove that he's a prolific scorer by getting 20 goals a season, not struggling to get into double figures.

If he can do that then that will go a long way towards West Ham being a competitive Premier League outfit in the years to come. But however they're doing, you know they will always have my support.

Julian Dicks
June 2013

Julian Dicks, nicknamed the Terminator for his committed and uncompromising style at left-back, made 328 appearances and scored 65 goals during his two spells as a West Ham player. He led by example when handed the captaincy and won the Hammer of the Year award on four occasions. He currently spends his time coaching and providing matchday analysis for BBC Radio London.

INTRODUCTION

'Redknapp was always going to be a tough act to follow'

THE summer of 2001 represented a major watershed in the history of West Ham United – for one obvious reason.

Harry Redknapp had managed the club for the past seven years, guiding the team to three consecutive top-ten finishes – not something the Hammers make a habit of – and a place in Europe in 1999.

That was always going to be difficult to sustain and in the 2000/01 season, during which star defender Rio Ferdinand was sold to Leeds United for £18m, West Ham struggled and could only finish in 15th place.

Redknapp did well to bump the figure up to what was, at the time, a British transfer record, but in retrospect that was the beginning of the end for the Hammers boss, who was severely criticised by chairman Terence Brown for the way he had been spending the club's money.

When a meeting took place to discuss the budget for the following campaign, the chairman and manager clashed – with disputes about the quality of recent signings, how much had actually been spent (with Brown including the value of contracts) and, supposedly, quotes that had recently appeared in the press – and a proposed new four-year contract for Redknapp was ripped up and replaced with a P45. And so on 9 May 2001, West Ham released a statement claiming the two parties had 'agreed to part company', although Redknapp would emphatically insist to this writer that he was 'pushed' out the club.

Brown used his annual report to highlight spiralling costs and 'expenditure [that] cannot be justified' under Redknapp, who described the attack as 'disgusting' when later discussing the matter at his luxury home on the Dorset coast.

Redknapp had succeeded Billy Bonds as manager in 1994 amid suspicions that he had cynically engineered events, to such an extent that the former close friends stopped talking to each other. And therefore some believed it was perhaps fitting that he should leave the club in similarly controversial circumstances.

The West Ham fans had always seen Redknapp, who had emerged from the club's youth ranks to spend seven years as a first-team player, as one of their own and they loved his Cockney wit and Arthur Daley-style wheeling and dealing when running the show.

His achievements at Upton Park have perhaps, in the eyes of some, dimmed slightly with the passing of time and his four-year spell in charge of bitter rivals Tottenham Hotspur, for obvious reasons, did little to improve his image in the eyes of many Hammers fans.

But he was always going to be a tough act to follow in 2001 and his departure from West Ham triggered a sequence of events that represent an undeniably turbulent, occasionally triumphant and often traumatic 12 years for the club.

In that time the Hammers have recruited six of their 14 permanent managers, had four different owners, appeared in three winner-takes-all play-off finals, endured two relegations, enjoyed as many promotions and played their part in one of the most epic FA Cup finals of all-time.

Add in the seemingly never-ending saga of the Carlos Tevez affair, the battle to win control of West Ham, the collapse of chairman Bjorgulfur Gudmundsson's financial empire and the tussle for the keys to the Olympic Stadium and it's fair to say there has rarely been a dull moment down Upton Park way over the past decade or so.

It is all in stark contrast to the club's history of having represented stability and steadiness, but it's a reflection of the new millennium times and how football has changed – with the financial pressures to remain competitive in the Premier League proving the dominant force – that West Ham have had to do whatever it takes to keep up with the Joneses.

In strictly playing terms, however, the Hammers have generally personified unpredictability, and perhaps that sense of never quite knowing what to expect next is what makes supporting the club such an exciting and frequently exasperating experience.

Evidence of that has certainly been provided over the past 12 years, which have been chronicled in this book from the point of view of a series of weekly columns produced for the local press, namely the *East London Advertiser* and *Barking & Dagenham Post*.

Combining critical comment, in-depth analysis and opinionated assessment, supplemented with reflections and observations from the present day, the material presents an alternative history – if you will – of West Ham's fluctuating fortunes since 2001 from the perspective of somebody who began supporting the team in the late 1970s and then first wrote about them in the mid-1990s when editing *Hammers News*, the club's official monthly magazine.

When working for the local press, the concept of constructing an opinion column originated from the desire to express personal views or address topics that couldn't necessarily be accommodated through straight news reporting.

Most events provoked a passionate response from somebody who cares about the club, while others demanded a touch of diplomacy. Sometimes extreme views needed to be aired, at other times a voice of reason was required when elsewhere people were reacting hysterically.

Throughout the entire period, however, there has always been the need for honesty – whether that has resulted in columns that readers agreed or disagreed with.

As they say, football is a game of opinions – and we should all be thankful that West Ham, whatever they're doing, just never stop inspiring them.

Kirk Blows
July 2013

SEASON 2001/02

'Yeah, we'll take that, thanks very much'

HARRY REDKNAPP had gone and West Ham's hopes of landing 'first choice' replacement Alan Curbishley (according to managing director Paul Aldridge) and Manchester United first-team coach Steve McClaren hit the buffers when the former decided to stay at Charlton and the latter thought his management ambitions would be better served at Middlesbrough (which said it all really).

Neither man seemed to be the most charismatic on earth, but the Hammers managed to hand the job to somebody who appeared to have even less of that particular commodity.

The fact that Glenn Roeder then compared himself to a horse (Foinavon) for being the 'last man standing' hardly inspired confidence and made some people wish the 1967 Grand National winner had got the job instead.

The former Watford and Gillingham manager, who had been on the West Ham coaching staff for two years, also quoted his old QPR boss Terry Venables when saying, 'If you're going to regret something, regret doing it rather than not doing it.'

That simply encouraged the view that we would all up end regretting that Roeder did indeed do something – decide to take the job.

One hundred fans apparently accepted the club's offer of a refund on their season tickets, while Trevor Brooking joined the board as a non-executive director.

Former Hammers striker Paul Goddard was appointed as Roeder's assistant while Ludek Miklosko replaced Les Sealey – who soon died from a heart attack at the age of 43 – as goalkeeping coach.

Frank Lampard junior was sold to Chelsea for £11m with the midfielder complaining that he couldn't remain at Upton Park following the departures of his father Frank and uncle Harry, which made him rather unpopular with the West Ham faithful – something of an understatement – for the rest of his career.

Hammer of the Year Stuart Pearce and fellow defender Igor Stimac also quit the club for Manchester City and Hajduk Split respectively, while foreign flops such as Kaba Diawara, Davor Suker and Christian Bassila would also figure no more.

David James arrived in a £3.5m move from Aston Villa but was ruled out until Christmas after suffering a knee ligament injury when clashing with team-mate Martin Keown in England's 2-0 home defeat to Holland before the domestic season had even begun.

The club broke its transfer record twice with the signings of Don Hutchison (£5m from Sunderland) and Tomas Repka (£5.5m from Fiorentina), while Sebastien Schemmel looked rather better value for money when turning his loan from Metz into a £465,000 move.

It was the start of a new era, but fans went into the new season with a high degree of scepticism.

WOW, SO FAR SO GOOD (30 August 2001)

It is early days but few who have witnessed the two West Ham games so far this season will disagree with the suggestion that there appears to be a new spirit of determination within the camp.

Plenty of fans might have viewed the opening fixtures with great trepidation and not many would have predicted much of a return from games against potential championship-chasers Liverpool and Leeds.

Yet a fully deserved first point was gained on Saturday as West Ham ended the 100 per cent record of Leeds with a goalless draw, while only the clinical finishing of Michael Owen deprived the team of a similar reward in the 2-1 defeat at Anfield.

Both performances have confirmed that the team is certainly playing for Glenn Roeder and the new boss deserves credit for that.

It is conceivable that the negative publicity surrounding the appointment of Roeder and predictions of possible relegation have served as a motivating force.

Or maybe Glenn himself has pinned a few press cuttings on the dressing-room wall to invoke a fighting response from his troops.

Fans also believe there is greater organisation on the pitch with players seemingly more comfortable within Roeder's 4-4-2 formation.

Central defenders Rigobert Song and Christian Dailly have impressed in the two games, while Sebastien Schemmel and Trevor Sinclair both posed a threat to Leeds down the right flank on Saturday.

And while striker Paolo Di Canio will always be a maverick, Roeder has insisted that Joe Cole's talents will be deployed in a more disciplined way.

As has been said, it's early days but the signs against top-quality opposition are that the Hammers are determined to prove a few people wrong this season.

Kirk now says: Indeed they did, although it wasn't all plain sailing and it didn't take long for serious doubts about Glenn Roeder's appointment to emerge, especially for those who never backed the decision in the first place.

ER, SO FAR SO NOT SO GOOD (20 September 2001)

Sinking to the foot of the Premiership table, a Worthington Cup exit at Second Division Reading, four games without a goal, Tomas Repka sent off on his debut ... it has not been the best of times for West Ham.

New manager Glenn Roeder stressed the need for a good start to the season and, despite his men showing early promise in games against Liverpool and Leeds, he now stands alone as the only Premiership boss without a win under his belt.

Roeder will feel as if he has not had much go his way so far.

New goalkeeper David James has been ruled out until Christmas, while injury has also deprived him of striker Frederic Kanoute for all but half a game.

Paolo Di Canio has also missed games through injury as Roeder seeks to integrate new signings Don Hutchison and Repka into the side.

And with the visit of Aston Villa being deferred to a later date, the Hammers have now seen the postponement of two Upton Park games at a time when a few extra points makes all the difference to the table.

There will be those, however, who feel that Roeder was too inexperienced to be handed the responsibility of solving the team's problems and the club is in exactly the position we all feared.

Roeder will insist he should only be judged once the new signings have settled in and his top strikers have returned to the side.

In Hutchison and Repka he has recruited players of quality and it is hard to imagine the team struggling for too long if all the key men are fit and available.

A victory against Newcastle on Sunday is now imperative with uninviting trips to Everton and Blackburn next on the list.

Results in those three matches are likely to determine what kind of season West Ham will have.

Kirk now says: West Ham did indeed pick up their first win of the season with a 3-0 success at home to Newcastle, but their fortunes were to get worse before they got better.

FORTUNES ALWAYS JEKYLL AND HYDE-ING (4 October 2001)

Paolo Di Canio wandered over to the distraught West Ham fans at the end of Saturday's 5-0 defeat at Everton and offered a gesture of apology for his side's abject second-half performance.

At least the Italian had the courage to face the suffering contingent, which is more than can be said for several others who quickly disappeared from view, too embarrassed to applaud supporters who deserve much better.

Not that Hammers fans would have built their hopes up too much before the match.

After all, West Ham had lost 12 of their previous 14 games at Goodison Park.

Joe Cole was still unavailable with a foot injury and record signing Tomas Repka was missing from defence through suspension.

Yet the Hammers were actually the better side during the early part of the game.

But after again failing to make possession count, they fell apart in catastrophic fashion against one of the Premiership's more ordinary teams.

Glenn Roeder described his side's defending as 'diabolical' and that is just one of many adjectives he could have used.

Don Hutchison's own goal when clashing with goalkeeper Shaka Hislop to put Everton 2-0 up was farcical.

Thomas Gravesen was then given the freedom to run from the halfway line for the third, Steve Watson was generously allowed two efforts for the fourth and Christian Dailly was dreadfully at fault for the fifth, scored by Thomas Radzinski.

Repka will be welcomed back but the Hammers are still in need of another quality central defender to play alongside him.

On paper the likes of Di Canio, Hutchison, Michael Carrick, Trevor Sinclair and Frederic Kanoute should have goals galore in them.

But the Hammers have failed to score in five of their seven matches so far – a worrying statistic.

Roeder has referred to his side's Jekyll and Hyde week following the 3-0 win against Newcastle just six days earlier.

And fans will be seeking immediate evidence as to which character reflects the true nature of West Ham's prospects this season.

Kirk now says: And just when you thought it couldn't get any more embarrassing …

THE BUCK STOPS WITH ROEDER (18 October 2001)

Glenn Roeder has been in football long enough to know that if results don't change, his position as West Ham's manager certainly will.

While any team playing five of their first seven games away from home is going to be disadvantaged, the fact is that results such as those at Everton (5-0) and Blackburn (7-1) are totally unacceptable.

Roeder is quickly realising what an unforgiving business football management can be.

His first big buy, goalkeeper David James, was crocked before making a single league outing and his most recent signing, defender Tomas Repka, has been sent off twice in three matches.

Roeder watched his side claw defeat from the jaws of victory to crash out of the Worthington Cup to Second Division Reading on penalties.

And now winger Trevor Sinclair has slapped in a transfer request, reflecting the dispirited mood of the club's star players since the £18m sale of Rio Ferdinand – certainly the turning point in West Ham's fortunes.

Roeder won't publicly admit it, but he feels handicapped by some of the players he inherited from former boss Harry Redknapp.

To be fair to Redknapp, he bought the likes of Svetoslav Todorov, Rigobert Song, Christian Dailly, Titi Camara and Ragnvald Soma at a time when the club was only prepared to invest up to £2m on any one player because of the uncertainty about the transfer system.

He also needed to bolster a squad desperately short on numbers.

None of that quintet has done enough to command a regular first-team place, leaving Roeder woefully short of options.

But that does not excuse recent performances and, while Roeder will feel badly let down by his players, the ultimate responsibility lies with him.

Kirk now says: The 7-1 defeat at Blackburn was undoubtedly the low point of Glenn Roeder's first season and it was tempting to put the boot in, but it was important to show some objectivity towards the manager.

PRAISE WHEN IT'S DUE ... WELL, A LITTLE ANYWAY (25 October 2001)

Glenn Roeder and his West Ham players deserve immense credit for the character shown in securing the 2-0 victory against Southampton.

Any side taking the field after conceding 12 goals in two games is going to be short of confidence.

But all parties showed the necessary resolve to gain three crucial points and a vital boost to morale – not that the Saints provided the toughest of tests.

The issue of character is a key one.

One former Hammers defender spoke off the record last week about how much he feared for the club's future because of the lack of players prepared to take on responsibility.

He also questioned Roeder's leadership abilities.

However, Roeder is showing himself to be an honest, decent man with principles and values. There is no doubt he has shown dignity while under pressure.

But he also needs to exude authority and the confidence of the supporters is undermined when he admits to finding the contrasting nature of West Ham's performances 'mystifying'.

After making that comment in the programme for the Southampton game, he reiterated the view in his post-match press conference.

Roeder may well be perplexed by the team's Jekyll and Hyde nature but admitting it in public is hardly going to inspire fans who want to believe the manager knows what is going on and is in control.

The win against Southampton will at least have shifted the media focus away from Roeder, who has received the backing of the board as well as support from various parties unlikely to send former boss Harry Redknapp a Christmas card.

However, fans will find it hard to buy into the wave of sympathy towards Roeder that has been growing recently, with the club's problems more than evident when the appointment was made.

With that said, there is the suspicion that the board totally underestimated the scale of the task facing Redknapp's successor.

Kirk now says: Roeder was often too honest for his own good when talking to the press, a duty he generally looked uncomfortable with.

ROEDER AND REDKNAPP TRADE 'PUNCHES' (1 October 2001)

It would be nice to think that not too many West Ham fans have been taken in by the games played by the national press in recent weeks.

Having presided over those big defeats at Everton and Blackburn, manager Glenn Roeder allowed his frustrations to extend to the point where he publicly questioned the quality of the new recruits last season.

He was entitled to do that, of course, with none of the players brought in following the £18m sale of Rio Ferdinand – with the possible exception of Rigobert Song – doing anything to suggest they merit regular first-team places.

But the papers then conveyed the message to former boss Harry Redknapp that Roeder had been critical of the squad he had inherited as a whole.

Provoked into a response, Redknapp rightfully defended himself by pointing to the success of bargain signings such as Paolo Di Canio, Frederic Kanoute and Trevor Sinclair, as well as the development of youthful talents like Joe Cole and Michael Carrick.

It quickly degenerated into a Redknapp versus Roeder bout with punches being traded on a daily basis as the press stoked the fires.

The reality, of course, is that both men were absolutely right in what they were saying.

Roeder would prefer quality to quantity – as seen in his own signings – while Redknapp did an excellent job of wheeling and dealing to raise his own transfer funds.

That often meant taking gambles on players and, as Redknapp frequently admitted, when you're rolling the dice you don't always win.

Neither man was really attacking the other – but that was the way in which their words were presented by the media.

It sells newspapers and makes great entertainment for the mass populace – but Hammers fans can hopefully see things for what they really are.

Kirk now says: Oh dear, a journalist being critical of the media … but there are times when the national press spin a story a certain way and those closer to the club feel obliged to set the record straight (or at least try to).

NUMBER'S UP FOR HARRY (15 November 2001)

West Ham fans will have been astonished by the contents of chairman Terence Brown's annual report last week.

Make no mistake; his statement presents a strong attack on the performance of former manager Harry Redknapp – especially in the transfer market.

To highlight recent failures such as Gary Charles and Davor Suker while overlooking the successes (Eyal Berkovic, Slaven Bilic, John Hartson, Trevor Sinclair, etc) during Redknapp's seven-year reign will emphasise the feeling that the board are trying hard to justify his departure.

It also ignores the conditions in which the manager had to work that involved taking gambles on out-of-favour players elsewhere and often generating his own funds.

Fans will particularly raise their eyebrows at the amount the club claims to have spent in the transfer market since 1994 – nearly £79m against a figure of just over £62m clawed back through sales prior to the departure of Frank Lampard.

It is fair to say that most supporters would struggle to think of how £55m was spent while the fact is that Redknapp's net expenditure during his last three years was nil.

This is at a time when the likes of Chelsea, Leeds and Liverpool have spent around £75m each.

Even if fans accept the published figures, that still only represents a deficit of just over £2m per year – about enough to purchase a Third Division player's toenail clippings.

The club may have the eighth highest wage bill in the Premiership but to rigidly judge performance against that and suggest West Ham should be qualifying for Europe every year is a touch harsh.

The salary level reflects not just squad quality but also the club's commitment to tying their best young players to long-term contracts to ensure there is no exploitation of the Bosman ruling.

That is more of an investment with monies being recouped when the club ultimately decides to cash in (as they did with Lampard and Rio Ferdinand).

The report rightly takes pride in the international recognition afforded the likes of Joe Cole and Michael Carrick, yet Redknapp will feel disappointed that it fails to acknowledge the role he played in reviving the club's youth policy.

And to make the point that West Ham had just finished 13th in the Premiership when Redknapp was appointed and only finished 15th last season – as if to suggest the club has gone backwards under his management – hardly displays a great appreciation of the environment in which the club operates.

It is also a rather negative message to want to project.

Some will therefore feel unsurprised that a frustrated Redknapp was reluctant to continue working in such unforgiving conditions.

And it doesn't bode well for current manager Glenn Roeder if he is to be judged by the same criteria.

Kirk now says: With West Ham struggling, it's clear that Terence Brown felt compelled to present a case against those mourning the departure of Harry Redknapp, who he believed had squandered much of the money received from the sale of Rio Ferdinand to Leeds. Fans might be a little more sympathetic to his thoughts than they were at the time.

JERM WARFARE (22 November 2001)

'This could crush him,' said a colleague when Jermain Defoe took the field as a 76th-minute replacement for hat-trick hero Paul Kitson at Charlton on Monday evening.

The 19-year-old's substitute appearance had the locals at The Valley foaming at the mouth despite moving West Ham closer to paying another instalment of the £1.4m 'compensation' fee set by a tribunal after the striker legged it through the Blackwall Tunnel two years ago.

Charlton have never forgiven the Hammers for luring the youngster away from the club that invested in his early development with manager Alan Curbishley complaining on Monday that the south Londoners had not been adequately compensated.

The fact that Defoe scored against his old team in the 4-4 draw would not have improved Curbishley's mood – or that of the home crowd.

The irony is that only the very smallest percentage of the Charlton support – if any – would ever have seen Defoe play in their colours with the youngster making not a single first-team appearance for the club.

But Glenn Roeder's decision to throw Defoe into the fray showed much belief in the teenager's character.

It is understandable that some might have feared for the young striker as he entered the arena to a crescendo of abuse.

But Roeder has already confirmed his intention to handle his valuable asset with care and he would not have exposed the player to such a hostile environment if he did not have total faith in the England Under-21 star's ability to deal with it.

Said Roeder, 'When you know Jermain as well as I do, you know that people booing won't bother him. If anything it would fire him up. He's got fantastic character and I'm sure he enjoyed his goal.'

Almost as much as Hammers fans did watching the smiles being wrenched off the faces of those barracking the youngster as he smacked in what could – and should – have been the winner.

Kirk now says: Never mind Charlton's grievances, Defoe would become even more reviled by West Ham fans following his poorly advised (and poorly timed) efforts to leave Upton Park in 2003.

FERGIE PAYS THE PRICE ... ONCE AGAIN (13 December 2001)

Glenn Roeder looked happier and more relaxed on Saturday evening than at any time since taking charge of West Ham in the summer.

But when you have just watched your side complete a deserved victory at Manchester United, of course, you can afford to smile.

'I had to laugh,' he said after the shock 1-0 win, 'when I heard Aston Villa boss John Gregory saying he was down to the "bare bones" when they played us the other night.

'They had a £9.5m striker in Juan Pablo Angel on the bench alongside £3.5m David Ginola!'

Roeder's substitutes that night cost a mere £1.5m in transfer fees as he struggled to name a full squad of 16 names.

Subsequently, he must have been shocked to see Sir Alex Ferguson omit the likes of David Beckham, Juan Sebastian Veron, Ruud van Nistelrooy and Andy Cole from United's starting line-up on Saturday.

Ferguson claimed that some of his men were 'tired' but, unless another reason for their exclusion comes to light, the only conclusion that can be drawn is that he thought the Hammers would pose little threat.

Certainly that's the message that would have been sent out to the United players that were selected, which might explain their complacency in a match they needed to win.

The resting of such attacking talent was especially hard to comprehend given the loss of key defenders plus Ryan Giggs to injury.

But it served to give the Hammers hope – and they duly responded by making United pay for their apparent arrogance.

Kirk now says: It's funny, but West Ham's second victory at Old Trafford in 2001 – courtesy of Jermain Defoe's second-half header, which brought a first win in six games – has almost been forgotten compared to Paolo Di Canio's winner in an FA Cup tie 11 months earlier.

CLARET AND BLUES ON THE BOOZE (27 December 2001)

Given recent events, many might be sick to the back teeth of reading 'soccer out of control' stories.

The press have predictably used the Lee Bowyer and Jonathan Woodgate controversy at Leeds United as a platform to stick the studded boot into the belly of any footballer guilty of indiscretion.

And with that in mind, it has to be said that the activities of certain West Ham players at the club's Christmas party represent a case of spectacularly poor timing.

Glenn Roeder recognised the point, going out of his way to remind his players of the dangers of letting their hair down a touch too much.

Not even in this columnist's hedonistic days as a rock journalist does he remember urinating against a bar (although there might have been a few other places ...).

Whether Hayden Foxe can actually remember doing so is another question.

The defender was not the most likely candidate when trying to guess the identity of the culprit despite the Australians having a reputation for enjoying a tinny or ten.

There were at least three other names in the current squad that sprang more readily to mind.

But let's not get too carried away here. The danger of overreacting and lumping all misdemeanours together in a bid to present an image of football staggering out of control is that the lines of distinction get blurred.

Of course, alcohol appears to be a common denominator and what Foxe did is hardly the greatest of public relations exercises.

But let's try and keep things in perspective.

Kirk now says: Not for the first time, West Ham players were reported to have over-indulged themselves with their festive frolics, with Hayden Foxe on this occasion earning the club some unwanted headlines. That's what happens when Glenn Roeder tells people to be on their best behaviour.

NO-GO FOR DI CANIO (7 February 2002)

Given the farcical nature of Paolo Di Canio's aborted move to Manchester United, we shouldn't be too surprised that the saga has continued to generate gossip despite the deal dying.

The Italian responded to the news of United dropping their interest by claiming he'd had no wish to leave West Ham in the first place and that it was the club's board that had been looking to push him out.

'They want to sell me,' he insisted, pointing his thumb in the direction of the directors, just because the Hammers had intimated that a figure of £3.5m would be enough to secure the striker's services.

Surely Di Canio's ego isn't so fragile as to be so fatally wounded by the idea that – like all players – he has his price.

Throughout the whole scenario manager Glenn Roeder's line has been that the club could not deny the 33-year-old's desire to finish his career on a glorious high with a batch of medals in his back pocket.

Fans might not share such a generous attitude towards granting the player's – and United's – wishes, but the fact remains that Di Canio offered not a single word of dissent when the move was still a possibility.

Indeed, it was strongly suspected that his agent had been prematurely sounding out the terms of contract with the Old Trafford board and was unhappy that only an 18-month deal appeared to be on offer.

If Di Canio really didn't fancy the move, he had plenty of opportunities to say so.

And West Ham could not have been that keen to cash in on the striker, given that they rejected United's only offer.

While most supporters are pleased that Di Canio remains a Hammer, many will also be aware of the bigger picture.

The player's contract expires in the summer of 2003 and unless it is renewed he will be worth exactly nothing.

Even if he does sign an extension, his value on the pitch might also be negligible given that he will be 35 next year.

Fans have questioned what kind of replacement the club could have bought for £3.5m but, given that new faces are still badly needed, that figure represents £3.5m more than will be available next summer.

Both Roeder and the board are well aware of that, of course, but that doesn't justify Di Canio's insecurities – or what some may perceive as his mind games.

Kirk now says: It seems strange to be arguing a case for Di Canio being allowed to join Manchester United, but it's worth pondering how West Ham's prospects would have been improved the following season had the club cashed in on the Italian maverick. Knowing the Hammers, they probably wouldn't have spent the money anyway.

HEADING DOWN THE RIGHT ROED? (14 February 2002)

The news of manager Glenn Roeder signing a new three-year contract with West Ham generates several interesting talking points.

The new agreement certainly adds weight to the belief that Roeder was offered only a one-year deal last summer.

If that was the case, it hardly displayed great confidence in the club's new appointment when it was made.

And if the club wasn't totally convinced, you can't blame the fans for having had major doubts either. As to whether Roeder has won the complete faith of the supporters remains a moot point.

A healthy home record, good purchases in David James and Tomas Repka, plus a growing confidence in front of the media all help his case.

But a dreadful away record, which includes a Worthington Cup defeat to Second Division Reading, leaves the Hammers still vulnerable to the potential threat of relegation with an upper mid-table position the best that can be hoped for.

Roeder has undoubtedly impressed behind the scenes, making changes that only the staff and players can fully appreciate.

He has certainly conducted himself in a dignified manner.

But you can't help feeling that Roeder has enjoyed a generous honeymoon period with certain parties still blaming former boss Harry Redknapp for all the current woes.

Managing director Paul Aldridge has praised Roeder's 'judicious spending' and 'encouraging results'.

A safe buying policy may save embarrassment but it is unlikely to produce the kind of player profits the club has so heavily relied upon in recent years. No speculation, no accumulation, as they say.

As for positive results, we can only assume the directors have been selective in which ones they considered – or maybe some of them only attend home games.

Kirk now says: The shock victory at Manchester United inspired a five-game unbeaten run, including draws against Arsenal and Liverpool, which eventually saw Roeder being rewarded for West Ham's upturn in fortunes. The folly of giving the manager a bumper three-year deal would be exposed the following season, of course.

INTERTOTO NO-GO IS A NO-NO (28 February 2002)

West Ham's decision to ignore this summer's Intertoto Cup competition may ultimately prove irrelevant given that clubs likely to finish higher in the Premiership table have expressed interest in taking a place.

But most Hammers supporters will be disappointed that the club is automatically closing a door on a route into European competition.

Glenn Roeder has explained that the current squad lacks sufficient depth to sustain the length of campaign we would see if the Hammers kicked off in the Intertoto at the end of June.

He therefore feels that hopes of a successful Premiership season would be undermined with players burning themselves out or exposing themselves to extra risk of injury.

There is a different argument, of course. For a start, West Ham's first-team squad is actually larger than it was when the club successfully used the competition to qualify for the UEFA Cup in 1999.

The strong start to the following league campaign suggested the Hammers had benefited from getting into gear ahead of those that had prepared for the season with a batch of low-key friendly matches.

And given that West Ham will be playing a number of pre-season friendlies in July anyway, just how many extra games are we really talking about?

It goes without saying that anybody involved in the World Cup finals would automatically be excluded from the squad – as indeed would any player that Roeder feels needs sufficient rest from a tough season.

But there are plenty of peripheral players – such as Ragnvald Soma, Richard Garcia and Hayden Foxe – and youngsters that could be used to get the club through the early rounds with Roeder dangling the carrot of more regular first-team football if they sufficiently impress.

It is not too much to ask, especially with players continuing to earn fantastic salaries every week throughout the summer for doing nothing but keeping themselves in reasonable shape and getting a suntan.

Surely the benefits of potentially playing in the UEFA Cup outweigh the few negatives.

Kirk now says: West Ham fans love their trips abroad and we'll never know how different the 2002/03 season would have been had the team warmed up with some competitive European action.

BEWARE A CRASH IN TV CASH (28 March 2002)

The threat to Football League clubs as a result of ITV Digital's hopes of renegotiating their current deal to avoid going bust has sent shockwaves not only through the Nationwide divisions but the Premiership as well.

Clubs are worryingly dependent on television revenue and some are beginning to realise that when that income is eventually reduced, they will be faced with major financial problems – and possible extinction.

To be fair to West Ham chairman Terence Brown, it is a scenario referred to in his end-of-year report before Christmas.

He made a special point of saying 'the growth of digital subscription television may be slowing' while expressing concern over the club's ever-increasing wage bill (£28.1m being the last published figure).

Turnover figures for most clubs are increasing but profits are not keeping in line – leaving clubs vulnerable if certain parts of their revenue were to take a turn for the worse.

There have already been reports of a possible player exodus at Leeds United in the summer if they fail to qualify for the Champions League and need to restructure their budget accordingly.

In this climate it is perhaps not surprising that West Ham are treading carefully, especially in the transfer market.

We are unlikely to see any major acquisitions before next season unless they have been funded by player sales first.

That will inevitably cause a sense of frustration for supporters, who are still a bit miffed at seeing just over half of the £18m received from the sale of defender Rio Ferdinand to Leeds 17 months ago paid in transfer fees for new players.

But with the club offsetting the rest against player contracts, they are clearly bracing themselves for the day when TV income starts to level off.

At least Hammers fans can take comfort from the fact that the club is being run on a relatively secure basis and its existence is unlikely to be threatened. But the margin for error is decreasing all the time.

Concerns about over-stretching finances could result in under-investment and eventual relegation.

It has happened before – in the late 1980s – remember.

So in walking along that tightrope, the club has to find the right balance.

Fans need to believe their club is showing ambition and have a genuine chance of competing for honours.

The reality, however, is that they will have to find reward in stability as the club rides out the turbulent times that may lay ahead for the sport in general.

Kirk now says: 'Concerns about over-stretching finances could result in under-investment and eventual relegation. The club has to find the right balance.' These words would prove prophetic and West Ham would admit the following year that they got it badly wrong.

KAN YOU BELIEVE IT? (2 May 2002)

As we know all too well, last week's disgraceful decision to disregard Frederic Kanoute's goal in the 2-0 defeat at Arsenal was not the first time West Ham have been victims of incompetence from match officials.

Yet it could almost have been anticipated that the benefit of any doubt was always going to go Arsenal's way.

Far better to deny West Ham, with relatively little hanging on their brave efforts, than risk costing the Gunners the championship.

It happened two years ago when Arsenal were allowed to score an injury-time winner despite the whole of Highbury – apart from the referee and his two assistants – spotting Emmanuel Petit's handball.

And now it has happened again, with it being claimed that Ashley Cole successfully cleared Kanoute's first-half shot – despite his foot being a good distance over the line.

As tennis legend John McEnroe would exclaim, 'The ball was in!!!'

Almost as astonishing was West Ham manager Glenn Roeder's insistence that he is against the use of video technology to clarify the accuracy of referees' decisions in such instances.

'I don't subscribe to stopping the game and using video evidence,' he said.

'I still think you have to have that little bit of excitement, mystery or romance in the game.'

Sorry, Glenn, but there was little romance hanging in the air as faces turned claret and blue with fury and frustration.

Roeder pleaded for the guilty linesman to admit his mistake but few Hammers fans will feel that offers any consolation.

The only crumb of comfort was that the decision would have brought little cheer to Manchester United boss Sir Alex Ferguson.

But even that will disappear if West Ham fail to claim seventh place from rivals Tottenham, with fans being left to wonder what might have been had justice been done.

Kirk now says: Arsenal easily won the title and West Ham finished above Spurs, so the result at Highbury made little difference, but that doesn't excuse a terrible decision – one that strangely never gets mentioned when the merits of goal-line technology are debated.

JAMES SHOULD GET THE VOTE (9 May 2002)

The Hammer of the Year award will be presented at Upton Park on Saturday – with goalkeeper David James and defender Sebastien Schemmel the favourites to poll most votes from supporters.

James showed great courage and conviction to return from the knee injury that delayed his Hammers career following the £3.5m move from Aston Villa last summer.

Since November, the England international has been a model of consistency, not only producing great saves but also providing a stabilising influence on the likes of Tomas Repka and Christian Dailly in front of him.

And while some say a goalkeeper receiving the award implies a mediocre season for the rest of the team, it should be remembered that Ludek Miklosko won the trophy in 1991 – a promotion season – while Shaka Hislop did so in 1999 when the Hammers finished fifth to qualify for the Intertoto Cup.

Frenchman Schemmel has won considerable support in his first full season following his bargain transfer from Metz last year, showing great commitment to the cause.

However, while he displays plenty of enthusiasm, his final ball when on the attack can let him down and it would surprise many if he were to follow in the footsteps of defenders such as Billy Bonds, Julian Dicks and Rio Ferdinand who have previously won the coveted award.

It has been a mixed season for many other Hammers players, with injuries affecting the likes of Joe Cole, Michael Carrick and Don Hutchison in midfield. Trevor Sinclair, meanwhile, has impressed while trying to gain a place in the England squad.

In attack, 19-year-old Jermain Defoe, who will surely win the Young Hammer of the Year award, has surged to the top of the West Ham scoring charts with 14 goals, despite not making manager Glenn Roeder's first-choice side.

It is an incredible feat for a boy with … incredible feet.

Frederic Kanoute's 12 goals in 27 games is a far more consistent return than last season, despite being in and out of the side with injury.

But partner Paolo Di Canio has disappointed in front of goal, scoring just six times excluding penalty kicks.

Departing left-back Nigel Winterburn will be acknowledged for his efforts in his final season at Upton Park while fans will hopefully recognise the tenacity of Steve Lomas, whose return to the midfield has coincided with the team's recent good form.

But this writer's vote goes to James, whose form is sure to win him a place in Sven-Goran Eriksson's squad for the World Cup finals when named this week.

Kirk now says: Sebastien Schemmel won the award ahead of David James, who did indeed go to the World Cup, while Glen Johnson was named the Young Hammer of the Year by academy boss Tony Carr, despite not having yet made a first-team appearance.

HAMMERS IN SEVENTH HEAVEN (16 May 2002)

So West Ham finished the 2001/02 season in seventh place, making it the club's fifth most successful top-flight league campaign ever.

Few would have credited the Hammers with the potential to finish so high, whoever had been in charge this season.

But for Glenn Roeder to guide the team to such an impressive placing in his first year as manager deserves special praise.

Most West Ham fans would have eagerly accepted the chance to finish just one place behind big-spending London rivals Chelsea if it had been offered at the start of the season.

Or to end the campaign just four places behind Manchester United. Yeah, we'll take that, thanks very much.

West Ham's success has been built on the foundations of a fantastic home record, bettered by just one point by second-placed Liverpool and equal to champions Arsenal.

That means the 34-point gulf that exists between West Ham and the Gunners is purely down to the difference in away results – so there's plenty of room for improvement there.

And the fact of the matter is that more points have been thrown away rather than won in fortuitous fashion.

So there could have been even more on the board, although the 11 points that separate the Hammers and Chelsea says much about how far clubs need to go if they are to break into the top six.

But a huge amount of credit must be given to Roeder.

It was always going to take a few months for his influence to truly show itself in the side, but he admirably stuck to his principles and can be proud of his achievements.

The West Ham board will also feel that their judgement has been vindicated.

Few can doubt that to invest the responsibility of turning things around in somebody with such limited managerial experience was a huge gamble last summer.

For many (not least this columnist), Roeder simply didn't have the credentials to succeed Harry Redknapp in the Hammers hot seat.

But the new boss worked diligently to apply his philosophies and has gained the rewards.

He now finds himself in a similar position to the former West Ham manager, in that the onus will be on him to generate his own funds for new recruits and find players at bargain prices.

Despite what the club might say about Redknapp's less successful acquisitions, his gambling instincts generally paid off and Roeder may also be tempted to 'take a punt' as he seeks to stretch his limited resources to the maximum.

That is unless a player is sold for big money, as was the case with Frank Lampard providing the new boss with £11m last summer.

The one disappointment is that the club effectively qualified for the Intertoto Cup yet turned its back on the competition for the sake of trying to earn a few more Premiership points next season.

Does Roeder really have so little faith in his squad?

Kirk now says: It was right to congratulate Glenn Roeder on his achievements but it just goes to show that managers – like players – can be one-season wonders, as the Hammers would discover to their cost.

REFLECTING ON SEASON 2001/02

Best signing: David James (Aston Villa), £3.5m

Worst signing: Vladimir Labant (Sparta Prague), £900,000

Best result: Winning 1-0 at Manchester United in December

Worst result: Losing 7-1 at Blackburn in September

Final position: 7th in the Premiership, 53 points

Manager and rating: Glenn Roeder 8/10

Best thing about season: A top-seven finish – what's not to like?

Worst thing about season: Conceding 12 goals in two games at Everton and Blackburn

SEASON 2002/03

'We won't take this anymore'

EVERYBODY knows the England squad needs to include three West Ham players if they want to win the World Cup – as was proved in 1966, of course – and Sven-Goran Eriksson must have realised as much when taking Joe Cole, David James and Trevor Sinclair to Japan and South Korea for the 2002 finals.

Cole subsequently became the first Hammer to play for England at a World Cup tournament since Alvin Martin had appeared in Mexico in 1986, although he was restricted to just 16 minutes against Sweden.

Sinclair played a much bigger role in his four outings but James remained on the bench as England – clearly having not put the three West Ham players to nearly enough use – crashed out at the quarter-final stage to Brazil.

Jermain Defoe, meanwhile, scored for the England Under-21s against European Championship host country Switzerland but couldn't stop his team from finishing bottom of their group.

Back home, former Hammer Kevin Keen was indeed brought back home when replacing the 'retiring' Peter Brabrook as coach of the club's Under-17s, while Anton Ferdinand secured a three-year contract with West Ham in the same week that older brother Rio completed his £30m British record transfer move from Leeds to Manchester United.

However, youngster Kieran Richardson decided against signing a professional contract with the Hammers and headed to Old Trafford instead, with Raimond van der Gouw making the opposite journey as a replacement for second-choice goalkeeper Shaka Hislop, who had moved to Portsmouth along with defender Hayden Foxe.

By and large, though, the Hammers did little in the summer market with their biggest signing being, er, Gary Breen on a free transfer. And what a waste of space he turned out to be.

CAN HAMMERS SURPRISE AGAIN? (15 August 2002)

Yet again West Ham head into a new season looking to prove the forecasters wrong.

A year ago, new boss Glenn Roeder was tipped to become one of the first managerial casualties while this time around the bookies seem to think there are just seven worse teams in the Premiership.

Ladbrokes are offering title odds of 250/1 – compared to an eighth-best 100/1 for Tottenham.

It is almost as if last season's seventh-place, when the Hammers finished above the likes of Spurs and Aston Villa, never happened.

But while Middlesbrough and Manchester City have each spent over £20m in a bid for European qualification, there are still plenty of reasons to believe that West Ham can enjoy another good campaign.

The Upton Park wage bill may have been relieved of squad players such as Steve Potts, Paul Kitson, Shaka Hislop, Rigobert Song, Ragnvald Soma, Gary Charles and Hayden Foxe, but the first-choice team has lost not a single vital component.

Indeed, Roeder now has added quality at his disposal with Republic of Ireland international Gary Breen and Frenchman Edouard Cisse arriving to increase the defensive and midfield options.

The Hammers began last season with David James, Ian Pearce, Joe Cole and Steve Lomas suffering from injuries.

This year Don Hutchison is the only serious casualty as the action commences.

Youngsters Cole and Michael Carrick can only improve as their development continues while 19-year-old striker Jermain Defoe – last season's top scorer – is set to shake off Roeder's protective arm from his shoulder and prove he is ready for a regular starting place.

There are high hopes for young striker Youssef Sofiane, another new signing who arrived for no fee, while outcast Titi Camara may well be allowed a chance to contribute to the attack if he proves his fitness.

The only potential problem on the horizon is that of temperamental striker Paolo Di Canio, who is sure to spark a few fireworks as soon as his place appears to be under threat from the emerging Defoe.

Keeping the Italian maverick happy is likely to prove Roeder's biggest test in the coming months.

But Roeder has a year of dramatic experience under his belt this time around and can only be better equipped to deal with whatever missiles the season throws at him.

Sadly, just like last year, West Ham have a tough start by facing two of the previous season's top four in their opening couple of games – at Newcastle and at home to Arsenal.

The third game, at Fulham, has been postponed so the Hammers could find themselves under increased pressure by the time they entertain Charlton at the end of the month.

The team will have to go some to match last season's impressive home record in the Premiership, which was equal to champions Arsenal and bettered only by Liverpool.

But the hope is that they can improve on their dismal away form, which produced just three league wins.

Assuming that key players remain fit, there is no reason why West Ham should not achieve another top-half finish and produce some exciting football in the process.

Kirk now says: Oops! It seems that seventh-place finish lulled everybody into a false sense of security. Gary Breen proved a disastrous signing and Glenn Roeder struggled to solve problems, not least with Paolo Di Canio who produced the 'fireworks' this column predicted.

KANOUTE MISS SO COSTLY (29 August 2002)

Julian Dicks may hide a pair of knackered knees behind the bar in which he now pulls pints and Ray Stewart may spend more time pursuing birdies on a golf course than he does kicking a ball about nowadays.

But West Ham fans must yearn for the days when the two former Hammers ruthlessly despatched penalty kicks with clinical precision – times when a spot-kick meant a near-certain goal.

That is not the case now, of course.

Hearts are in mouths when Paolo Di Canio walks up to the spot, with the Italian feeling the need to embarrass the goalkeeper by chipping the ball over his head rather than slotting it into the corner.

And when Di Canio is not around, the job is left to whoever fancies the task when the opportunity arises.

Manager Glenn Roeder admitted that was the case on Saturday after watching Frederic Kanoute feebly waste a chance to restore West Ham's two-goal lead against Arsenal.

One Sunday newspaper described the Frenchman's effort as being 'so weak that goalkeeper David Seaman could have batted it away with his ponytail' and highlighted it as the turning point of the match.

They weren't wrong. And the reality is that fans would have had far greater faith in Hammers goalkeeper David James successfully converting the spot-kick than the nervous-looking Kanoute.

It is over five years since a memorable dispute between John Hartson and Paul Kitson as to who should take a crucial penalty against Everton – Kitson missed and Everton rescued a two-goal deficit – when Dicks subsequently revealed that it was 'down to the players' to sort out penalties in his absence.

Clearly not much has changed, with Roeder confessing in Saturday's post-match press conference that Kanoute had volunteered on the pitch rather than having been designated in advance.

This might be acceptable if West Ham were playing on Hackney Marshes but in the Premiership there can surely be no place for such a haphazard idea.

It is one that seems at odds with the meticulous approach that Roeder has otherwise shown in his management.

It should be known in advance who is taking penalties – somebody who is champing at the bit to add to his goals tally rather than having the option to bottle it and hand the ball to somebody else.

The captain should also be on hand to ensure things are done properly – except the skipper for the day was stuck in his own penalty box at the other end of the pitch.

If ever the idea of having a goalkeeper as captain was proved to be a bad one, it was on Saturday.

As West Ham reeled from Kanoute's poor kick, with the inevitability of Arsenal scoring again staring everybody in the face, some leadership outfield might just have made the difference.

Arsenal duly equalised to confirm punters' views that they had been watching the same old Hammers.

And Roeder will hopefully be the first to admit that lessons have got to start being learned.

Kirk now says: Many still believe that West Ham would never have been relegated in 2003 had Kanoute put them 3-1 up against Arsenal instead of having to wait until the end of January for a first home league win.

IT'S THE WORST EVER START (26 September 2002)

First, the facts and figures: Two points from the opening six games represents West Ham's worst-ever league start.

The Hammers are the only Premiership side without a win this season with just one other club in the entire Football League – First Division Grimsby Town – yet to taste victory.

The team has failed to score in their last three home games, which is particularly depressing when considering that Charlton, West Brom and Manchester City were the opposition.

Against the corresponding fixtures last term – with promoted sides replacing those relegated – the Hammers are already nine points down on last season's tally.

And if West Ham fail to beat Chelsea at Stamford Bridge on Saturday, it will be the longest wait for a win since 1973 when fans were starved of victory until the 12th league game in a season that somehow saw the team finish fifth from bottom.

You can't blame the supporters for feeling tense.

It makes one wonder how the club's board of directors are feeling right now.

This time last year their patience with new boss Glenn Roeder was eventually rewarded with a top-seven finish, despite the team earning just five points from the opening seven games.

However, five of those matches were away from home while at Upton Park the side remained unbeaten until November – by which time they had just won three league games in succession.

A similar run may well be required this time around to stop speculation about Roeder's position from spiralling out of control.

One Sunday newspaper has already suggested that former Arsenal boss George Graham is being lined up should Roeder fail to improve the situation in the near future.

And once the Chelsea game is out of the way, the results against Birmingham, Sunderland, Fulham and Everton – not to mention the tricky Worthington Cup tie at Second Division Chesterfield – will surely determine how calm the club's directors remain.

Roeder has proved himself to be a man of honour and principle. Fans may be losing confidence but they still want him to succeed. But with relegation from the Premiership resulting in the severance of a club's financial lifeline, it is inevitable that while the Hammers remain bottom there will come a time when the board will panic.

Roeder has to find solutions to the team's problems before that moment arrives – or face the consequences.

Kirk now says: George Graham? Well, at least he would have sorted out the defence.

CHAIRMAN HAS BOOS COMPLAINT (3 October 2002)

So what to make of West Ham chairman Terence Brown's recent complaint regarding the home crowd's alleged abusive treatment of the club's young stars?

Admittedly, Brown would probably not have anticipated his words – written in response to a letter from a season-ticket holder – being published in the national newspapers.

But he made his comments to a member of the public and so it has to be assumed that he stands by them.

It is a dangerous situation when a chairman starts criticising his club's supporters, even more so when the team is struggling.

With the Hammers at the bottom of the Premiership table, he should be asking questions of his management staff and players rather than the disgruntled paying public. Goalkeeper David James admitted last week that he empathised with the fans.

'Damn right they should boo us if we're not performing,' he said.

Brown has the right to defend young players such as Michael Carrick, but the reality is that the Upton Park crowd have shown far more patience and understanding that many other fans might.

Given the home results so far, the players have got off relatively lightly with any jeering generally being reserved for manager Glenn Roeder's substitution decisions more than anything else.

It is certainly not right to suggest that the likes of Jermain Defoe have received abuse.

Sadly, this whole episode has simply cemented the national media's view that Carrick and his colleagues have become targets for the boo boys when that's not been the case.

And even if it was, the highly paid, over-sensitive players of today need to recognise that if they happily take the plaudits for their good displays, they also have to accept a bit of stick for the bad ones.

Kirk now says: Brown's criticism of the fans in this instance was very unfair and gave a totally misleading view of what was happening at Upton Park.

DI CANIO TRIES TO CALL THE SHOTS (24 October 2002)

Paolo Di Canio may not have had his most inspirational of games on Sunday against Everton, but that did not stop his name being at the centre of debate among West Ham fans afterwards.

The Italian's contract expires at the end of the season and he has asked the Hammers board to advise him by the end of October as to whether his services will be required beyond next summer.

By last weekend the club had said nothing and manager Glenn Roeder even responded to an innocent inquiry about the striker's future after the last-minute penalty winner against Fulham last week by insisting the question was 'below the belt'.

The club may not like being issued with ultimatums or pressed into making public statements, but most will feel that any player with just seven months left on his contract is entitled to know where he stands.

In the absence of the club initiating talks or Roeder making a statement that he would like Di Canio to stay, the only conclusion that can be drawn is that the player is likely to be allowed to leave.

The situation might have been different had the striker not irritated the board with premature requests for contract talks last autumn and strained his relationship with Roeder by kicking up a fuss when substituted on several occasions.

The directors may well be concerned about paying large wages to a player who will be 35 next summer while Roeder knows that life will be a lot more comfortable next season without an irascible Italian bending his ear every time he is left on the bench.

We now have to ask ourselves how Di Canio will respond if he does not get the answers he is looking for, while also wondering what effect it might have on the rest of the squad at this delicate time.

West Ham have not got so many players of such unique talent that they can afford to let one slip away so easily.

They would certainly miss his showmanship and the mood of the support won't be helped if it is suspected that the club is compromising the appeal of its product for the sake of its wage bill.

Kirk now says: Little did we know that the problems with Di Canio had only just started.

CLOCK IS TICKING FOR GLENN (14 November 2002)

As Mark Viduka tucked the ball into the West Ham net on Sunday to give Leeds a 4-1 half-time lead, Glenn Roeder must surely have known that his days as manager were numbered.

Ever the positive thinker, even Roeder must have realised his position is becoming increasingly untenable.

Just as the team ultimately failed to salvage anything from the game, despite a spirited second-half performance that saw them score twice, Roeder is unlikely to claw himself back from the position in which he finds himself.

The Hammers have lost six of their eight home games this season – an astonishing statistic.

The return of two points from the first seven league games at Upton Park is the worst in the club's entire history.

Leeds had not won any of their last half a dozen Premiership matches but here they were banging in goals for fun.

God only knows what thoughts were running around the head of West Ham chairman Terence Brown and his fellow directors as they looked on. Whether they will be shared with Roeder remains to be seen, with the manager claiming that he had not discussed the team's present plight with the club's board.

'I'm sure they will talk to me as and when they feel they need to,' said Roeder, while denying that he feared for his position.

Roeder has many qualities but the simple fact is that his methods are no longer working.

Four consecutive home defeats – including an embarrassing Worthington Cup exit to Second Division Oldham – prove it.

Roeder may have certain coaching abilities but his motivational skills have to be called into question.

The players have undoubtedly let him down but that is because they have stopped responding to his commands. And when that happens a change of management is usually inevitable.

Kirk now says: Roeder appeared to have run out of ideas by November, so it seems incredible that he was allowed to see out the season.

ROED TO HELL (5 December 2002)

It has been anticipated for weeks that a home defeat by Southampton would be considered not so much the straw that breaks the camel's back at West Ham but the slab of concrete that squashes it flat.

As we saw on Monday night, the patience of the long-suffering Hammers supporters has certainly snapped.

'We won't take this anymore,' they screamed, while chanting for chairman Terence Brown to step down.

It is interesting that the fans decided to target the club's hierarchy for abuse instead of struggling manager Glenn Roeder.

The supporters clearly hold the view that the team is now paying the price for years of under-investment – the very thing former manager Harry Redknapp complained about and which led to his sacking.

The board themselves are now paying the price for making that unnecessary change and appointing a coach with no top-flight managerial experience.

The methods that worked so well for Roeder last season have achieved nothing this time around and results speak for themselves.

Astonishingly, Roeder refused to concede on Monday night that there might come a time when it would in the club's best interests for him to call it a day, declaring his determination to carry on.

The popular view is that his fate rests in other people's hands.

The protests outside the Boleyn Ground after the 1-0 defeat by Southampton were vociferous and venomous.

Past experience tells us that when fan hysteria builds to such a high level of hostility, a response of some sort from the club under fire is generally inevitable.

The chairman must realise that decisions made at this pivotal point in West Ham's history will determine the club's entire future.

The pressure is on Brown to make the right ones – and be accountable for them.

Kirk now says: So what did the board of directors do? Sit on their hands and do nothing about the management position, simply hoping that the transfer window would allow the club to stage a rescue act.

SO THAT'S WHAT IT FEELS LIKE! (9 January 2003)

Hallelujah! West Ham have finally won a home game this season – at the 13th time of asking.

For the majority of Hammers fans, the 3-2 FA Cup win against Nottingham Forest on Saturday represented their first taste of success in what has been a thoroughly miserable campaign so far.

Many had forgotten what the experience felt like and the same can be said of the West Ham players.

Of course, it is now vital that, having finally overcome a major psychological barrier, they use that victory as a platform to achieve the results needed to secure Premiership survival.

Aside from taking the Hammers into the fourth round of the FA Cup, the success against Forest extended the team's unbeaten run to four games, with just one defeat – at Manchester United – in the last six.

There is certainly no shortage of spirit. But while it is hoped the players are growing in confidence, there is still much that needs to be rectified.

Saturday's match exposed all of the team's current frailties, faults and failings – particularly defensively.

The Hammers have not kept a clean sheet since the 1-0 win at Fulham on 23 October and in the 13 games since they have conceded 25 goals – almost two a match.

David James is dropping costly clangers and was the victim of ironic cheers from the Upton Park crowd whenever he collected the simplest of balls.

Glenn Roeder has replaced Tomas Repka with Gary Breen but the defence looks no better for it.

And the merits of deploying defender Ian Pearce as an emergency striker have to be considered as much for what the team loses in defence as for what it gains in attack.

Meanwhile, the side continues to look vulnerable at set-pieces.

It can be hoped the Hammers have turned the corner but the fact is that, unless these problems are addressed, they will always struggle.

Kirk now says: The cup win against Forest was West Ham's first in 13 games but the next seven outings would produce just one victory.

BOWYER DEAL SHOULD BE CELEBRATED (16 January 2003)

West Ham's cut-price signing of Lee Bowyer represents the bargain of the season, yet his arrival at Upton Park has prompted reactions of pure hysteria in some quarters.

Glenn Roeder snapped up the controversial midfielder for a reported figure of around £300,000, but his purchase has been criticised as being morally unjust.

Such claims are unfounded. Bowyer's dubious past has nothing to do with West Ham.

Had the player signed the £40,000-a-week contract that was on offer at his former club Leeds, nobody would have complained about the Yorkshire outfit retaining his services.

And did Liverpool receive flak for agreeing a £9m fee to buy him last summer before the move broke down?

No. So why the outcry when the Hammers sign him for peanuts?

As Roeder admits himself, nearly half the Premiership's managers were queuing up to acquire the player – and if he's good enough for them he's surely good enough for West Ham.

The team certainly needs him.

The criticism reveals one thing – that certain sections of the media have their own agenda.

For example, one 'campaigning' national tabloid went to great lengths to hastily manufacture a hostile reaction to the deal.

Yet did anybody stop to consider that such claims were put into print before it was possible for them to gauge genuine public opinion?

Hammers fans should have just two immediate concerns about the player.

One is that Bowyer might be so keen to keep his nose clean that his game will be robbed of the natural aggression that he relies upon so much, as we saw on his debut against Newcastle.

The other is that he is unlikely to be treated fairly by referees.

More worryingly, Roeder has confessed that the signing of the England international will deny him the opportunity to recruit a defender while the transfer window is open, with his remaining funds allocated to a new striker.

With the Hammers leaking an average of two goals a game, fans can only hope that reinforcements in midfield and attack will help take the pressure off the defence.

Otherwise the relegation quicksand will continue to engulf the side as it seeks to secure its Premiership status.

Kirk now says: So much for 'bargain of the season'. Bowyer, carrying an ankle problem, was restricted to 11 outings for the Hammers, having little influence and failing to score while collecting five bookings.

BOOK ALLEGATIONS RAISE EYEBROWS (20 February 2003)

The allegation in a newspaper book serialisation last week that West Ham chairman Terence Brown paid former manager Harry Redknapp a £300,000 bonus, encouraging him not to buy players following the £18m sale of defender Rio Ferdinand in November 2000, has left fans scratching their heads in bewilderment.

So too the suggestion that Redknapp ignored the alleged agreement to spend regardless, as if the club could do nothing to stop him.

Harry insists the money was simply 'a gift' and we might never learn if there were strings attached to the payment.

Whatever the case, those in the know have always believed that Redknapp's dismissal had far more to do with finance than it did with football.

If taking the team down to 15th in the Premiership table was a sackable offence, then current boss Glenn Roeder would have been fired ten times over by now.

But these stories will have confirmed many people's suspicions as to why Roeder was chosen as Redknapp's successor in June 2001.

The West Ham directors clearly felt he was somebody who would operate strictly on corporate lines, as well as being a character who was unlikely to rock the boat.

That is not something the current manager would acknowledge, but there's very little evidence to support claims to the contrary.

For example, he has won few battles when it comes to gaining funds for new players, having had to rely on virtual free transfers and short-contract deals.

The club may well be happy with how Roeder conducts himself when it comes to matters off the field but, sadly for all of us, he's proved himself less capable of winning football matches this season – and that's easily the priority as far as the supporters are concerned.

Kirk now says: Needless to say, Tom Bowyer's Broken Dreams: Vanity, Greed And The Souring Of British Football *book stirred up all kinds of controversy.*

YET ANOTHER PR DISASTER (27 February 2003)

West Ham chairman Terence Brown won't have been happy when he picked up the *News Of The World* before the game at West Brom on Sunday.

Not for the first time this season, a written response to a disgruntled supporter – this time in the form of an e-mail – has found its way into the newspapers.

On this occasion, Brown defended the work of Glenn Roeder, pointing an accusing finger at players that have under-achieved this season and denied that the manager has only kept his job because the club could not afford to pay him off.

The reply has gained a mixed response from Hammers fans. Some feel the chairman simply cannot win at times. If he ignores letters from fans he is accused of showing a lack of respect. And if he replies the message invariably makes headlines.

That is partly because Brown is so reluctant to make any public comment, preferring to shun publicity and keep a low profile.

There are those who feel that the chairman has simply been honest in this case and is entitled to express his opinion.

Others, meanwhile, will feel as if he has scored an own goal by naming the players he feels have let Roeder down – David James, Trevor Sinclair, Christian Dailly and Tomas Repka are those mentioned.

We all know which men have struggled this season, but even Roeder himself has avoided public criticism of individuals after games.

We can only wonder what impact this story will have in the dressing room and Brown may well reflect on the matter by feeling that he could have shown a little more diplomacy.

But what will astonish many is the blatant contradiction between his latest message and one revealed back in September, when the chairman criticised fans for booing players during poor performances.

Yet now Brown says, 'What never ceases to amaze me is that the supporters will blame everyone (myself, the board, the manager) for what has happened and totally excuse the players.'

It is little wonder that the fans are confused, while such incidents simply suggest the club still has much to learn in the public relations department.

Kirk now says: The BBC website jokingly compared Terence Brown to legendary recluse Howard Hughes during this particular season and, given the stories that appeared whenever the chairman said anything, perhaps he was better off keeping a low profile after all.

DI CANIO MUST REMAIN ONSIDE (6 March 2003)

Two successive wins for the first time since October, the end of a 21-game stretch without a clean sheet, the Premiership safety margin reduced to just goal difference … it's no wonder the mood at Upton Park is considerably more buoyant than for some time.

Indeed, with recent recruit Les Ferdinand scoring his first goal for West Ham in the 2-0 win against his former club Tottenham last Saturday and forging an exciting-looking partnership with Jermain Defoe up front, it is even being suggested that the team can happily survive without the services of Paolo Di Canio.

The volatile Italian is once again in the news for criticising manager Glenn Roeder and many are becoming increasingly weary of the striker throwing his toys out of his pram every time he feels there has been an injustice.

However, some will feel he is entitled to be aggrieved by the way the club have allowed his contract to run down this season.

Whatever the rights or wrongs of that particular matter, the key issue is whether Di Canio will be allowed to contribute to West Ham's relegation fight in the remaining nine games.

Roeder has already insisted that Ferdinand and Defoe will retain their places in the next match at Everton – and rightly so – but it would be wrong for the Hammers boss to totally exclude Di Canio from the picture.

The manager has always picked the talented Roman when fit in the past and it is vital that none of the squabbling is allowed to interfere in his team selection as the chase for points intensifies.

Likewise, Di Canio has to prove he really does have the club's best interests at heart by accepting decisions – because Premiership safety may well depend on it.

Kirk now says: After angrily describing Roeder as a 'young manager who makes mistakes' following his substitution in a 2-1 win at West Brom, Di Canio would not appear in one of his squads ever again.

ROEDER'S RISKY GAME (17 April 2003)

West Ham may have finished the game against Aston Villa with three strikers on the pitch, but one was conspicuous by his absence – Paolo Di Canio.

The controversial forward has not featured in a first-team game since late February.

And the fact that he failed to even make the substitutes' bench last Saturday is the biggest indication yet that manager Glenn Roeder intends to freeze the Italian out of the picture for the rest of the season.

It is a decision that could decide West Ham's Premiership fate – as well as Roeder's as boss.

In batting away questions about Di Canio's future, the Hammers chief has made it obvious that he is resentful of the player's unsettling antics and would like to exclude him from the team if circumstances permit.

Results have conveniently allowed Roeder to stick with Jermain Defoe, Les Ferdinand and Fredi Kanoute as his main forwards, with the team going six games unbeaten since Di Canio last stomped off the pitch. But Saturday's 2-2 home draw with Villa allowed Di Canio the perfect opportunity to insist he should have been involved.

West Ham manufactured at least 15 goalscoring chances, yet contrived to misfire the final bullet that would have shot down Villa and dragged them into the relegation dogfight.

Few fans would argue against the idea of having two strikers available as substitutes for a must-win game.

Yet Roeder mysteriously decided that two midfielders – Don Hutchison and Edouard Cisse – would dominate the bench.

Hutchison saw just six minutes of action at a time when it would have made more sense for a forward to replace the departing Kanoute.

Yet Roeder obviously feels he can afford to dispense with Di Canio's mercurial talents.

He might prefer that to be the case, but the reality is that if any two of Defoe, Kanoute and Ferdinand were to suffer injury – and two of the three are worryingly fragile – he will suddenly need to ask the Italian to produce the goods.

Di Canio may not fancy taking a place on the bench but it is Roeder's job to exploit his playing assets to the maximum.

And if the club is relegated as a result of the manager failing to do so, he will only have himself to blame.

Kirk now says: Roeder effectively gambled with West Ham's Premiership status to win a personal battle against Di Canio and assert his authority, undermining the club's survival hopes in the process.

GET WELL SOON, GLENN (24 April 2003)

The news of Glenn Roeder's collapse and hospitalisation on Monday evening will have come as a great shock to West Ham fans and all of them will hope he makes a speedy recovery.

Glenn has suffered a great deal of criticism for the team's poor performances this season and his position appeared to be in considerable jeopardy prior to Christmas.

But the manager weathered the storm and his perseverance was rewarded with a six-game unbeaten run that gave the Hammers hope of retaining their Premiership status.

Just a few weeks ago this column acknowledged Roeder's courage by saying that his resolve was certainly to be admired, especially considering the pressure he has been under.

Whatever the critics have said – and this writer is certainly among them – there is no doubt that he has faced up to the demands placed upon him and retained his dignity in trying circumstances.

Some of his decisions may not have been popular with certain players or fans, but there is no denying his fortitude or work ethic.

The 1-0 defeat at Bolton on Saturday represented a serious blow to the club's hopes of staying up, however, and fans heckled Glenn as he attempted to board the team bus afterwards.

His reluctance to issue instructions from the touchline during the 1-0 win against Middlesbrough on Monday was noticeable and this can be attributed more to him feeling unwell than an attempt to avoid flak from fans.

Some felt he wasn't quite his normal self in the post-match press conference and it was later discovered that he was rushed to hospital shortly after saying goodbye to journalists.

Thankfully, Glenn's condition was reported on Tuesday morning as not being heart related and all that's left to say is that everybody wishes him a successful return to health.

Kirk now says: Roeder had suffered a brain tumour and underwent successful surgery before returning to his position for the start of the following season.

IT'S CLEVER TO CALL ON TREVOR (1 May 2003)

The West Ham board had just three options following manager Glenn Roeder's hospitalisation last week.

The most daring would have been to seek an emergency candidate such as Terry Venables to act as Red Adair to try and keep the Hammers in the Premiership.

The least inspiring would have been to simply allow the weight of management responsibility to fall on the shoulders of coaches Paul Goddard and Roger Cross.

It may just prove that in taking the third option – that of asking non-executive director Trevor Brooking to oversee things – they have gone for the cleverest. Admittedly, it's not easy to imagine this most polite of characters throwing his weight around the dressing room – but then again he probably doesn't need to.

Having personified elegance and style during 635 appearances for West Ham and 47 England games, Brooking has already won the respect of the current Hammers squad.

His intelligence, communication skills and understanding of the game will ensure the players will go into the remaining two matches of the season as prepared as they possibly can.

The key, as far as Brooking was concerned when accepting the new role, was to maintain continuity at the club.

Roeder had collected 15 points from his last eight games prior to his collapse and with so little time remaining it was imperative that a solution was found that caused as little disruption as possible.

The 1-0 win at Kevin Keegan's Manchester City provided Brooking with an excellent start as he seeks to keep West Ham in the Premiership.

As the caretaker manager admitted himself, the game could have gone either way but you just sensed that it was going to be decided by a late goal – and fortunately it went the visitors' way as it finished Kev 0 Trev 1. Whether West Ham survive in the top flight or not remains to be seen – but how fitting it would be if one of the club's finest ambassadors could help engineer a miraculous escape.

Kirk now says: Well, it was worth fantasising about.

BROWN ADMITS HE GOT IT WRONG (8 May 2003)

How fitting that Paolo Di Canio should score the winning goal for West Ham against Chelsea on Saturday – on the day that chairman Terence Brown apologised to supporters for the club's misjudgements.

Following the Hammers' failure to beat Aston Villa three weeks ago, this column made the point that having Di Canio frozen out of the first-team picture was against the club's best interests.

And the Italian's precious winner against the Blues, in what is almost certain to be his final appearance at Upton Park, proved that very point with it always being likely that his mercurial talents would be needed at some stage.

We should therefore thank caretaker boss Trevor Brooking for following his own instincts by bringing Di Canio back in from the cold.

Sadly, we shall never know what difference Paolo might have made in the 2-2 draw with Villa or in the subsequent 1-0 defeat at Bolton had he played – results that will be sorely regretted if the club is relegated on Sunday.

Brown used the word 'misjudgement' not in the context of the club's handling of Di Canio in the final year of his contract but the board's 'belt-tightening' in recent years.

He acknowledged that such a financial strategy would be a key factor if the club is indeed relegated and admitted that 'with the benefit of hindsight one could argue that the board might have acted differently'. For that, he said sorry.

While it is gratifying to see the chairman admit the board's failings, such a confession will simply add weight to the case of those fans that believe the club is lacking in vision of leadership.

Supporters will feel the problem has been reflected not just in the club's lack of net expenditure on players over the last five years but also the decision to oust successful boss Harry Redknapp and name a replacement with such restricted managerial experience.

Whatever his shortcomings, Redknapp succeeded in keeping the club in the Premiership despite limited resources.

And if the board is now regretting its lack of player investment, it should also doubt the wisdom of pushing out a man who proved he could work with little funds.

It is at least reassuring that Brown has pledged that, in the event of relegation, the club will do its 'utmost to retain as strong a playing squad as possible in order to have the best chance of returning to the Premier League'.

Let us just hope that Sunday's results mean that nobody has to worry about the club needing to fulfil that specific commitment.

Kirk now says: Sadly, a 2-2 draw at Birmingham on the final day proved meaningless with Bolton's 1-0 home win against a disinterested Middlesbrough condemning West Ham to relegation with a record 42 points.

DEFOE NO-GO A STATEMENT OF INTENT (15 May 2003)

As the full impact of West Ham's relegation from the Premiership begins to sink in, fans can at least draw comfort from the messages transmitted from Upton Park in the past week or so.

A huge statement of intent was made when the Hammers defiantly rejected striker Jermain Defoe's poorly timed transfer request.

Meanwhile, both caretaker boss Trevor Brooking and managing director Paul Aldridge have insisted that the club's strategy is to try to retain as many of its best players as possible in order to hopefully ensure a speedy return to the top flight.

The worry among supporters was that relegation would result in most of the top earners being offloaded, but thankfully it has been recognised that selling the club's best assets would be counterproductive and only create bigger financial worries in the long term.

It is also reassuring that director Brooking has continued to influence first-team decisions since the end of the season, while Aldridge declared that the wage bill had been considerably reduced by the departure of several fringe players as well as Paolo Di Canio.

That may indeed be true but it should not be overlooked that eight of the players confirmed for release last week were members of the first-team squad and those places will still need to be filled before the 46-game First Division programme commences.

There will inevitably be other departures in the summer and just who will actually stay at the club remains to be seen.

But while many mistakes have been made in recent years, it is hoped that – for the time being at least – supporters can take heart from the policy the club is trying to adopt during this crucial period.

Kirk now says: Needless to say, the fans believed they had been lied to with Joe Cole and Glen Johnson being sold to Chelsea for a total of £12.6m, while Frederic Kanoute moved to Tottenham and Trevor Sinclair went to Manchester City for £4m and £2.5m respectively.

REFLECTING ON SEASON 2002/03

Best signing: Rufus Brevett (Fulham), undisclosed

Worst signing: Gary Breen (Coventry), free

Best result: Winning 3-2 at Chelsea in September

Worst result: Losing 6-0 at Manchester United (FA Cup) in January

Final position: 18th in the Premier League, 42 points

Manager and rating: Glenn Roeder 2/10

Best thing about season: Paolo Di Canio telling Glenn Roeder exactly what he thought of him

Worst thing about season: Being relegated after the club failed to remove Glenn Roeder from his position

SEASON 2003/04

'At best a soap opera, at worst a total farce'

IT seems unkind to refer to someone who was recovering from brain surgery at this time as a 'dead man walking' but the reality was that it was always going to be only a matter of time before Glenn Roeder was told his services as manager would be no longer required.

Roeder returned to work on 1 July and was seen on the club's pre-season visit to Sweden sporting a shaven head as evidence of the unfortunate trauma he had experienced.

As a club, the Hammers were also feeling wounded following relegation and knew that their own return to full health would not be swift or painless.

The arrival of Russian billionaire Roman Abramovich at Chelsea in the summer of 2003 allowed them to pay £6.6m for Joe Cole and £6m for Glen Johnson, while Fredi Kanoute and Trevor Sinclair were also sold to help rescue the Hammers, whose (most would say overpaid) hierarchy agreed salary deferrals of nearly 50 per cent to ease the financial problems.

Paolo Di Canio penned a one-year deal with Charlton Athletic while Lee Bowyer and Gary Breen headed up the A1 to sign for Newcastle and Sunderland respectively. Sebastien Schemmel was also on his way after being fined for publicly criticising Roeder and the frustrated Frenchman rejoined former boss Harry Redknapp at Portsmouth.

Jermain Defoe was going nowhere, however, after seeing his poorly advised transfer request – stupidly submitted the very day after relegation – rightly binned, and new personnel arrived in the shape of striker David Connolly (£285,000 from Wimbledon), former Hammers trainee Kevin Horlock (£300,000 from Manchester City) and lifelong fan Robert Lee (free from Derby County).

It was a miserable time for West Ham fans as they saw the quality of the squad downgraded, but they could at least smile when the question of faith was raised with the revelation that departing midfielder John Moncur was a committed Christian who described Jesus as a bloke who got 'battered' and was 'the strongest geezer I've ever known'.

Suddenly there was hope after all.

SAY ONE THING, DO ANOTHER (7 August 2003)

Last week's pre-season friendly defeats by Second Division Wycombe and Dutch champions PSV Eindhoven will have done little to lift the mood of West Ham supporters still reeling from the club's relegation from the Premiership.

But fans that followed the entire pre-season programme will have been even more concerned by the shallowness of the Hammers squad used for those games.

This has seen the likes of Anton Ferdinand, Elliott Ward, Trent McClenahan and Daryl McMahon from last season's Under-19 squad elevated into the first-team picture.

None of this should particularly surprise anybody, though.

While the release of Paolo Di Canio, Lee Bowyer, Les Ferdinand, Edouard Cisse, Nigel Winterburn, John Moncur, Gary Breen, Scott Minto and Raimond van der Gouw eased the club's wage bill, it was obvious that many of these players would need replacing.

This week's sale of Joe Cole plus the recent departures of Glen Johnson, Trevor Sinclair and Frederic Kanoute may have raised the sums required to keep the banks at bay, but it has left West Ham sadly short of the quality required on the pitch.

This column praised the club for acknowledging that the sale of its best young players would be totally counterproductive as it seeks to gain an immediate return to the Premiership.

Fans also purchased season tickets on the basis of the board's declared strategy. So to suddenly reverse this policy, especially when the Hammers hierarchy must have been able to anticipate this situation back in May, is a bitter pill for the supporters to swallow.

Kirk now says: Chairman Terence Brown later admitted that sales were necessary because 'by November we would have run out of cash and cheques would have bounced'. He added, 'I have been told by supporters that I should have been more open [but] had I done so my former Premier League colleagues would have smelt blood in the water.' So that's alright then.

COMMUNICATION BREAKDOWN (14 August 2003)

Reporters leaving Preston's ground on Saturday were left feeling that everything involving West Ham at the moment represents at best a soap opera and at worst a total farce.

Forget the sale of star players and the speculation surrounding the future of striker Jermain Defoe.

It was the allegation by new hitman David Connolly that manager Glenn Roeder had forced him on to the substitutes' bench because of an agreement with Liverpool that loan signing Neil Mellor would definitely start games during his year at Upton Park.

The Hammers boss quickly refuted this idea, saying he had no idea why Connolly held such a belief and that he wasn't the least bit bothered about the player's grievance.

This is a problem entirely of Roeder's making. Either he failed to clearly communicate with the former Watford and Wimbledon striker as to why Mellor was preferred – leaving Connolly the victim of a misunderstanding – or he was less than honest with the press about the exact deal with Liverpool.

Either way, it allowed the media to continue its 'club in crisis' coverage, despite West Ham's morale-boosting 2-1 win on the season's opening day.

While Connolly was unprofessional in rushing into the press room to air his complaint, any disciplinary action against him would obviously be detrimental to the club's prospects.

But if he is not punished, fans are entitled to wonder why the likes of Paolo Di Canio and Sebastien Schemmel were considered persona non grata after complaining about Roeder's questionable style of man-management.

Such inconsistencies in how players are treated do nothing to encourage their respect and it took Connolly barely a week to lose any he had for Roeder.

Maybe people are now beginning to understand why so many West Ham stars under-performed last season.

Kirk now says: Roeder comically referred to Connolly as 'an angry ant' for his rant, but the striker would eventually weigh in with 14 goals that season while Neil Mellor scored just twice in 21 outings.

THE FANS ARE REVOLTING (21 August 2003)

The West Ham fans who staged a protest outside the Boleyn Ground following the goalless draw with Sheffield United on Saturday would surely think there was a misspelling on the cover of *Hammers News*.

The magazine claimed the club has 'New Ambitions', whereas 'No Ambitions' would be more like it.

Inside the ground, supporters deemed it necessary to boo as the final whistle blew, despite the fact that a four-point return from the first two league games and a Carling Cup victory against Rushden & Diamonds would have been willingly accepted in advance.

After watching the side labour its way to a point against one of the division's grittier sides, those who had paid anything up to £39 for the privilege clearly felt they had been delivered a sub-standard product.

This time last year the Hammers were stylishly out-playing champions Arsenal (despite being held to a draw), yet here we are now watching a skeleton of a squad creak its way to a point against a team featuring such household names as Nick Montgomery, Chris Morgan and Robert Kozluk.

Striker Jermain Defoe and inspired signing David Connolly may have a glut of goals in their boots, yet without a genuinely creative midfielder – thanks to the sale of Joe Cole – you are left wondering who is going to supply the ammunition, especially when sides such as Sheffield United come to Upton Park determined to defend for a point.

Meanwhile, chairman Terence Brown's well-intentioned statement last week represented yet another public relations disaster for the club.

In trying to appease supporters by setting the record straight about the club's finances and the summer sale of players, he ended up being accused by the national media of confessing to a pack of lies.

Furthermore, the chairman's decision to quote from the *Oxford English Dictionary* as to the definition of 'supporter' is likely to achieve nothing apart from leaving the fans feeling patronised and insulted.

Kirk now says: There was a black cloud hanging over the Boleyn Ground, but the skies were about to brighten.

ROEDER SACKING LONG OVERDUE (28 August 2003)

A respected newspaper reporter who has known Glenn Roeder for many years and supported him to the hilt was forced to privately concede after West Ham's 6-0 FA Cup defeat at Manchester United back in January that the manager 'can't survive this and has got to go'.

Seven long months later, having somehow got a squad including England internationals Joe Cole, Trevor Sinclair and David James plus Under-21 stars Michael Carrick and Jermain Defoe – not to mention foreign strikers Paolo Di Canio and Frederic Kanoute – relegated from the Premiership, Roeder has finally left Upton Park.

Inevitably, there will be those who will criticise the club for sacking a hard-working and likeable man just four games into the new season after having seen 13 first-team players pushed through the exit gates.

The likelihood, of course, is that the board of directors had lost confidence in Roeder many months ago but could not take action earlier in the summer when he was recovering from brain surgery.

To sack him at that point would have prompted widespread condemnation and even Roeder's harshest critics would have found it difficult justifying the timing of his removal as he concentrated on regaining his health.

Had Roeder won his first four games this season – as indeed the club would have hoped – then he would have bought himself more time.

Yet the team's performances so far, particularly during the embarrassing 1-0 defeat at Rotherham on Saturday, have done nothing to suggest that he had turned the corner in terms of getting the best out of his players.

That fact is that Roeder wasn't fired after four games but 86 – including his one game as caretaker boss and excluding those when Trevor Brooking filled in – of which he failed to win 57.

He left the club in 12th place in the First Division, their lowest position since 1990.

He inherited a good nucleus of players two years ago and was given a £15m head start in terms of cash to spend on new recruits.

He only has to look at the squads he started and ended up with to realise his best efforts simply weren't good enough.

Of course, players were sold as a must during the summer, but those who feel that Roeder has had his hands tied of late must remember that everything that has happened recently has been as a direct consequence of his own failings – particularly in terms of his inability to construct a decent defence last season.

There is no doubt that Roeder is a man of great integrity who worked diligently in an effort to prove he was capable of managing West Ham, despite his obvious lack of credentials when given the job.

But his refusal to acknowledge that it might be in everybody's best interests for him to resign last year, when his methods were clearly not working, suggested he was simply trying to prove a point to himself, ultimately at the club's expense.

Additionally, the West Ham board have to accept responsibility for gambling on his appointment and not taking action earlier last season, when Roeder's position became increasingly untenable.

In an effort to impose his authority he fell out with several players, most notably Di Canio and Sebastien Schemmel.

The recent bust-up with new striker David Connolly was another public relations disaster.

Fans can only hope now that the next manager is somewhat better equipped to deal with the task.

The future of the club depends on it.

Kirk now says: The funny thing about Roeder's sacking was that the story appeared on the club's website with a picture of the former manager beneath the logo of new sponsors JobServe with the tagline 'Looking for a new job?' No, you couldn't make it up.

PARDEW IN POLE POSITION (11 September 2003)

Several names were initially linked with the West Ham managerial post following the sacking of Glenn Roeder, but Reading's Alan Pardew would appear to have been the club's preferred choice.

This was confirmed last weekend with the news that the Royals had snubbed the Hammers' first official approach for the 42-year-old, who was doing nothing to deny his interest in the vacancy.

West Ham caretaker boss Trevor Brooking has been quick to stress that there was not much point in appointing a manager with Premiership experience if West Ham can't actually get back into that league.

Winning promotion this season is absolutely crucial and it is clear the Upton Park board have looked at last season's First Division table to see which bosses were developing their reputations where it matters.

Hence the club has been linked with the likes of Pardew, who guided Reading to fourth place in May, and Paul Hart of Nottingham Forest who finished sixth.

Former Crystal Palace, Charlton and Barnet midfielder Pardew assumed control of Reading in October 1999 and won promotion from the Second Division in 2002.

He has achieved success without spending a fortune in the transfer market and that is something that won't have gone unnoticed in the cash-conscious Boleyn boardroom.

Reading are unbeaten in the league this season and sit in second place ahead of their visit to Upton Park on Saturday.

And the top two is certainly where the Hammers need to finish come the end of the campaign.

Kirk now says: The choice of Alan Pardew made perfect sense – and it can be assumed that caretaker boss Trevor Brooking had plenty to do with the decision.

PARDS HAS TIME TO PREPARE (25 September 2003)

The agreement for Alan Pardew to officially become West Ham's tenth manager on 18 October is by far the best outcome to what was becoming a protracted saga.

With Reading chasing a High Court injunction against their former manager being allowed to take up any other post, the situation could have dragged on indefinitely. Fortunately, common sense has prevailed and a compensation package was agreed between the two clubs, allowing Pardew to move to Upton Park next month.

Caretaker boss Trevor Brooking may well have preferred to hand over the reins more immediately, but the current situation might just work to the Hammers' advantage.

Given Brooking's excellent record in charge, many fans were hoping he would consider taking the job permanently and it will be interesting to see how he fares in his remaining five league games.

To introduce Pardew just a day or so before last Saturday's trip to Gillingham would simply have unsettled the team on the back of a four-game winning run – although that might not have been a bad thing considering the way they played.

Pardew can at least spend the next three weeks or so preparing for the task ahead and, while the 2-0 defeat at Gillingham was a setback, the hope is that Brooking can maintain West Ham's position among the promotion chasers so that the new boss can inherit a winning team.

Kirk now says: Brooking did indeed hand over a Hammers side in fine form, taking 12 points from his final six games against Cardiff City, Millwall, Crystal Palace, Derby County, Norwich City and Burnley. But Alan Pardew did not find things easy when he took charge.

A REAL HAMMER HORROW SHOW (13 November 2003)

What an absolute disaster. The arguments raged as stunned West Ham fans left the Boleyn Ground on Saturday evening trying to work out what had been the key turning point in the 4-3 defeat by West Brom.

Was it Jermain Defoe's failure to put the Hammers 4-0 up when clean through with just goalkeeper Russell Hoult to beat?

Was it the communication breakdown between defender Christian Dailly and goalkeeper David James that gifted Albion a lifeline with their first goal?

Or was it Defoe's sending off just moments before half-time with West Ham's lead already cut to 3-2?

Ultimately, of course, all those incidents were contributory factors as the Hammers shot themselves in the foot in a way that perhaps only they can.

It was a devastating defeat that will haunt the fans, the players and manager Alan Pardew for weeks if not months to come.

Even if the psychological harm can be repaired, the damage to West Ham's promotion prospects is obvious, with the club now seven points adrift of table-toppers West Brom instead of the one they should have been.

Defoe certainly has to take a major share of the responsibility, needlessly sliding late into Sean Gregan with just seconds remaining on the first-half clock. His rash decision-making is costing the team valuable points. The performance of referee Mike Dean was also a talking point as supporters left the ground. He rushed to thrust the red card into Defoe's face with such eagerness that it was difficult to believe he didn't enjoy the moment.

And why was Defoe yellow-carded earlier for 'diving' outside the penalty box when Albion's Paul Robinson was allowed to escape unpunished for throwing himself to the floor in a bid to win a spot-kick?

This column last week insisted that new boss Pardew's influence could only be judged over a period of months rather than weeks.

That remains the case but Saturday's outcome will have severely damaged confidence in West Ham finishing in the top two come May.

Kirk now says: The Hammers drew six of their first seven games under Pardew, with the only defeat coming when a first win under the new boss seemed an absolute certainty after they went three goals ahead against West Brom in the opening 18 minutes only to then collapse.

FANS FED THE BROWN STUFF (20 November 2003)

The annual statement from West Ham chairman Terence Brown has not always resulted in a favourable reaction from the club's supporters.

Two years ago Brown unconvincingly pointed to a handful of Harry Redknapp's less successful signings to try and justify the dismissal of a manager that had kept the club in the Premiership for seven years.

Last year the chairman insisted the club was not prepared to 'gamble on 107 years of hard-earned history in the vain hope of achieving some unprecedented success on the pitch' – a 'belt-tightening' policy he later admitted the board had sadly misjudged.

And this year is no different, with Brown drawing irrelevant parallels between seasons 2000/01 and 2002/03, in which the first team accumulated 42 points on both occasions, in an effort to suggest that last term's relegation was simply 'unfortunate'.

Yet there is a big difference between waiting six games for a first home league victory and 13 games, as the club did last season.

In 2000/01 the side had won seven of its opening 20 Premiership games before then sliding towards danger, whereas it took manager Glenn Roeder a painful 31 outings to reach that tally last time around as the team languished in the drop zone for virtually the whole campaign.

The warning signs were therefore flashing so much earlier, brighter and louder last season and yet the club chose to back its struggling manager – a gamble that never looked like paying off.

Roeder rightfully paid the price, albeit nine months too late, but the club's hierarchy remains despite admitting to mistakes.

Of course, the directors may enjoy backslapping sessions over West Ham avoiding the kind of financial collapse that has threatened the likes of Ipswich, Derby, Bradford and Leicester following relegation.

But that is largely down to being able to cash-in on such playing assets as Joe Cole, Glen Johnson, Frederic Kanoute and Trevor Sinclair – to the tune of £18m – whereas those other outfits went down with poor squads of relatively low value.

The fact that West Ham were relegated with such quality players may have saved them financially but it also emphasises how it should never have been allowed to happen in the first place.

Last weekend saw the full England squad include three former Hammers youngsters sold for over £23.5m – and that's without omitted £18m defender Rio Ferdinand – while the chairman's statement confessed to the existence of a £48m 'borrowing facility'.

It is therefore difficult not to believe that public confidence in the club's leadership has diminished to a disturbingly low level.

Kirk now says: The fans knew that West Ham had been mismanaged to relegation – from the boardroom down to the coaching staff – and no amount of spin would convince them otherwise.

FA'S GAIN IS WEST HAM'S LOSS (4 December 2003)

Trevor Brooking's appointment as the Football Association's director of football development was announced just 24 hours after West Ham's 4-0 win against Wigan.

And Hammers fans are entitled to ponder how much the club director's departure from Upton Park will be felt in the long term.

The former England midfielder returned to West Ham as a non-executive director in 2001 to help bridge the gap between the boardroom and the training ground as the new management team of Glenn Roeder and Paul Goddard got their feet under the table.

How much influence he exerted during Roeder's reign is open to debate, but we can assume Brooking would have sought to offer his expertise to the club without being seen to interfere in the manager's affairs.

If anything, he probably offered too much of a defence for struggling Roeder by emphasising the team's troubles, whereas others would have focused more on the manager's inability to deal with those problems.

Brooking's efforts to keep a low profile fell by the wayside when he twice accepted the club's invitation to assume temporary control of first-team affairs this year and on both occasions he won instant acclaim. There is no doubting the man's in-depth knowledge of the game and great intelligence, but just as important was the common sense and simple logic he brought to the job.

He quickly proved he had far more to offer the game than had previously been exploited and the FA has now provided him with an ideal platform to use his skills.

All at West Ham wish him well in his new role and while some supporters have suggested that new manager Alan Pardew will now feel a greater sense of freedom, that's not necessarily the case. If anything, he has lost an ally.

Pardew secured his first win in eight games as Hammers boss on Saturday but was quick to emphasise that 'there's still a lot of work to do'.

He knows that in Jermain Defoe, David Connolly, Marlon Harewood and Brian Deane he has a strike-force that will frighten the rest of the First Division to death.

Fans will worry about the team's defensive lapses – and yet the clean sheet against Wigan last weekend saw the Hammers match Sunderland for having conceded the least number of goals in the division.

Which leaves the midfield as the biggest cause for concern, with a lack of width and creativity being the obvious obstacles to overcome.

If only Pardew had a certain Mr Brooking in his playing prime at his disposal.

Kirk now says: Brooking would be knighted the following year and the Boleyn Ground's Sir Trevor Brooking Stand, branded as such in 2009, serves as a reminder of one of West Ham's finest footballers and greatest ambassadors.

WILL CASH BE SPLASHED? (22 January 2004)

Football fans naturally get nervous when they see their clubs selling players.

They obviously wonder how much those men will be missed and what percentage of the transfer fees received will be re-invested in the first-team squad (if any).

Some reports have suggested that West Ham's agreements to sell David James and Ian Pearce (to Manchester City and Fulham respectively) were as a result of a financial crisis, with the club desperately offloading high earners to pay off debts.

Alan Pardew has acknowledged that the club's wage bill – the highest in the First Division – is a major consideration, but insists his chief motivation has been to raise funds for team rebuilding.

It was obvious after the recent home defeats by Stoke, Ipswich and Preston that the present team is unlikely to suddenly start showing the sort of form needed if automatic promotion is going to be achieved.

So Pardew has had to do something to shake things up, admitting the need to take 'educated gambles' as he wheels and deals.

And unless a club offers the £10m required to buy striker Jermain Defoe, he is going to be restricted to a limited budget, especially if the Hammers are looking to reduce their outgoings.

Therefore the club itself now needs to take 'an educated gamble' by deciding how much can be spent in the pursuit of promotion while considering the long-term implications if another season in Division One beckons.

The West Ham board faces a huge dilemma while the manager is presented with a massive challenge.

Only time will tell which parties pass their respective tests.

Kirk now says: West Ham did at least sign influential midfielder Nigel Reo-Coker for a bargain £500,000 at this time, although the less said about Jobi McAnuff and Adam Nowland (who also arrived from Wimbledon) the better.

WAS IT RIGHT TO SELL JER-MAIN MAN? (5 February 2004)

The decision to sell Jermain Defoe to Tottenham just hours before the Premiership transfer window closed represents a huge gamble by West Ham.

Up until that point the majority of Hammers fans had been feeling relieved that the window looked set to pass without a club making a sufficient bid for the want-away striker.

For many, it was imperative that Defoe stayed at Upton Park for the rest of the season because his goals were considered essential if West Ham were to win instant promotion back to the top flight.

That was certainly the club's stance when turning down the player's transfer request last summer and many will now consider the chances of going up to have been severely jeopardised.

There has, of course, been a growing feeling that, with the Hammers sliding out of promotion contention, it might be necessary to sacrifice Defoe in order to fund Alan Pardew's team rebuilding.

Such logic would have been accepted had the deal taken place three weeks ago, with Pardew then having time to target players from Premiership clubs.

But to sell the 21-year-old hitman at such a late stage seems pointless, with the Hammers now restricted to chasing players at First Division level or below.

This will increase the fear that the bulk of the £7m received will disappear into the black hole that has swallowed up so much other cash following the sale of the club's top players.

What will also disturb fans is Defoe's strange choice of destination.

Had he agreed to join the likes of Manchester United, Arsenal or Chelsea it would have been understandable. But to move to a mid-table outfit with little chance of playing Champions League football suggests far too much desperation on his part.

The pressure is now on West Ham to prove they have made the right decision – and the only way they can do that is by winning promotion in May.

A failure to do so will leave fans feeling that the club has once again shot itself in the foot, with the question forever remaining, what if Jermain Defoe had stayed?

Kirk now says: By the time this column was published, it had been announced that Spurs striker Bobby Zamora had made the opposite journey as a replacement for Jermain Defoe.

BOBBY COULD BE A DAZZLER (12 February 2004)

Bobby Zamora's appearance as a half-time substitute at Bradford saw the striker become the 22nd player to make his debut for West Ham this season – a quite astonishing statistic.

The members of that particular group include a clutch of seasoned professionals, a handful of youngsters, some loan signings who have come and gone, most of Wimbledon's midfield and players who can genuinely be considered as the faces of tomorrow.

Zamora certainly comes into the latter category and, of all the new recruits, is the one who perhaps holds the biggest key to West Ham's future – and not just because he finds himself stepping into the shoes of the latest big name to have been sold off by the club.

The 23-year-old striker, who arrived in part-exchange as Jermain Defoe moved to Tottenham, enjoyed a great start to his Hammers career by scoring on his debut in the 2-1 win at Bradford and it is obvious that manager Alan Pardew considers Zamora to be a huge talent.

Indeed, it's possible to believe the Hammers boss genuinely believes that Zamora, who scored 79 goals in 134 games for Brighton, can boost West Ham's promotion bid just as much as Defoe would have done upon his return from a second five-game suspension.

In which case, Pardew will feel he has secured an excellent deal for West Ham, not least because the manager clearly places a huge emphasis on his players wanting to represent the club – with Defoe failing miserably in that respect.

Zamora is a Hammers fan, having been a junior at the club before making his name elsewhere, while Defoe's enforced presence – for all the goals he would probably have scored – might have undermined the team spirit that Pardew is working so hard to develop.

That is why it is possible to understand the gamble that West Ham have taken in selling Defoe as the club seeks to gain promotion this season, although only time will tell if the right decision has been made.

Kirk now says: The signing of Bobby Zamora softened the blow of Jermain Defoe's departure, although his five goals in 20 outings were sadly not enough to win promotion for the Hammers.

HAMMERS THEIR OWN WORST ENEMY (26 February 2004)

West Ham's 1-1 draw at top-of-the-table Norwich may have extended the team's unbeaten run away from home to an impressive dozen games – but it was also the 12th time this season that they have failed to win a match after leading.

On most of those occasions, the Hammers have needlessly chucked away the points – with the Norwich game a classic example.

Marlon Harewood produced a great 20-yard strike to put West Ham ahead, only for Tomas Repka to undo all his good work during the game by heading the ball down for Darren Huckerby to equalise.

And it's been a similar story on most trips to other promotion contenders – a crazy Hayden Mullins own goal costing victory at West Brom and a misjudgement from goalkeeper Stephen Bywater allowing Sheffield United to recover from a 3-1 deficit.

Of course, we mustn't forget the home game against West Brom, with a 3-0 lead incredibly evaporating into a 4-3 defeat. Despite everything, with West Ham leading and second-placed Albion losing at 4.20pm on Saturday, the gap between the two sides could have been down to just six points – the Hammers also having a game in hand.

Sadly, with the way results eventually turned against them, West Ham are now 11 points adrift of an automatic promotion spot.

Needless to say, the team has given itself a huge mountain to climb.

The Hammers got relegated last season because they failed to deny fellow strugglers Bolton a win at the Reebok; this year an instant return to the Premiership will probably be lost because of the points foolishly given away to their closest rivals.

Kirk now says: The Hammers failed to win any of their games against the teams that ultimately secured automatic promotion, namely Norwich and West Brom.

IT'S TIME TO START PRAYING (15 April 2004)

West Ham manager Alan Pardew always tries to project an image of positivity yet few fans share his optimism at the moment.

The team have slipped out of the play-off positions after collecting only one point from three games, in which they have failed to find the net.

The 1-0 defeat at Crystal Palace on Monday means the Hammers have lost four successive away games.

Several players face suspension in the coming weeks, while injury problems make it impossible to find any continuity or build momentum.

Certain men are playing out of their favoured positions, there's an obvious lack of midfield creativity and defensive mistakes are costing the side dear.

It is little wonder that there's a growing feeling among fans that even if the Hammers were to somehow claim a play-off position, the odds would probably be against them winning them.

Pardew said he reckoned his men needed to win four of their last half a dozen games to make the top six, so that now means the Hammers need to win ALL of their remaining matches.

That is not likely to happen on current form.

And a final-day fixture at fellow play-off hopefuls Wigan has a rather ominous look about it.

As this column has previously stated, another season in Division One may not be a disaster from a football point of view, yet it certainly would be from a financial one.

It is time to start praying for a bit of good fortune because the Hammers certainly need some right now.

Kirk now says: Thankfully West Ham found a bit of form when most needed because they won their next three games, scoring eight goals without conceding, before heading to Wigan on the final day.

RELIEF GIVES WAY TO BELIEF (13 May 2004)

Alan Pardew may not admit to feeling a sense of relief at seeing his West Ham side finish fourth to secure their place in the promotion play-offs – but the club's supporters surely will.

It has been a long, hard season for the Hammers, with three managers naming 36 players – 24 of whom have made their first-team debuts this term – across 53 league and cup games.

The mid-April defeat at Crystal Palace saw the team slip to eighth in the table following a run of three games without so much as a goal.

Yet West Ham travelled to Wigan last weekend knowing a play-off place was secure as long as they avoided a four-goal defeat.

Given the club's habit of snatching defeat from the jaws of victory, there will have been some fans fearing the worst at the JJB Stadium.

The mathematical circumstances clearly had a huge influence on the team's performance and it is to the players' credit that they pursued a positive result, rather than simply accepting a 1-0 defeat that would have seen both Wigan and West Ham into the play-offs.

Brian Deane's 90th-minute equaliser determined that the Hammers now travel to Ipswich in the semi-finals rather than return to the JJB.

Pardew seemed pleased about not having to face a Wigan side that would have had the psychological advantage of their recent win as well as returning striker Jason Roberts in their favour.

The general belief is that Ipswich's relatively open style of play will suit the Hammers, but nothing can be taken for granted.

Pardew knows from his own experience at old club Reading that qualifying for the play-offs means little if you don't go on to win them.

So while it's a time for relief, it's not really one for celebration – for a few weeks at least.

Kirk now says: Wigan boss Paul Jewell, not surprisingly, looked a broken man after Deane's late header denied his side a play-off place and lifted Crystal Palace into the play-offs at their expense.

PUMP UP THE VOLUME (20 May 2004)

West Ham's win against Ipswich on Tuesday is likely to be remembered as one of the great Upton Park nights – for both the 2-0 scoreline that secured a place in the play-off final in Cardiff as well as the magnificent atmosphere generated by the club's loyal supporters.

The credit for both must go to Alan Pardew. The Hammers boss is nothing if not astute and it could be argued that his shrewdest decision at the beginning of the week was not one relating to team selection but how he played the media.

Pardew entered the press room following his side's 1-0 semi-final first-leg defeat at Portman Road preferring to avoid detailed analysis of the game for the sake of using the occasion to try to influence events still to come.

Psychology plays a major part in Pardew's weaponry and, having just witnessed the fantastic role played by the Ipswich fans in willing their team ahead, the West Ham manager was quick to warn the opposition of the hostile environment awaiting them in the return game.

Not only did this serve to intimidate those playing under Ipswich boss Joe Royle, who complained that some of his players mysteriously 'froze' at Upton Park, but also it threw down the gauntlet for Hammers fans to make their vast numbers heard.

They duly responded in brilliant fashion and with the pre-match pyrotechnics helping to create a winning atmosphere, the only concern was that the intensity would fade if West Ham failed to make an early breakthrough.

With Steve Lomas hitting the crossbar and Ipswich goalkeeper Kelvin Davis making great saves from Bobby Zamora and Christian Dailly in the first half, fans could have been forgiven for beginning to think it might prove to be one of those unfortunate nights.

The pace was frantic, frenetic and frenzied.

But justice was done when Matthew Etherington's superb drive and Dailly's less potent but just as rewarding effort confirmed West Ham's superiority.

Whatever happens in the play-off final against Crystal Palace, it can't be denied that Pardew's experience of play-off scenarios with former club Reading has already been put to great use.

Kirk now says: The atmosphere for the second leg against Ipswich was indeed like the bubbling Boleyn of old.

DON'T YOU HATE THAT THING CALLED FATE (3 June 2004)

As West Ham manager Alan Pardew reluctantly conceded this week, it seems as if some things are preordained.

From the moment that Brian Deane scored the equaliser at Wigan to hand Crystal Palace a last-gasp play-off place, it seemed inevitable that the Hammers would meet them in the final – and live to regret it.

For the last two months, Palace have enjoyed as much good fortune as it is possible to have.

They collected seven points from three games in which four members of the opposition were sent off.

They won their final home game thanks to a ridiculous last-minute penalty decision.

They then secured their play-off place as a result of events they had no control over.

In the semi-final second leg against Sunderland they levelled the aggregate score with a 92nd-minute goal that should have been ruled out.

The subsequent penalty shoot-out lottery then just happened to throw up Palace's numbers.

You always had the feeling that any luck being dished out in the final would land in Palace's lap.

And so it proved, courtesy of referee Graham Poll's refusal to award the Hammers a penalty when Michael Carrick was clearly fouled by Mikele Leigertwood.

Had West Ham equalised with eight minutes remaining, anything could have happened – but they would certainly have had the momentum behind them.

Poll only had one major decision to make during the game and yet he still managed to get it wrong.

The problem with Poll is that he always seems to have a personal agenda that is in direct conflict with the interests of the game.

He originally tried to make a name for himself by throwing out yellow and red cards like confetti.

Now he's eager to prove he won't be fooled into blowing just because a player has hit the deck – whether they have been fouled or not. Either way, it's all about Poll displaying his authority and showing us who is boss.

Losing a play-off final is bad enough but to feel cheated at the same time makes it much harder to stomach.

Of course, we mustn't lose sight of the fact that West Ham's performance on the day in the 1-0 defeat – courtesy of Neil Shipperley's second-half strike – was dreadfully disappointing.

They fell well short of their best, with several players letting the side down badly.

Pardew's decision to withdraw three strikers in the shape of Bobby Zamora, Marlon Harewood and David Connolly also left many scratching their heads as the final whistle approached.

So now the manager will be forced to offload his highest earning players while trying to build a team capable of making a stronger promotion challenge next season.

As this column has previously suggested, another season in Division One may not be a disaster from a football point of view.

Financially, however, it is a massive blow and it remains to be seen how long it will take for the bruises to heal.

Kirk now says: The only consolation – and it wasn't much of one – was that everybody knew that Palace would probably be relegated the following year. And they duly obliged.

REFLECTING ON SEASON 2003/04

Best signing: Marlon Harewood (Nottingham Forest), £500,000

Worst signing: Adam Nowland (Wimbledon), undisclosed

Best result: Winning 2-0 at home to Ipswich (play-off semi-final) in May

Worst result: Losing 1-0 to Crystal Palace (play-off final) in May

Final position: 4th in the First Division, 74 points

Manager and rating: Trevor Brooking 9/10, Alan Pardew 7/10

Best thing about season: Glenn Roeder being sacked

Worst thing about season: Failing to win promotion

SEASON 2004/05

'Failure could condemn club to years of mediocrity'

ALAN PARDEW took a huge gamble in the summer of 2004 when he decided to sell striker David Connolly to anticipated promotion rivals Leicester for £500,000 and replace him with veteran England international Teddy Sheringham on a free transfer from Portsmouth. Connolly, 27, had scored 14 goals the previous term and it seemed a crazy idea to sell him to the Foxes, who would be strengthened by West Ham's need to fund the acquisitions of the 38-year-old Sheringham and former Spurs team-mate Sergei Rebrov.

If West Ham missed out on promotion the following year, it was likely to be because Leicester had finished above them.

Yet these fears thankfully proved unfounded, with Leicester ending up a lowly 15th despite Connolly's 13-goal contribution, while Sheringham scored 21 goals for the Hammers to prove he still knew where the net was and how to make it bulge.

Winger Luke Chadwick arrived on a free transfer from Manchester United, while Jobi McAnuff was sold to Cardiff for £500,000 and Kevin Horlock and Brian Deane were both released.

The most high-profile departure – and one that seemed horribly inevitable – however, was that of Michael Carrick, who joined Tottenham in a paltry £2.75m deal that hardly reflected his quality (thanks to having just one year left on his contract) given that the midfielder would move to Manchester United for a fee of £18.6m just two years later.

Director Scott Duxbury had insisted he would try to secure 'the best transfer fee' for the Hammers but the club foolishly neglected to negotiate a sell-on figure, which must go down as one of the silliest things they have ever done (and that's really saying something).

TITLE TALK OR TITTLE-TATTLE? (16 September 2004)
Most managers are generally coy about revealing their true aspirations but Alan Pardew has repeatedly been open about the fact that West

Ham have one goal in sight this season – to win the Championship trophy.

No aiming for second place, no hoping for a play-off position, just the insistence that the Hammers finish top of the pile come next May.

For such a suggestion to be remotely convincing, it was imperative that the club did everything it could to enable the team to actually play a good game rather than just allow the manager to talk one.

Thankfully, in providing Pardew with the funds to recruit four new players prior to the away game at Sheffield United at the weekend, the board appear to be investing in the belief that automatic promotion is attainable.

Just a few weeks back, there was a suspicion that new recruits were going to be kept to the bare minimum, as the financial impact of a second season outside of the Premiership began to hit hard.

Gates are badly down on last year's figures and, with it being revealed that the £2.75m from Michael Carrick's recent sale to Spurs was needed as security in case the club missed out on promotion, there was the genuine fear that little or nothing would be spent on the team.

The likes of Coventry, Derby and Sheffield Wednesday splashed nothing when offloading their high earners following relegation.

But a defensive injury crisis and the realisation that a third term in football's second tier would represent another catastrophe – not least due to the loss of parachute payments – have prompted the board to push the boat out as far as they feel they can.

Admittedly, two of the four signings are loan deals (including Chris Powell), but the £575,000 spent on Malky Mackay and Carl Fletcher can be put into perspective by recognising how little cash was exchanged by the majority of Premiership clubs during the recent transfer window. And the temporary acquisition of £3m defender Calum Davenport from Tottenham represents a clever bit of business, despite the needless moaning from his former club Coventry.

West Ham's hierarchy hasn't got much to be proud of in the last few years, so let's be grateful for small mercies.

Whether Pardew has recruited the right players or filled the right holes in the team is a matter of debate. Few can argue with the view that the defence badly needed reinforcing, although some will still worry about Hayden Mullins being forced to play in a right-back role.

Pardew believes his squad can win the division – now it's time for the players and management to deliver.

Kirk now says: The suggestion that West Ham could win the division seems laughable in retrospect considering they ultimately finished a massive 21 points adrift of top-of-the-table Sunderland.

IT'S ROUGH ON CLOUGH DAY (30 September 2004)

West Ham fans travelled to Nottingham Forest at the weekend with two pieces of hard-earned knowledge.

Firstly, that when it comes to party pooping, the Hammers are one of the worst teams around.

And secondly, when a side hasn't won at home in recent memory, they only need to get West Ham down for a game to virtually guarantee themselves a welcome three points.

The events at the City Ground on Sunday will have done little to change their view that, given the circumstances, defeat was sadly inevitable.

With Forest boss Joe Kinnear confessing that the recent death of former manager Brian Clough acted as a huge motivational tool – in terms of wanting to reward the Nottingham public for their show of respect and support – it was always going to be a difficult outing for the visitors.

Add the fact that Forest had yet to win a league game this season and the script was clearly written long before the Hammers' bus turned into the car park.

One only needs to recall the time when West Ham meekly surrendered to a Bolton side that hadn't won in the previous ten home league games two years ago to realise how accommodating they can be to struggling opposition when the mood takes them.

With just 120 seconds of injury time signalled on Sunday, most would have thought the Hammers could have held on for at least one of the three points that looked fairly safe until Forest wiped out Marlon Harewood's opener with six minutes of the game remaining.

But long-time West Ham fans knew better – and their fears were realised when substitute Marlon King curled in the winner with virtually the last kick of the match.

The one consolation was that the goal would have brought a smile to the late Mr Clough, for whom both sets of supporters impeccably observed a minute's silence before kick-off.

For Hammers fans, however, the result simply confirmed that certain leopards can never change their spots.

Kirk now says: The recent death of Brian Clough made it a memorable – if still a rather disappointing – day and plenty of Hammers fans bought into the emotion of the occasion by snapping up the merchandise on offer in tribute to the great man. Wonder if it's now worth anything …

ONE COIN CAN'T CAUSE CANCER (4 November 2004)

The headlines following West Ham's Carling Cup defeat at Chelsea last week were dominated by references to the 'outbreak of violence' in the section of Stamford Bridge reserved for away supporters.

On the basis of a few photographs of the police making their presence felt among Hammers fans, national newspapers indulged themselves in producing the predictable rhetoric of the game sinking back to the dark ages of the 1970s and 1980s as the 'cancer' of 'hooliganism' reared its ugly head again.

What a shame that more people couldn't have paid more attention to the actual facts.

Of the 41,774 paying spectators at the match, just 16 were arrested – only SIX of which were West Ham fans.

There was no fighting whatsoever between rival supporters, as one would expect to be the case if the game had regressed the 25 years that had been suggested.

The only scenes of friction in the lower tier of the Matthew Harding Stand took place after the police had decided to make themselves busy.

Of course, it mustn't be forgotten that Chelsea striker Mateja Kezman was struck by a coin during the game.

Thankfully, he preferred not to exploit the incident in a way that many other players surely would have had they been given half a chance. Hats must be taken off to the man.

But with the Serb being surrounded by half a dozen Hammers players at the time, it's impossible to draw definite conclusions as to which person the coin was aimed at and by whom it was thrown.

West Ham goalkeeper Jimmy Walker was also reported to have been the target of various objects, so are we to believe that he was the victim of his own supporters?

Furthermore, it should not be forgotten that missiles appeared to be thrown from the top tier, inhabited by home fans looking down on visiting supporters below them.

In this context, it would seem ludicrous for the Football Association to meet the hysterical demands of the media for West Ham to be penalised for something over which they had no control.

Nobody is suggesting that guilty parties should not be punished.

It was indeed the responsibility of the police and Chelsea's stewards to ensure that nobody broke the law.

But that doesn't mean that innocent fans should be indiscriminately labelled as 'thugs' just because of the team they support or the actions of a few morons. Or that the image of the game should be unnecessarily tarnished because of the deep-rooted desire of the national media to exaggerate, distort and manipulate situations to suit their own ends.

Kirk now says: It is easy to get accused of bias when defending the behaviour of West Ham fans after headlines have been made for the wrong reasons, but if the local press aren't going to set the record straight when the national media are whipping up hysteria and trotting out the same old cliches, then who the hell is?

MORE MISERY AT MILLWALL (25 November 2004)

Alan Pardew may not have had the look of a broken man after the 1-0 defeat at Millwall but the West Ham manager certainly had the demeanour of a battered one.

Whether it was more the result, the show of dissent of unhappy Hammers fans or the injustice of seeing his side reduced to ten men following Marlon Harewood's sending off is open to debate.

But whereas Pardew would usually enter press conferences with a spirit of fortitude, resolutely standing arms folded behind a desk, on this occasion he sat down with almost an air of resignation, as if the afternoon's events had knocked the stuffing out of him.

Nobody could blame him, of course, with the feeling being that little is going West Ham's way this season.

Pardew has been deprived of key players through injury and lost games because of red cards, with Harewood becoming the fifth Hammer to have received his marching orders this term.

There are things that managers cannot legislate for, with referee Peter Walton showing no benefit of the doubt to Harewood as he swung the pendulum of fortune in Millwall's direction.

Where Pardew can occasionally be questioned are the matters he does have direct control over, namely his purchase of players, team selection and match strategy.

His decision to deploy a five-man midfield against Millwall was understandable given last season's 4-1 disaster at The Den, the recent defeat at Cardiff by the same scoreline and the fact that Darren Powell and Mauricio Taricco were making their debuts in defence.

But his substitution of Luke Chadwick, who was enjoying his best game for the Hammers, angered fans that are still trying to fathom out why three strikers were taken off during the play-off final defeat in May when the team was a goal down to Crystal Palace.

The fact that these unlikely decisions rarely work in the team's favour, as was the case on Sunday, is doing nothing to improve Pardew's relationship with the supporters.

That is not to say the former Reading chief has not achieved much in his year at West Ham.

Pardew has been forced to build a brand new team, selling the likes of Jermain Defoe, David James and Michael Carrick in the process to reduce the wage bill and raise money to ease the club's debts.

Some 24 players made their West Ham debuts last season and another 13 have already done so this term as he tries to point the Boleyn's ship in the right direction.

At the same time, the manager is trying to impose his own character on the team while trying to consider the club's traditional philosophies, prompting some to wonder whether they are indeed compatible with each other.

Given time, Pardew's methods may well succeed but, as he acknowledges all too readily himself, he hasn't got much of that ticking stuff on his side at the moment.

And if the promotion that's been demanded – and he indeed expected of himself – is not delivered next May, he will sadly be considered to have failed.

Kirk now says: The result at Millwall – coming after a 1-0 home defeat by Brighton – meant that West Ham had won just once in five league games and a sense of desperation was beginning to creep in. Mauricio Taricco left the field after 27 minutes in his one and only appearance for the Hammers (apparently injured but looking more hurt at being substituted) and duly ripped up his contract.

AND NOW FOR THE SNOOZE (6 January 2005)

Rumour has it that Alan Pardew took his West Ham players into the club's press room a couple of hours before the game against Sheffield United on Monday to play them a video tape on the TV monitors.

One can only speculate as to what was screened, be it an episode of *Emmerdale* to prepare the Hammers for visitors from Yorkshire or a programme on stress relief through self-hypnosis.

Either way, it appeared to send the players into a deep slumber from which they struggled to escape during a 2-0 defeat that saw the team produce not a single shot on target.

This would be disappointing enough at any stage of the season but to come just two days after a morale-boosting win at table-toppers Ipswich is difficult for supporters to accept.

The week began with reports of West Ham considering a move for former Tottenham chief David Pleat if results and performances did not start to show a consistent improvement.

The insipid display against the Blades on Monday hardly suggested the players were trying too hard to keep their existing manager in a job.

There is no disputing the fact that Pardew faced a huge challenge in trying to build a promotion-winning side while selling top players and reducing the club's wage bill at the same time.

But the former Reading boss was always well aware of the need to win promotion within his first two seasons and it would seem that the Hammers board have become increasingly nervous as they consider the financial consequences of another possible year of failure.

Pardew has worked tirelessly in his quest to bring the club success and is entitled to believe that those calling for his head at the beginning of the week should have displayed far more patience.

And he's got a point, particularly with a change of management at this stage representing a massive gamble by West Ham. What happens next is anyone's guess but the fact remains that the margins for error are becoming ever more slender as the weeks of the season pass by.

Kirk now says: Defeat dropped the Hammers down to sixth in the Championship table and speculation about Alan Pardew's future was beginning to pick up steam.

PRESSURE BUILDS ON PARDS (27 January 2005)

Minutes after West Ham's 2-1 home defeat by Derby on Sunday, this columnist asked Alan Pardew if the club's directors had reassured him about his position in the wake of stories that another loss – following the 4-2 disaster at Wolves – would cost him his job.

'I haven't asked the question,' he responded, not looking too pleased at the spotlight being turned on his face.

Pardew may not have contacted his bosses before the game but it was also evident that they had not approached him either to put his mind at rest.

This paper understands that Pardew's position is indeed safe for the remainder of the campaign, with it being believed that a change at this point of time would undermine the club's promotion chances.

The manager's task was to try and return the club to the Premiership within his first two seasons and the feeling is that he should at least be given that period of time to prove himself.

There is also the recognition that it's now virtually impossible for the Hammers to claw back the 12-point gap that exists between the club and the automatic promotion spots, whoever is in charge.

So it's now a case of everybody pulling together to mount an assault on one of the play-off places, which given the fact the team has now slipped down to ninth is by no means a formality.

Maybe it's hoped by some that Pardew may achieve more if he suspects his job is on the line.

But it would surely be in everybody's best interests if the club publicly declares their backing of the manager and let's hope it happens sooner rather than later.

Kirk now says: No such declaration from the club was forthcoming, so Pardew and the fans were left to hope that improving results would secure the manager's future.

'NOT MANY PEOPLE LIKED ALAN PARDEW' (17 March 2005)

Make no mistake, West Ham's 3-1 defeat at Reading on Saturday represents yet another huge embarrassment for the club.

The Royals had not won a league fixture in 2005, going some 11 games without victory and failing to score more than once in any of their last 14 outings.

Yet a woeful lack of organisation at the back and little inspiration going forward saw the Hammers make Steve Coppell's side look like Champions League winners by comparison.

It was obvious that Reading were going to be hungry to repeat last season's home success against former manager Alan Pardew, with goalkeeper Marcus Hahnemann warning, 'This game for us is like Rangers against Celtic.'

That is something of an overstatement, yet the Hammers once again failed to match their opponents in terms of spirit and determination.

It is little wonder that fans are asking big questions of Pardew, who is clearly failing to get the best out of his under-achieving players.

Perhaps Hahnemann offered a clue as to why that may be when he revealed, 'Not many people liked Alan Pardew when he was at Reading. There were guys who didn't see eye to eye with him.'

The West Ham boss would insist he's not interested in making friends, simply winning football matches.

That is fine, but he's not winning enough football matches at the moment – and that certainly won't help him gain friends.

And it's still hard to argue against the belief that a good relationship with his players can only help any manager.

It has been rumoured that Pardew's authoritarian approach has rubbed a few people up the wrong way.

So while he may indeed have the respect of the players as a coach, it might require a bit more than that to get them performing at their very best. Conversely, it's suspected that former Hammers boss Glenn Roeder was liked but not particularly respected, which might explain how he managed to relegate a side containing such talents as Joe Cole, Michael Carrick and Jermain Defoe.

It might not be coincidence that Sir Trevor Brooking – a man clearly liked AND respected – had the best record of the lot of them during his short period as caretaker boss.

Kirk now says: Pardew's critics within the club would later accuse him of arrogance, with the manager putting several noses out of joint behind the scenes as he tried to make his presence felt at Upton Park. Long-time photographer Steve Bacon has plenty of good stories to tell.

TC WANTS TO BE TOP CAT AT UPTON PARK (24 March 2005)

Reports that former West Ham striker Tony Cottee has been looking to spearhead a possible takeover of the club in the summer will inevitably be greeted with enthusiasm from supporters.

After all, fans have made their feelings about the current Hammers hierarchy clearly known over the last couple of years.

They question why the board of directors jeopardised the club's top-flight status by dismissing a manager whose methods were proven (Harry Redknapp) and then appointed a near novice whose inexperience proved costly (Glenn Roeder).

They question how a club can produce such homegrown talents as Rio Ferdinand, Frank Lampard, Joe Cole, Glen Johnson, Michael Carrick and Jermain Defoe – the best crop of youngsters from one academy since the emergence of Manchester United's teenagers during the early 1990s – and ultimately find themselves relegated from the Premiership.

They question how a club can raise around £60m through the sale of its top players in three years and yet still find itself £33.8m in debt.

The supporters will therefore hardly be crying into their beer over the potential demise of a board that has presided over these spectacular failings and one that many believe has been driven by far too much self-interest.

Of course, there is no point in new investors inheriting control of a club if they don't have sufficient funds to initiate significant change once they have taken over.

Incoming parties would first have to persuade chairman Terence Brown to relinquish power by selling his large stake in the Hammers – far more likely if the club fails to secure promotion via the play-offs – and then try to reduce the debt while funding team rebuilding.

That represents a mountainous task and only time will tell if these parties really have the resources to see the project through.

But the popular view amongst the support is that the club certainly requires a new regime – one with vision, ambition and a genuine knowledge of football – if it is to stand any real hope of achieving meaningful success in the future.

Kirk now says: Cottee's efforts were sincere and well intended but he was unable to raise sufficient funds to turn his dream of securing a position of power at the club he supported as a boy into reality, although he would continue to work on the project for another 18 months.

IT'S A MASOCHIST'S DREAM (5 May 2005)

The fact that following West Ham involves the conflicting emotions of agony and ecstasy was highlighted in this column a week ago – and the point was proved yet again at the weekend.

Both the Hammers and closest play-off rivals Reading fell to depressing 2-1 home defeats to slip out of the all-important top-six places following their games on Friday and Saturday respectively.

Yet both outfits experienced the delight of moving up into them without actually playing at the time.

Thankfully, the situation leaves West Ham on the right side of the dotted line, having scored more goals than the Royals who have the same points total and goal difference.

It arms the Hammers with the knowledge that they simply have to match Reading's result at automatic promotion hopefuls Wigan when they travel to Watford on Sunday to secure a chance of a lifeline to the Premiership.

What it promises is that the final weekend of the Championship season will produce even more pain and pleasure for supporters.

And with fifth-placed Derby suffering a heavy loss at Coventry, it also means that both West Ham and Reading could be celebrating if final-day wins for them coincide with a victory for Preston at Pride Park.

It all looks so much more positive for Hammers fans than it did on Friday, when the 2-1 defeat by champions Sunderland left them contemplating a near-certain third season of football outside the top flight.

In many ways the result summed up exactly why some 21 points separate the two clubs, with Sunderland stealing a late victory with a typically workmanlike but effective and efficient performance.

A comparison of the line-ups would leave most West Ham fans keen to transfer no more than three players from north to south.

The Black Cats squad included Hammers cast-offs in the shape of veterans Gary Breen and Brian Deane, for example.

Yet it's obvious that Sunderland's teamwork has ultimately proved so much more valuable than the combined worth of West Ham's individual talents over the course of the season.

The reasons behind that can be debated at another time, however.

All that currently matters is that the Hammers deliver what's required of them at Vicarage Road on Sunday – and keep hopes of a much-needed return to the Premiership alive.

Kirk now says: A column that sounds surprisingly optimistic given that so much rested on the final-day trip to Watford, but thankfully the Hammers duly held their nerve to secure a 2-1 win that saw them finish sixth in the table and book their place in the play-offs for a second consecutive year.

AN UNHAPPY ROYLE (12 May 2005)

Ipswich manager Joe Royle had a face like thunder on the evening of 18 May last year.

Not only had his men just been defeated in the second leg of their play-off semi-final at West Ham to be condemned to another season in the Championship, but also his team bus had embarrassingly become wedged between the gates of the Boleyn Ground car park.

Poor Royle cringed in the front seat as Hammers fans gleefully chanted, 'We'll never play you again!'

But play them again West Ham did, with defeat in the play-off final against Crystal Palace leaving them to battle it out against Ipswich all over again for a place in the Premiership.

Town recovered well from their setback, pushing hard for an automatic promotion spot before losing out to Wigan on the final day of the league campaign.

And so here we are again, with both the Hammers and Ipswich set to meet in another play-off semi-final and both legs taking place on the very same dates as last year.

Once again it's impossible to predict the outcome.

Many believe that Ipswich's attacking approach will suit West Ham's style – as was the case last year.

That theory is supported by the fact that the Hammers are unbeaten in the two league games between the sides this season and that they won convincingly at Portman Road on New Year's Day.

Yet West Ham's Jekyll and Hyde nature will always leave fans unsure of what characteristics are going to be displayed on any given day.

All we can do is keep our fingers crossed that a certain Ipswich manager is looking rather glum come 18 May because the gates of promotion have closed on him once again.

Kirk now says: Gates of promotion? Geddit? The fact that West Ham had squeezed past Ipswich the previous year gave the team the serious belief that they could once again progress through the play-off semi-final stage to claim a winner-takes-all place in Cardiff.

URIAH HEAP OF TROUBLE (19 May 2005)

Allocating referees to games may not be the most exciting job in the world – but that doesn't mean that somebody from the Football League should have a bit of fun at West Ham's expense.

The decision to name Uriah Rennie as the official in charge of the Hammers' play-off semi-final first leg at Upton Park last weekend defied all logic and common sense.

Here is a man whose incompetence once saw him dropped from the Premiership list, who has been frequently accused of arrogance by managers and players and is renowned for inconsistency, erratic judgement and poor decision-making.

As one reporter mentioned during Saturday's game, the only thing you're guaranteed with Rennie in charge is a (Uriah) heap of controversy.

So you would assume the Football League would play things safe by appointing a 'steady Eddie' for one of the Championship's most important matches of the season.

Instead, they go for a 'silly Billy', a man whose flexible interpretations of the rules of the game appear to be dictated by which way the wind is blowing at any given point in time.

No wonder some of us were holding our heads in our hands when we saw Rennie's name on the team-sheet. Needless to say he lived up to his reputation, with his contentious free-kick award to Ipswich in the final minute of the first half proving a bitter pill to swallow.

Not only did he move the ball forward following Tomas Repka's dissent (strange how he never took such action whenever Town disputed his calls), but also he then made a complete mess of the situation by forcing the Hammers wall back at least 12 yards.

The resulting goal, with Tommy Miller's shot hitting a post and rebounding off goalkeeper Jimmy Walker, knocked the wind out of West Ham's sails and swung the momentum of the game firmly in Ipswich's favour.

Town duly took advantage to level after the break and it left West Ham having to travel for Wednesday's second leg with the score delicately poised at 2-2.

The Hammers had gone 2-0 ahead through goals created by lively winger Matthew Etherington, who manager Alan Pardew insisted had been targeted for some heavy treatment by the opposition.

One late challenge from behind went unpunished and yet when Etherington then committed a foul he was promptly booked.

Rennie's performance had both managers fuming after the game, with Pardew complaining, 'The inconsistency of the referee was a problem all day. It was so frustrating.'

It was all so predictable, of course – maybe even to the gentleman from the Football League who might even have chuckled as he assigned Rennie to the game at Upton Park.

Kirk now says: And to think that Rennie is supposed to give you pain relief, not a headache.

DELIVER ... OR DIE (26 May 2005)

It is incredible to think that West Ham once had a team featuring such high-calibre stars as Trevor Brooking, Billy Bonds, Alan Devonshire, Alvin Martin, Phil Parkes, Paul Goddard, Frank Lampard, David Cross and Ray Stewart playing Second Division football.

Back in those days – 1980/81 to be exact – clubs could pursue the dream of promotion to the top flight in the knowledge there would be a good chance of survival (the Hammers finished in the top ten three years in succession after going up).

That is not necessarily the case now, of course, with a huge gulf in quality having opened up between teams in the top two divisions.

The structure of the professional game has changed over the last two decades and what it means is that securing a place in the Premiership is not about football now but about finance.

Indeed, it's probably not overstating the case to say that the outcome of West Ham's Championship play-off final against Preston on Monday will determine the club's entire future.

Victory at the Millennium Stadium in Cardiff would secure an immediate £20m windfall and provide the financial security that has been in doubt since the Hammers were relegated two years ago.

Defeat, however, would see the loss of parachute payments and the severance of the financial umbilical cord that has helped keep the club alive since 2003.

With the club a reported £30m in debt, the banks are likely to start getting nervous and it will again be suggested that the threat of administration looms large.

Whether that's the case or not, failure to win promotion at this attempt could condemn West Ham to years of mediocrity in football's wilderness.

Next week's meeting with Preston is likely to prove pivotal in the club's history.

There are those who have suggested that, from a football point of view, the Hammers are not quite ready to take on the Premiership.

That may be right, but they're missing the point. Even if immediate relegation back to the Championship was a cast-iron certainty, it's still imperative that West Ham reclaim their place among the game's elite – if only to set itself on a stable financial footing once again.

It is funny to think that when the likes of Brooking and Bonds were plying their trade as players, relegation to football's second tier probably meant increased income as a result of higher gates when winning games.

The Hammers' average home attendance actually grew after suffering the drop in 1978.

That was before television rights, sponsorship and merchandise became vital revenue streams for clubs.

Needless to say, West Ham simply MUST deliver the goods against Preston on Monday.

Kirk now says: Crikey, talk about cranking up the pressure ahead of the big game.

THE CYCLE OF MISERY IS OVER (2 JUNE 2005)

West Ham began life in the Championship two years ago with an opening-day fixture at Preston North End.

How fitting that the Hammers should escape from the division following victory against the same club.

West Ham supporters were, perhaps unusually, feeling optimistic about the play-off final at the Millennium Stadium on Monday.

Whereas last year's final carried an air of inevitability about Crystal Palace emerging victorious, the strong feeling this time was that the Hammers were going to make their superiority really count.

Fans drew extra confidence from small omens.

Supporters of the League 1 and League 2 play-off winners – Sheffield Wednesday and Southend United – had also occupied the South Stand of the Millennium Stadium, so the trend simply had to continue.

Southend finished fourth in their division and Wednesday fifth. So with West Ham coming home sixth, the pattern had to be completed.

Such observations seem trivial now, but sometimes fate throws up sequences of coincidence that fans can hang their hats on.

Yet for all the anticipation and expectation, it still took time for the fact that West Ham are a Premiership club again to fully sink in once the final whistle on the 1-0 win had blown.

It has been a long, painful two years for the club, but it's time to pay credit where it is due.

Alan Pardew was recruited with the instruction to return the club to the top flight within a two-year period and that's exactly what he has done.

It may not have been in the totally convincing fashion we would have liked, with automatic promotion never really looking likely and a play-off place only being secured on the final day of the league season.

Pardew's performance has come under heavy scrutiny, with punters and pundits often questioning whether his methods were going to work.

He has now admitted that he began to develop his own doubts as the Hammers spent the whole of March and April outside the play-off zone.

But Pardew stayed focused, displayed resilience and remained positive.

Ultimately, he has fashioned a promotion-winning team while reducing the wage bill and the club's debts – and for that we should all be grateful.

West Ham are back in the Premiership where the club and their supporters belong – and boy does it feel good.

Kirk now says: Pardew literally bounced into the press room after the game and slapped this writer on the back – as if to say, 'Ha! Proved you wrong, didn't I?' He was entitled to look just a little bit pleased with himself, though, admitting that had West Ham not won 'the biggest game in our history', the club would have been 'trapped in the Championship for years'. He conceded that 'it got very close to the directors having to make a decision about me' during the season when there was huge pressure to succeed. However, with a place in the Premiership now secure, the 'cycle of misery' was finally over.

REFLECTING ON SEASON 2004/05

Best signing: Teddy Sheringham (Portsmouth), free

Worst signing: Sergei Rebrov (Tottenham), free

Best result: Winning 1-0 against Preston (play-off final) in May

Worst result: Losing 1-0 at Millwall in November

Final position: 6th in the Championship, 73 points

Manager and rating: Alan Pardew 8/10

Best thing about season: Winning promotion

Worst thing about season: Watching the side under-perform to scrape into the play-offs

SEASON 2005/06

'An explosion of tears, cheers and a few beers'

PERHAPS the most amusing moment after West Ham's 1-0 play-off final victory in Cardiff came when 'interviewing' Preston assistant boss David Kelly at the Celtic Manor Hotel.

There was no real need to speak to the former West Ham striker, who seemed to spend half his time at Upton Park on his backside rather than scoring goals, but there was something sadistically satisfying about asking Kelly to reveal the painful emotions of seeing promotion slip away by a single goal (as the Hammers had the previous year).

Let us just say he didn't look happy …

Hammers chairman Terence Brown told Alan Pardew that he had a budget of £20m to cover new signings including salaries and he spent well on the likes of defenders Paul Konchesky (Charlton), Danny Gabbidon and James Collins (both Cardiff), plus Israeli playmaker Yossi Benayoun (Racing Santander).

Goalkeeper Roy Carroll arrived on a free transfer from Manchester United and Shaka Hislop returned from Portsmouth, while Teddy Sheringham and Tomas Repka remained on board despite question marks about their futures. Meanwhile, Don Hutchison, Malky Mackay and Steve Lomas jumped on the tube to join Millwall, Watford and QPR respectively, while Rufus Brevett and Chris Powell were released.

Pardew was listed as 5/1 second favourite for the sack behind Newcastle boss Graeme Souness (who lasted until February) and his hopes for success were not boosted by his failure to secure the big-name striker he had been looking for.

However, the Hammers went into the new campaign on the back of an eight-game unbeaten pre-season run (ignoring the penalty shoot-out defeat by Osasuna) and this columnist was in unusually optimistic mood when predicting that the team might just 'surprise a few people' – and so it proved.

HOW HEAVY WILL BENNI BLOW BE? (8 September 2005)

A lucky 13 Premiership clubs were successful in signing at least one new player on transfer deadline day on Wednesday.

Sadly, West Ham were not one of them, with the club's attempts to sign striker Benni McCarthy ending in failure after Porto refused to accept a bid of £6.1m for the South Africa international.

Hammers boss Alan Pardew admitted that he felt 'a mixture of anger and disappointment' after seeing the deal collapse at the death despite the player indicating his wish to move to Upton Park.

It was the second time the club had experienced such frustration in the summer, with Emmanuel Adebayor seemingly heading the Hammers' way before Monaco performed a U-turn and pulled the plug on the transaction.

West Ham certainly don't appear to have had too much in the way of luck in their efforts to sign a big-money striker as they embark on their return to the Premiership.

The club was also unsuccessful in bids for Peter Crouch and Milan Baros before they signed for Liverpool and Aston Villa respectively.

Some fans will inevitably question if West Ham's hierarchy could have handled things differently, believing that a price for McCarthy should have been established long before the day the transfer window closed. The real concern, however, is how the Hammers will overcome the handicap of having to soldier on throughout the first half of the campaign without the striking reinforcement they obviously feel they need.

Frenchmen David Bellion and Jeremie Aliadiere have been recruited on season-long loans, but if Pardew genuinely believed they could be relied upon to score goals on a regular basis he wouldn't have been making £6m bids for other forwards.

As the deadline for signings neared, the fear was that West Ham's promising start to the season had convinced the manager that perhaps a new hitman was not so vital after all.

That appears not to have been the case, though.

The fact remains that while four points have been collected from the opening three fixtures, the Hammers have averaged just a goal a game and their failure to convert chances against Bolton last time out resulted in the club's first defeat.

We are now left keeping our fingers crossed that Teddy Sheringham, Marlon Harewood, Bobby Zamora and the aforementioned Bellion and Aliadiere can score enough goals between them to keep West Ham in a comfortable position before the transfer window opens again in January. By that time we'll know exactly how damaging the lack of a new big-money striker will have proved to be.

Kirk now says: McCarthy remained at Porto for another season before signing for Blackburn, where he remained for nearly four years and eventually joined the Hammers, for whom he failed to score in 14 outings and was heavily criticised for his weight and fitness problems. As suspected, Aliadiere and Bellion made next to no impact, but thankfully Harewood, Zamora and Sheringham were able to shoulder the weight of goalscoring responsibility for the first half of the campaign.

HAREWOOD ENDS EIGHT-YEAR WAIT (15 September 2005)

Hat-tricks from West Ham players at Upton Park are as rare as the buses in Green Street running on time, so fans should treasure Marlon Harewood's superb treble against Aston Villa on Monday evening.

For the record, the previous Hammer to achieve such a feat in a Premiership game at the Boleyn Ground was Paul Kitson, who scored three times in a 5-1 victory against Sheffield Wednesday back in May 1997.

In September that year his strike partner John Hartson notched a treble in a Coca-Cola Cup outing against Huddersfield Town, while Frank Lampard did likewise in the same competition against Walsall two months later.

Kitson also scored three in the 4-4 draw with Charlton at The Valley in November 2001, while Jermain Defoe and Matthew Etherington both claimed hat-tracks during the 2003/04 season, with Cardiff and MK Dons on the receiving end.

But it has been EIGHT long years since any Hammers player dared score more than twice in a top-flight league match at Upton Park and such a statistic puts Harewood's hat-trick against Villa in true perspective. The striker's performance as he inspired West Ham to a 4-0 romp was in stark contrast to his last outing when he squandered a number of good opportunities during the 2-1 home defeat by Bolton.

Manager Alan Pardew admitted the 26-year-old had not exactly enjoyed one of his better days, with fans also recognising that the Hammers are hardly in a position to go wasting chances as they try to re-establish themselves in the Premiership.

Many may have anticipated a similar scenario in the televised clash against Villa and when Etherington, Paul Konchesky, Tomas Repka and Yossi Benayoun all failed to net with the game's early opportunities, the fear was that the opposition would make them pay.

Enter Harewood, who promptly despatched three of his four chances into the back of the net in ruthless fashion.

Had Michael Owen struck such goals, we would all have been acknowledging why Newcastle paid £16m to bring the England striker back to his homeland.

The difference between Owen and Harewood, of course, is that the former has made his name through sheer consistency while the latter has often frustrated supporters with his erratic nature.

As Hammers boss Alan Pardew rightly pointed out, Harewood has always scored goals and his career record now shows that he has netted 95 times in 303 first-team outings.

Harewood has scored several brilliant goals in the claret and blue but also left fans tearing their hair out over some of his wastefulness.

The game at Sheffield United last season springs to mind, with the striker missing a virtual open goal from a few feet out only to then smack one in from 25 yards a short while later.

Having helped the Hammers to promotion last term with 22 goals, Harewood certainly deserves his chance in the Premiership.

He has hit back at the critics by showing what he is capable of, so it's now up to him to prove that he can maintain the high standards he has set himself.

Kirk now says: Marlon was a confidence player but he was also much better when reacting instinctively rather than trying to think, if you catch the drift.

MAKING PLANS FOR NIGEL (6 October 2005)

It is not uncommon for Nigel Reo-Coker's name to be heard being sung on the platforms of Upton Park station once a few pints have been guzzled following a successful West Ham home outing.

So fans will surely have celebrated the news of the midfielder signing a new five-year contract with a few cheers and beers.

The announcement was somewhat timely, with the 21-year-old's name being mentioned as a potential target for Manchester United following Roy Keane's announcement that he fails to see himself remaining at Old Trafford beyond the end of the campaign.

It is unlikely that United boss Sir Alex Ferguson would consider the West Ham youngster as being quite ready to take on Europe's finest as he looks to make Champions League progress.

But Reo-Coker has so far made a career out of showing maturity well beyond his limited years in the game.

He captained the club formerly known as Wimbledon at the age of 19 and has since skippered both West Ham and England's Under-21 sides with success.

And many hold the view that he will inevitably progress to captain his country at full level at some future point in time.

Having arrived at Upton Park in January last year, it didn't take long for Reo-Coker to suggest that Alan Pardew had made an astute signing for a fee believed to be around the £500,000 mark.

It is fair to say that Nigel struggled to consistently impose himself on games in the Championship last season, to the point where he occasionally found himself on the substitutes' bench in the second half of the campaign.

This season has been a different story, however, with the midfielder playing a key role as the Hammers have quickly adapted to life back in the Premiership.

Now that he has started making those surging runs through the midfield on a more regular basis, supporters feel optimistic that there is a lot more to come from the player as he continues to develop.

Consistency will surely come with age, while it's hoped that he can show more precision with his final pass and greater potency in front of goal. As Reo-Coker progresses, though, he will only attract greater interest from bigger outfits and Hammers fans are no strangers to seeing the club's best young talents heading off to pastures new.

Some reassurance can be gained from the fact the player has committed himself to West Ham until 2010, but few believe he will still be gracing the Boleyn Ground turf on a regular basis at that time.

As the club have proved on many occasions, they have simply protected their investment by ensuring that a huge transfer fee can be commanded once the time comes around for a key player to move on.

It is the right thing to do, of course, with the funds from the sales of Rio Ferdinand, Frank Lampard, Glen Johnson and Joe Cole, for example, helping to safeguard the club's financial future once things went wrong on the pitch.

As was the case when those players were still wearing claret and blue shirts, the supporters will hope that West Ham can hold on to their best youngsters for as long as possible and enjoy some success with them before the club eventually decides it is time to cash in.

Kirk now says: Reo-Coker captain the full England team? Ha ha ha ha ha ha ha ha ha ha ha ha ha ha ha ha ha ha ha ha ha ha ha ha ha ha ha ha ha ha ha ha ha ha ha ha ha ha ha ha ha ha ha ha ha ha ha ha ha ha ha ha ha ha ha ha ha ha ha ha ha ha ha ha ha ha ha ha ha ha ha ha ha ha ha ha ha ha ha ha ha ha ha ha ha ha ha ha ha!

PARDS POCKETS PAY-RISE PRIZE (5 November 2005)

The news that Alan Pardew has agreed a new five-year contract should come as no surprise. After guiding West Ham to promotion in his first full season, the former Reading boss has steered the team into the top half of the Premiership table.

The temptation will be to believe that the Hammers hierarchy have conjured up the new contract on the basis of the campaign's opening stretch of games, which has produced four league wins and 15 points.

But as chairman Terence Brown has stated, the club appreciates the job that Pardew has performed as a whole since his arrival in October 2003.

He achieved promotion within the specified time-span while reducing the club's wage bill and raising money in the transfer market.

Pardew has implemented an entirely new structure behind the scenes, recruiting his own coaching and back-up team as he looked to stamp his own ideas on the club.

He retained his dignity during a period of intense pressure last season when it appeared that the Hammers could even miss out on a play-off place.

And he has dug up gold nuggets such as playmaker Yossi Benayoun while placing the emphasis on building the team around players whose best days will surely be ahead of them (former England striker Teddy Sheringham excepted, of course).

It was therefore inevitable that Pardew would be rewarded for his efforts with a bumper new contract.

That is not to say there's not an element of risk involved in the club producing a deal that ties the manager to the club until 2010.

Many supporters, particularly those who have only recently warmed to Pardew since winning the play-off final against Preston back in May, will be wondering where that leaves the club if the Hammers happen to lose their next ten Premiership games.

Or what if things go badly wrong at any time in the next 18 months?

Would the Hammers find themselves in the position of considering a change of management yet being prohibited by the cost of settlement?

It may sound like negative thinking but it's happened before, with many believing that former boss Glenn Roeder only clung on during the relegation season of 2002/03 because of the financial penalties involved.

Indeed, there was great speculation that Pardew himself may have found himself looking for new employment had West Ham failed to secure promotion last term.

Only the club's board of directors will really know how close they came to pulling the claret and blue rug from under the manager's feet.

But on the basis of this season's encouraging progress, the chairman will feel that his patience has been vindicated.

He clearly has great confidence in Pardew continuing the club's upward trajectory (and may even wonder if England could one day come calling).

And even though such optimism may be a little more reserved in some areas of the support, it's hoped the club have got this crucial decision spot on.

Kirk now says: The answer to this question was sort of yes, er, maybe not, as the events of the following year or so would prove.

RAISE A GLASS OF VINTAGE SHERI (10 November 2005)

Former West Ham boss Harry Redknapp was on the box on Sunday, singing the praises of Teddy Sheringham following reports that the Hammers hitman was being considered for England's World Cup finals party as a member of the backroom team.

'I dunno about that; he could still do a job for his country as a player!' Redknapp quipped of the former international who will turn 40 two months before the tournament begins next summer.

Just a day earlier, Sheringham had claimed his fourth goal of the season to secure a 1-0 victory against West Brom, prompting Alan Pardew to rave about the veteran's all-round contribution.

'Teddy was terrific,' he said. 'You need lieutenants in your team and he's one of the best.'

Not that anybody expected the striker to be catapulted back into Sven-Goran Eriksson's England squad for the friendly against Argentina.

For the record, Sheringham won the last of his 51 caps as a late substitute in the World Cup quarter-final defeat to Brazil nearly three-and-a-half years ago.

Since then he has spent another season at Tottenham, helped shoot Portsmouth into the top flight and done the same for West Ham.

His goal against Blackburn on the opening day of the season saw Sheringham become the Premiership's oldest goalscorer – inheriting the honour from, ironically, another Hammer in Stuart Pearce.

He might be considered too old for England but that doesn't mean he's not good enough, especially when the likes of Peter Crouch are getting the nod.

The Liverpool striker has failed to score in any of his 16 outings for club and country this term, yet Eriksson appears to be keen to take him to Germany next summer.

Bizarrely, the England coach has described the 6ft 7in Crouch as 'more special than any other player I've had' – from which we can only deduce that 'more special' is Swedish for 'tallest'.

All this is of great interest to West Ham supporters, remembering that their club failed in a £5m-plus bid for the former Southampton skyscraper before the season began.

There wasn't much disappointment among fans when the Hammers lost out, but any sentiment now must surely be one of huge relief as Crouch struggles for the Reds.

At 24 he's got age on his side and, of course, he's an entirely different kind of player to Sheringham. But if a striker's job is to score goals and create chances for others, the West Ham man is clearly head and shoulders above Crouch – metaphorically at least.

Kirk now says: Of course, there was to be no England call-up for Teddy Sheringham, despite chipping in with seven goals as the Hammers acclimatised to life back in the Premiership.

THE FERD DEGREE (24 November 2005)

Anton Ferdinand admits he is relishing the prospect of playing against his older brother Rio when Manchester United visit the Boleyn Ground on Sunday.

The West Ham defender brushed aside the disappointment of seeing his England Under-21 side fail to qualify for the European Championship by scoring an injury-time equaliser at Tottenham at the weekend.

The 1-1 draw will have boosted the whole team as they anticipate the arrival of the Red Devils at Upton Park.

But Ferdinand will go into the game in buoyant mood after enjoying an excellent start to his first Premiership season.

Some might have doubted the 20-year-old's ability to quickly adapt to the demands of the top flight, despite his key role in helping the Hammers to promotion last term.

Ferdinand established a successful partnership with fellow youngster Elliott Ward as West Ham suffered just one defeat in their final 13 games last season.

This time around, he has forged a great understanding with new recruit Danny Gabbidon, with their ever-present centre-half partnership allowing just 11 league goals to be conceded so far.

That figure is better than United can boast as they travel to east London for Sunday's highly anticipated encounter.

It has not been easy for Ferdinand. While Rio was tipped for the very top from his days as a West Ham youth-team player, Anton has been inevitably – and at times unfavourably – compared to his brother, who is six years his senior.

In the player's defence, Hammers academy boss Tony Carr told this columnist 18 months ago, 'Anton is not as mature or physically developed as Rio was at the same age, so everybody has to be patient because he's developing at a different rate. But I believe in him.'

That belief – and the faith shown in him by Alan Pardew – has proved well founded in recent times and Anton has fully convinced supporters of his true potential.

It is unlikely to see him breaking British transfer records in the way his brother did but if that means a longer stay in Hammers colours then few will be complaining.

And so Anton is set to meet Rio on Sunday and he will be desperate to come out on top – not just for himself but the club as a whole.

United boss Sir Alex Ferguson once famously accused West Ham of an 'obscene' amount of effort when his side lost at Upton Park in the early nineties to see their title hopes blow up in smoke.

Needless to say, a certain Hammer won't be keeping much in reserve at the weekend.

Kirk now says: The suspicion was that Tony Carr was being kindly diplomatic when saying that Anton was 'developing at a different rate' to Rio, because he could hardly admit that the younger Ferdinand was never going to be as good as his brother. To be fair to Anton, he did earn the Hammers a fee of £8m when sold to Sunderland.

SIMPLY THE BEST (GEORGE NOT CLYDE) (1 December 2005)

It is perhaps fitting that Manchester United found themselves visiting West Ham on Sunday, in their first outing following the death of their former star George Best.

After all, whenever we see TV footage of the brilliant Best producing a piece of magic to score a wonder goal, it seems the Hammers are invariably on the receiving end.

Indeed, *The Sun* published a picture on Friday of the player swerving past West Ham's Billy Bonds during a 4-2 victory at Old Trafford in September 1971 in which he helped himself to a hat-trick.

In total, Best scored 11 goals in his 16 outings against the Hammers between 1964 and 1972, so it's fair to assume he probably enjoyed meeting the boys in claret and blue.

And with West Ham fans appreciating footballers with flair and flamboyance as much as anybody – Paolo Di Canio coming closest in recent times to representing such maverick spirit in our own colours – we can safely say Best's talents would have been fully admired and applauded by the Upton Park faithful.

Such a view was endorsed by Sir Bobby Charlton – one of his former team-mates – who, along with Hammers legend Sir Trevor Brooking, made a short speech prior to Sunday's kick-off.

A minute's applause replaced the traditional 60 seconds of silence in Best's memory – and, incredibly, West Ham fans were up on their feet again just moments later when Marlon Harewood registered the fastest goal of the Premiership season.

The Hammers snatched the lead after just 52 seconds but, although they did well to retain the lead until half-time, it was always suspected that they had scored too early to rely purely on that single strike.

And so it proved, with Wayne Rooney and John O'Shea netting within nine minutes of each other shortly into the second period to claim victory for the Red Devils.

On the day, West Ham fell short of being able to inflict further woe on the visitors who had endured a miserable week ahead of the game.

Roy Keane's acrimonious departure, their failure to beat Villarreal at Old Trafford, Vodafone's withdrawal of sponsorship and Best's death meant it was imperative that Sir Alex Ferguson's men produced a fighting display at Upton Park – and they duly delivered.

The Hammers can at least console themselves with the fact they gave United a huge fright and remained in the game until the end.

They are back among the big boys now and examinations are unlikely to prove much more testing than the one posed by United.

| *Kirk now says: Now there's a rarity, being philosophical in defeat.*

A REAL YEAR TO CHEER (5 January 2006)

No matter how you look at it, 2005 was a great year for West Ham United.

For the club to win promotion back to the Premiership last season and then see December out with a top-half placing can be considered nothing but a huge success.

The previous year had ended with the Hammers one place outside the Championship play-off zone following a 2-2 draw at Rotherham.

Yet a fine 2-0 win at table-toppers Ipswich on New Year's Day and a 1-0 FA Cup victory against top-flight opposition in the shape of Norwich confirmed the ability was there, if not the consistency.

By that stage of the season a play-off place was the only realistic route to promotion – and even that looked unlikely following successive defeats by Leeds, Preston and Reading.

But the 3-1 loss at the Madejski Stadium proved something of a watershed, with the introduction of defender Elliott Ward and goalkeeper Jimmy Walker helping the Hammers to build an impressive 13-game unbeaten run that culminated in the play-off final success against Preston in May.

Predictably, West Ham were listed as the bookies' favourites for the drop during 2005/06, especially after the club failed to land the big-money striker they had been looking for.

But that was to underestimate the signings of Yossi Benayoun, Roy Carroll, Danny Gabbidon and Paul Konchesky, who played key roles as the Hammers consolidated their return to the Premiership by remaining in the top half of the table as 2005 came to a close. With the exception of Benayoun, the midfield and attack was comprised of players who had struggled for consistency in the Championship.

Therefore much credit must also go to the likes of Nigel Reo-Coker, Hayden Mullins, Matthew Etherington, Marlon Harewood and Bobby Zamora, who collectively had such little experience at the top level.

Of their 48 league and cup fixtures in 2005, the Hammers claimed victory in 20 games and were unbeaten in another 11, scoring 69 goals and conceding 59 in the process.

Those figures may not look spectacular on paper but, given they include a period in which the team was re-acclimatising to a higher standard of football, they make for very positive reading.

Sadly, the year ended on a disappointing note, with the final four games producing just a single point (at Portsmouth).

But with Alan Pardew set to take advantage of the transfer window, it's hoped the squad will get the boost necessary to quickly reach the recognised 40-point safety mark.

Kirk now says: West Ham had 26 points by the turn of the year but staying up was still the priority, although a fantastic run of seven consecutive league and cup wins would see them looking up the table not down.

ASH CASH NOT JUST A FLASH GESTURE (26 January 2005)

Fans must surely be delighted to see West Ham smash their transfer record with the £7m signing of striker Dean Ashton from Norwich.

The deal represents a huge statement of intent by the Hammers as they look to consolidate their Premiership place and build for the future.

Many have questioned the club's ambition over the last five years – not least after relegation in 2003 – but Ashton's signing is clear proof that West Ham are not content to simply make up the numbers following their return to the top flight.

Inevitably, there will have been eyebrows raised over the huge fee agreed for the 22-year-old, for whom Norwich paid Crewe just £3m a year ago.

With the Canaries relying on Ashton to fire them back into the top flight, it was always going to take a massive bid to persuade them to release their top scorer, who has bagged 11 goals so far this term.

Indeed, this columnist was present when Norwich boss Nigel Worthington insisted it would take a 'crazy offer' to sanction the striker's departure.

Some may indeed suggest that the £7m fee – which will rise by a further £250,000 if Ashton plays for the full England side and helps West Ham into European competition – is way too excessive.

The figure was certainly more than the Hammers were initially prepared to pay and the Canaries' demands were high enough to frighten off Manchester City and other clubs interested in the striker.

West Ham's finance director Scott Duxbury has described the deal as a potential 'steal', although it's unlikely the club was using such language when they were in the process of negotiating the price.

There is no doubt that there is an element of risk when making such a financial commitment for a player – even more so when he has made only 16 Premiership outings to date.

But if he's the right player for West Ham, he's the right player – whether he's costing £5m or £7m.

Ashton's record of 92 goals in 223 club appearances is an impressive statistic and, given that he has always beaten his previous season's tally, there's a reassuring consistency to his upward trajectory.

He will have to perform miracles to beat last season's total of 27 goals this term, but West Ham clearly feel they have a full England player in the making, with Ashton having won several Under-21 caps.

So the Hammers have finally secured their big-money striker, after moves for Benni McCarthy, Peter Crouch, Milan Baros, Emmanuel Adebayor and Andy Johnson all failed to come to fruition.

And Ashton is set to make his debut in the home FA Cup tie against Blackburn on Saturday, having not played against West Ham in the third-round game at Carrow Road because of an alleged groin strain.

Alan Pardew has been pushing his superiors to back him in his pursuit of the striker – and they have not let him down.

Kirk now says: The club-record signing of Dean Ashton was the first time that Hammers fans had been genuinely excited by the arrival of a new player for several years and he certainly looked the business.

GREENWOOD SET THE STANDARDS (16 February 2006)

West Ham legends such as Sir Trevor Brooking and Billy Bonds MBE have rightly paid tribute to the many qualities and huge influence of former manager Ron Greenwood MBE, who sadly passed away last week.

Former defender John McDowell may not be as highly revered as those two distinguished players but his reflections on Ron, who enjoyed a successful 16-year association with the Hammers before taking charge of the England team in 1977, are no less valid.

'I'm certain I heard Ron turn round one day and say, "I'd rather see us lose 4-3 and play well than win 1-0 and play badly,"' John once told this columnist, before recalling when the West Ham chief admonished him for denying a team a certain goal by conceding a late penalty.

'The bloke missed his kick and we went on to win the match, but Ron came into the dressing room afterwards and said, "If I see you do that in another game you'll never play for West Ham again."

'I told him that it helped us to win the match but Ron replied, "It's not the way we play football at West Ham."'

Needless to say, Ron Greenwood was a man of great integrity and high standards – commodities sadly lacking in a later England manager.

He didn't make headlines for having affairs with TV celebrities or FA staff. He didn't negotiate with clubs behind his employer's back or hold clandestine talks with fake sheiks in Dubai.

That is because Ron was in a different class.

For him, football wasn't worth playing unless his team performed with style, dignity and discipline.

His progressive thinking about the game not only cemented the foundations of all the good things associated with West Ham but also helped England to win the World Cup in 1966.

He treated his players with respect and subsequently commanded it himself.

And when he became general manager at Upton Park in 1974, he proved himself as being ahead of his time by acting as a director of football some 20 years before the role became popular.

Like the rest of the human race, of course, he wasn't perfect.

Not all of his players enjoyed a close relationship with him, but then the same could be said of any football club manager.

Former striker Brian Dear is not a member of that group, however, remembering, 'Ron was a fine and tender man. He got hurt easily. He didn't like hangers-on and if people took liberties with his players he used to get upset.'

So let's put things into context.

Another former West Ham manager, Glenn Roeder, last week claimed that 'people were reasonably impressed' by him taking the club to their 'third highest finish' of seventh in 2002.

Sorry, Glenn, but you've got it wrong.

Ron took the Hammers to their third best finish of sixth in 1973 – their equal highest placing at the time – and he never embarrassed himself with relegation, something that will always destroy Roeder's CV.

The two bosses cannot be compared and it's beyond belief that they have both occupied the same office at the Boleyn Ground.

Ron Greenwood was a true icon and West Ham supporters have so much to thank him for.

Now that's something to be 'impressed' about.

Kirk now says: It seems strange to pay tribute to a former Hammers boss by sticking the boot into another one, but it proves that Glenn Roeder was still getting up people's noses even after leaving the club.

WENGER TALKS A LOAD OF ARSE (16 March 2006)

For a man so highly intelligent, Arsene Wenger can certainly talk some nonsense when he wants to – as West Ham supporters well know.

First the Arsenal boss dismissed Hammers striker Fredi Kanoute's wrongly disallowed goal at Highbury in 2002 by insisting his side 'would have won the game anyway', despite the score being 0-0 at the time.

One year later, he laughably claimed that Dennis Bergkamp's blatant elbow into the face of midfielder Lee Bowyer was simply a case of the Dutchman 'protecting the ball'.

Now he has accused Alan Pardew of making 'racist' remarks after the Hammers boss said that Arsenal's progress in Europe could hardly be considered a British success when their team is made up of foreigners.

Pardew added, 'It's important that top clubs don't lose sight of the fact it's the English Premier League and that English players should be involved. We could lose the soul of British football – the English player.'

He is absolutely right, of course.

Yet Wenger bizarrely responded by saying, 'We have Kick Racism Out Of Football but racism starts here. I was very, very disappointed to hear what Alan Pardew said.'

He then pointed out that West Ham had taken Arsenal's French forward Jeremie Aliadiere on loan without worrying about his nationality.

The media made the most of Pardew's comments, with both *The Sun* and the *Daily Mirror* splashing the story across their back pages a couple of days after Arsenal's two-legged victory over Real Madrid.

Pardew's words had topicality and were portrayed in a way that suggested he was attacking Arsenal's methods.

But for Wenger to suggest that Pardew is guilty of racism – and hypocrisy – is absolute rubbish.

There is nothing racist about saying English football needs successful English players.

It is vital that every country generates its own talent and it would be interesting to hear what Frenchman Wenger would be saying if his own country was totally over-run by foreign imports.

Pardew has since tried to play down the furore and said he'll be far more cautious in future when discussing matters relating to other clubs.

He might be a little naïve at times but it would be disappointing if he couldn't express his opinion on a topical issue.

Pardew's honesty has been refreshing for the game and maybe that's something Wenger could learn to appreciate.

Kirk now says: This little spat between Wenger and Pardew wasn't the last of their confrontations, which took a more physical nature the following season.

TEARS, CHEERS – AND JUST A FEW BEERS (27 April 2006)

Sports writer and Sky pundit Paul McCarthy admitted on television that he had been hanky handed and wiping his eyes following West Ham's 1-0 FA Cup semi-final victory against Middlesbrough on Sunday.

And he wasn't the only fan – in the Villa Park stands or the press box, for that matter – having difficulty containing his emotions as the Hammers booked both their place in Europe and a Cup Final clash with Liverpool next month.

The delirious scenes of joy and jubilation at the final whistle will live long in the memory of all those present, with a quarter of a century of FA Cup hurt suddenly culminating in an explosion of cheers, tears and, later, the sinking of a few beers (okay, lots).

Not since 1980 have West Ham appeared in an FA Cup Final, when Trevor Brooking's header earned a 1-0 triumph against hot favourites Arsenal.

The Hammers were a Second Division side, but manager John Lyall formulated a brilliant tactical and strategic ploy to thwart the Gunners and claim victory.

Lyall sadly died of a heart attack last week, of course, and it was fitting that West Ham should mark his untimely passing by securing a place in the showdown against Liverpool.

The fixture is a repeat of the 1981 League Cup Final when, again as a Second Division side, the Hammers fought back to wipe out the Reds' highly controversial opener in the 118th minute with a last-gasp Ray Stewart penalty.

European champions-elect Liverpool won the replay 2-1 but West Ham were firmly in the ascendancy as a club, with the two cup final appearances being followed up with promotion and three successive top-half finishes.

This year's march to Cardiff is genuine proof of the club's development and growth over the past two years, with Alan Pardew's men having reached the Millennium Stadium via a strenuous route involving tough trips to Bolton and Manchester City as well as other all-Premiership ties against Blackburn and Boro.

And the reward for battling through to the final is a guaranteed place in the UEFA Cup.

For that reason, there was unbearable tension during the semi-final, with such a huge prize awaiting the eventual victors.

It was always going to be a tight encounter but the Hammers have often saved their best for the second half of games this season.

The look of emotion on Marlon Harewood's face said it all as he tore off his shirt and hurled it towards the turf in a fit of uncontrolled ecstasy after scoring the winner.

The victory clearly meant as much to West Ham's players as it did to the supporters and the post-match celebrations had Villa Park seriously rocking in its foundations.

So the Hammers are back in Cardiff for the third consecutive year, after their two Championship play-off final outings following the arrival of manager Pardew.

And who's to say he can't follow in John Lyall's footsteps by masterminding another shock FA Cup Final success?

Kirk now says: But first there was the little matter of West Ham's final league game.

HAMMERS HAVE STOMACH FOR THE FIGHT (11 May 2006)

Tottenham might have been complaining about the effects of food poisoning but that didn't stop West Ham from savouring the taste of a great season after the 2-1 win against their big rivals on Sunday.

The victory left Hammers fans reflecting on a stunning campaign that has seen the club secure a ninth-place finish upon their return to the Premiership, reach their first FA Cup Final in 26 years and claim a place in the UEFA Cup.

Add in the fact that the result prevented Spurs from finishing fourth and securing a Champions League place and those of a claret and blue persuasion were left thinking that life just can't get any better.

But then it's remembered, of course, that there's the small matter of a Cup Final against Liverpool this weekend.

Can West Ham really round off the season by seeing off hot favourites Liverpool – the current European champions, no less – to win their first major trophy in more than a quarter of a century?

The answer, of course, is that they can.

That doesn't mean they necessarily will but Hammers boss Alan Pardew will make sure his troops begin the game at the Millennium Stadium with no sense of inferiority.

Liverpool finished third to qualify for the Champions League but, with the bookies making West Ham 4/1 outsiders to win the FA Cup, it has been overlooked that just six league places separate the two clubs.

The memorable scenes of celebration at Villa Park following the semi-final success against Middlesbrough recognised the fact that a major prize had been secured in the form of European qualification.

Now the final itself is upon us, however, the club's focus is very much on completing the job by lifting the FA Cup – and many believe there has been a sense of destiny attached to the route to Cardiff.

Pardew has some big decisions to make, although some are dependent on the fitness of Dean Ashton and Matthew Etherington.

In defence, he has to decide whether to stick with his recognised first-choice central partnership of Danny Gabbidon and Anton Ferdinand – as many would prefer – or move the latter out to right-back at the expense of Lionel Scaloni and recall James Collins.

With Hayden Mullins suspended, it's expected that Carl Fletcher will start alongside skipper Nigel Reo-Coker.

What is certain, however, is that the team's key men – such as Marlon Harewood and Yossi Benayoun – must perform to their absolute best and that players take any chances that come their way.

If West Ham play to their full potential, then maybe it will be Liverpool – instead of Spurs – feeling sick this time around.

Kirk now says: The myth of Tottenham's players being poisoned by a dodgy lasagne has been written into football folklore – with all sorts of conspiracy theories doing the rounds – but the truth is that they simply fell victim to a stomach bug that had infiltrated their training camp.

NO LOSERS ON DAY OF HEARTBREAK (18 May 2006)

One half of the Millennium Stadium usually empties within moments of a game finishing – and it's never the part where fans are celebrating.

But that was not the case on Saturday, with the West Ham faithful staying behind to acknowledge the magnificent effort by their team in taking Liverpool all the way in what has been described as one of the best ever FA Cup finals.

Ninety minutes were on the clock when Steven Gerrard's second great strike of the day rescued a 3-3 draw for the Reds to take the game into extra-time prior to their subsequent penalty shoot-out success.

West Ham had been just four minutes of injury time away from claiming a shock victory against a Liverpool side that went into the occasion on the back of an amazing 11-game winning run.

The bookies had such little faith in the Hammers that this columnist was able to place a bet at 13/2 that they would win in normal time.

Yet West Ham's performance made a complete mockery of such odds as they raced into a 2-0 first-half lead and then went ahead again after being pegged back in the second period.

Indeed, they led Liverpool – last season's European champions, remember – for some 59 minutes in total, but Gerrard's late effort saw an FA Cup Final produce six goals for only the second time since 1953.

It is no overstatement to say the game was an absolute classic and, as Hammers boss Alan Pardew admitted, football was certainly the winner on a day in which neither team deserved to lose.

Some believed it would be West Ham's destiny to win the FA Cup for the first time in 26 years in the season that former managers Ron Greenwood and John Lyall had passed away.

The victory may have just eluded the team but both legends would have been immensely proud of their former club's efforts.

There was, of course, an element of good fortune about all three of West Ham's goals on the day.

Liverpool defender Jamie Carragher opened the scoring with an own goal, goalkeeper Pepe Reina fumbled to allow Dean Ashton to extend the lead, while Paul Konchesky found the net with a cross that somehow sailed into the top right-hand corner.

Yet the goals were a deserved reward for the way in which the Hammers took the game to Liverpool.

There were some outstanding performances, with Yossi Benayoun, Danny Gabbidon and Dean Ashton all particularly impressing.

Lionel Scaloni also gave everything, although he must surely regret putting the ball out of play – to allow Liverpool's Djibril Cisse to receive treatment – just moments before Gerrard's second leveller.

That saw the momentum swing heavily in Liverpool's favour and, when striker Marlon Harewood collected an ankle injury that left him hobbling around and Reo-Coker saw a late header pushed on to a post, you feared that it wasn't quite going to be West Ham's day.

When the penalties arrived one always sensed that Liverpool's experienced players would find it easier to hold their nerve – and so it proved as they claimed a 3-1 shoot-out victory.

It was heartbreaking for West Ham fans to witness, but at least there is the consolation of a place in the UEFA Cup next season.

And while Liverpool snatched the FA Cup trophy, it was the Hammers who won many thousands of new friends.

Kirk now says: The passage of time has done little to diminish the memory of a classic FA Cup encounter, although the fact that it's been dubbed the 'Gerrard final' will irritate West Ham fans. The match-day programme is worth a few bob as well.

REFLECTING ON SEASON 2005/06

Best signing: Dean Ashton (Norwich), £7.25m

Worst signing: Yaniv Katan (Maccabi Haifa), £100,000

Best result: Winning 2-1 at home to Tottenham in May (to deny them a place in the Champions League)

Worst result: Losing 4-1 at Bolton in March

Final position: 9th in Premier League, 55 points

Manager and rating: Alan Pardew 8/10

Best thing about season: Taking part in an epic FA Cup Final

Worst thing about season: The deaths of former managers Ron Greenwood and John Lyall

SEASON 2006/07

'Issues must have distracted the manager's focus'

THE sight of a Ferdinand brother breaking down in tears following the heartbreak of a penalty shoot-out defeat became something of a recurring theme in the summer of 2006, with Rio mourning England's World Cup quarter-final exit at the hands of Portugal in the same way that Anton was left wiping his eyes after West Ham's FA Cup Final failure against Liverpool in May. Hankies all round then …

The Hammers had only one player on duty at the finals in Germany, with goalkeeper Shaka Hislop playing against England as his Trinidad & Tobago side suffered a 2-0 defeat in June – and even he was to leave Upton Park for the second time the following month.

England midfielder Frank Lampard did his best to upset West Ham fans again by declaring in his autobiography, 'When Joe Cole joined me at Chelsea he would turn away in disappointment if West Ham had lost but I would smile. I wanted them to lose.'

And he justified his efforts to leave Upton Park in 2001 by saying, 'This wasn't about football any more, this was family.'

He had always said his relationship with Harry Redknapp and Frank Lampard senior was irrelevant to his career and yet he played the family card when it suited him. And he wonders why he still gets abuse …

Back at the Boleyn, it was confirmed in July that winger Shaun Newton, who had arrived from Wolves in March 2005, had failed a drugs test and been served with a seven-month suspension that would rule him out until Christmas.

You would have thought the 30-year-old with three young children would have had more sense than to act like a teenager drunk on new-found celebrity status, but clearly not.

'We will stand by Shaun through this difficult time,' said Alan Pardew, before packing him off to Leicester the following March.

Also on his way out of Upton Park was defender Elliott Ward, who was sent to Coventry for a £1m fee, while Tomas Repka had returned to the Czech Republic earlier in the year when signing for former club Sparta Prague.

TOP SEVEN WOULD BE HEAVEN (17 August 2006)

Terry Venables believes that West Ham are going to finish seventh this season, one place behind Newcastle and ahead of the likes of Everton, Middlesbrough, Blackburn and Manchester City.

Of course, most Hammers fans would gladly accept the position predicted by England's new assistant manager.

For starters, it would represent an improvement on last term's impressive ninth-placed finish, with Bolton and Blackburn being the clubs overtaken according to El Tel's crystal ball.

Whether it's possible to make a serious challenge for a UEFA Cup place via the Premiership is likely to depend on how West Ham deal with the demands of playing in Europe this season – the prize claimed thanks to reaching the FA Cup Final last term.

So we must look at the summer signings of Lee Bowyer, Carlton Cole, John Pantsil, Tyrone Mears, Jonathan Spector and George McCartney – plus the securing of England goalkeeper Robert Green – and hope the squad has been sufficiently strengthened, although boss Alan Pardew admits there could still be at least one more new face in the coming weeks.

The overall quality of the squad has certainly been greatly improved, with the likes of Clive Clarke and Carl Fletcher returning to their natural habitat of the Championship following moves to Sunderland and Crystal Palace respectively.

Of course, Pardew will be aware there's so much more to come from several of last season's stars, with youngsters such as Nigel Reo-Coker and Anton Ferdinand expected to continue their development to the point of challenging for full England call-ups this term.

Such recognition has already been handed to Dean Ashton this week and the striker is likely to prove West Ham's key man this season.

The 22-year-old scored six times in 16 outings for the Hammers last term following his club record £7.25m switch from Norwich in January. But despite winning much general acclaim, Ashton still looked distinctly leaden at times – with a bulky build that was more John Hartson than Alan Shearer.

The hope was that he would benefit from enduring a Pardew pre-season programme for the first time, but we can now see that the club's fitness gurus have gone substantially further.

Indeed, the Hammers chief declared, 'We've worked on changing Dean's shape and making him much more mobile. He looks fantastic and now has all the attributes of an England player.'

There should certainly be no shortage of goals from the Hammers this season, with Marlon Harewood, Carlton Cole, Bobby Zamora and Teddy Sheringham competing for a place alongside Ashton.

If Ferdinand and Hammer of the Year Danny Gabbidon can quickly find full fitness following their pre-season injuries then West Ham should continue to be defensively sound – especially with the full-back departments being strengthened and the conclusion of Green's signing from Norwich.

Pardew admits he needs more genuine wide men in the squad, especially with Shaun Newton banned until December and Matty Etherington injured for the start of the campaign.

But if he can solve that one remaining problem before the transfer window closes then West Ham fans will have every reason to believe the team can continue to make progress and once again enjoy a highly successful season.

And maybe that 'Venables verdict' might not be such an eyebrow-raiser after all.

Kirk now says: West Ham fans were entitled to be optimistic. But nobody could predict the traumatic and turbulent season that West Ham would suffer over the next nine months, with changes of ownership and management, the controversial signing of two Argentina internationals, an FA inquiry and record fine, Dean Ashton suffering long-term injury, plus a nail-biting battle against relegation making this campaign the most dramatic in the club's history.

WHU IS BEHIND TAKEOVER TALKS? (7 September 2006)

It was just a couple of weeks ago that this columnist happened to find himself involved in a heated debate with a Chelsea fan about the merits of his club's two recent Premiership title successes.

'But surely it can't be remotely satisfying knowing that such achievements have been bought rather than earned,' he was told.

Incredibly, West Ham fans have been questioning such a principled point of view following confirmation that the club has begun 'exploratory discussions' regarding its possible sale and elevation into football's elite.

The Hammers were understandably not at liberty to reveal who the potential purchaser would be, but it was widely reported that Kia Joorabchian's Media Sports Investment – linked with a bid for the club last year and responsible for bringing Argentina stars Carlos Tevez and Javier Mascherano to Upton Park on Thursday – was the interested party.

The takeover story hit the tabloid front pages on Saturday, with one newspaper generating headlines such as 'I'm Forever Blowing Roubles', 'West Hamski' and 'Hammer & Sickle' amid claims that Russian oligarch Boris Berezovsky and Georgian businessman Badri Patarkatsishvili were funding the venture.

Indeed, it was even alleged that Chelsea owner Roman Abramovich had some kind of financial stake in MSI – a suggestion that has been strenuously denied by all key parties.

Sunday's newspapers saw the Russian interest in West Ham being downplayed, with it being claimed that a 'Middle East consortium' was behind the takeover initiative.

The sense of mystery and intrigue was growing by the day, with bewildered Hammers fans feeling a mixture of excitement and uncertainty about the future of their club – not to mention their very own philosophies.

If West Ham is to change hands, how much would the supporters care about the identity of the new owners and what would their reactions be to the idea of buying success by way of a Chelsea-style revolution?

Surprisingly, Joorabchian last week told the BBC, 'MSI is a company that will not invest in European football as such by investing in a club.'

On reflection those words make sense, with the implication being that there's plenty of easier money to be made from the movement of players – with it being speculated that it would be MSI, as opposed to West Ham, that would receive the lion's share of the transfer fees when Tevez and Mascherano come to leave Upton Park.

It is inevitable that such theories will have been generated when there's an Irons curtain of secrecy surrounding the specifics of the deal that sensationally brought the Argentina internationals to the club.

West Ham's initial announcement simply stated that Tevez and Mascherano had signed 'permanent contracts' with the club but that 'all other aspects of the transfers would remain confidential and undisclosed'.

As if the budget-conscious Hammers go swooping for World Cup superstars worth in excess of £30m on a regular basis …

And manager Alan Pardew's confession that 'the chairman came to me on Monday and gave me the opportunity to go for Carlos and Javier' hardly dismisses the belief that the concept of the purchases was originated more in the boardroom than the dressing room.

Not that Hammers fans will really give a hoot.

The transfers may initially have had a somewhat cynical, financially motivated feel about them – with the popular view being that the players have been brought to Europe to suit MSI's needs – but there's been absolutely no suggestion that any regulations have been contravened.

And if the unique arrangement stands to benefit all parties – West Ham, its supporters, MSI and the players themselves – both in football and financial terms, then the only people really left to complain about it will be other clubs that failed to show such initiative themselves.

Kirk now says: The West Ham soap opera at this time was less like an episode of EastEnders *and more like a Cold War documentary, with the various names associated with funding a possible takeover of the club creating an unlikely link between Green Street and Red Square. Berezovsky and Patarkatsishvili (try pronouncing those names after a few beers) have both since been found dead in their British homes.*

PARDS SHOWS WHO'S BOSS (14 September 2006)

Sky Sports must surely have been cracking open the champagne when they heard that West Ham had signed Carlos Tevez and Javier Mascherano ahead of their televised game against Aston Villa last weekend.

At exactly the same point last season, the TV cameras had been present at Upton Park to witness Marlon Harewood claiming a superb hat-trick against Villa to mark his arrival as a Premiership striker.

And now, 12 months on, Sky suddenly had the opportunity to show two Argentina stars making their debuts for the Hammers following their shock move from Corinthians.

With West Ham's supporters equally desperate to get an immediate glimpse of Tevez and Mascherano, you can imagine the kind of pressure Alan Pardew must have been under as he pondered his starting line-up for the game. With that in mind, some might have considered it a brave decision to point the two internationals towards the substitutes' bench as the game against Villa kicked off – causing disappointment in the stands and on the television gantry.

The gossip amongst the newspaper hacks was that Pardew had made a deliberate 'statement' that he and he alone dictates first-team affairs at West Ham, whatever moves are made in the boardroom.

The Hammers chief quickly denied the suggestion, insisting it was a 'football decision' to omit the two Argentines from his team.

As a result of the international break, the fresh recruits had enjoyed just two days of proper training with their new team-mates and it could be a few weeks before both players are back in peak condition following their post-World Cup vacations.

If Pardew did make a conscious statement, however, then it was to the players who have served him so well over the last two seasons.

West Ham have made a decent start to the campaign and to have dropped either Harewood or Bobby Zamora up front and defensive midfielder Hayden Mullins for the new men would have betrayed the manager's long-standing philosophy that if you're playing well you keep your shirt – barring tactical restructures, of course.

In showing loyalty to those players, Pardew has dismissed the notion that Tevez and Mascherano will enjoy any kind of special treatment or favouritism during their stay at the Boleyn Ground.

And in doing so, the manager will have preserved the spirit and camaraderie that has proved to be such a vital ingredient in the club's success in recent times.

That is not to say that the presence of the two new players on the pitch from the very start of the game would not have helped propel the Hammers to victory against Villa last weekend.

The excitement of the supporters would probably have given the team an added zest, as opposed to the strange feeling of apprehension that allowed Villa to take an early lead and kill any sense of euphoria that existed in the ground before kick-off.

Ironically, it was Zamora – who might have feared for his place following the arrival of Tevez – who claimed the second-half equaliser as West Ham battled to a 1-1 draw.

That means Zamora tops the Premiership goal charts with five goals in four outings this term, whereas Harewood – who made way as Tevez was brought on as a 60th-minute substitute – has yet to open his account for the season.

Meanwhile, Carlton Cole got on the field for just the final eight minutes while Teddy Sheringham failed to even make the bench.

Needless to say, Pardew will have plenty of selection dilemmas in the coming months – not least when record signing Dean Ashton is fit again.

But, as we saw at the weekend, the Hammers boss is prepared to risk short-term pain for long-term gain.

And for that he deserves much credit.

Kirk now says: After the game, Pardew comically claimed, 'The two new guys were the icing on the cake … but the cake needs to taste nice in the first place' with the suspicion that Tevez and Mascherano had been planted at West Ham as a sweetener for a possible takeover by MSI, who owned part of the players' economic rights.

SICILIANS RELY ON THE ROUGH STUFF (21 September 2006)

West Ham have a mountain to climb when they visit Sicily next week – and we're not talking about the island's Mount Etna – as they look to overturn a 1-0 deficit in their UEFA Cup first-round tie against Palermo.

Thursday's home defeat by the Serie A outfit left everybody associated with the Hammers with a bitter taste in the mouth.

The evening had begun in positive and friendly fashion, with joint West Ham-Palermo scarves being sold down Green Street way.

But the scissors were probably being taken to those souvenirs just two hours later, with any sense of goodwill disappearing as a result of the visitors' cynical and surprisingly aggressive approach to the game.

Indeed, it's no overstatement to say that Palermo displayed a menacing mentality that was more stomach churning than the pink shirts they wear for home outings.

Coach Francesco Guidolin confirmed that he had taken the physical reputation of British football seriously by stating, 'We knew that we would have to fight to get a result here.'

And that's what his players literally did, although they did so in a manner that suggested that the rough stuff, not to mention all the old tricks of the trade, came very much as second nature.

Guidolin also claimed his men had not relied on any luck, although his side had clearly benefited from all the good fortune handed out on the night as they stole a precious first-leg victory.

Andrea Caracciolo's 45th-minute goal came just moments after the ball had appeared to run out of play and the Sicilians frequently enjoyed the leniency of Swedish referee Stefan Johannesson, who booked just three of the visitors despite their strong-arm tactics, while confirmation that it was never going to be West Ham's night came when Marlon Harewood's late effort hit a post.

That is not to say that some fans were not left questioning Alan Pardew's strategy, with the Hammers surrendering the early initiative with what appeared to be a 4-1-4-1 formation, with midfielder Javier Mascherano sitting deep in front of the defence and his Argentine compatriot Carlos Tevez starting wide on the left rather than alongside the isolated Bobby Zamora up front.

Pardew later confessed that he had adopted a more cautious approach in order to avoid conceding an early goal, but the experiment failed against opposition who were able to draw on their experience of having reached the last 16 of the competition last year.

So, can the Hammers stage a repeat of their fine comeback against Metz in 1999 when they wiped out a first-leg home defeat with an emphatic 3-1 away win to clinch the Intertoto Cup?

Pardew insists the tie is 'evenly poised', claiming Palermo have a psychological dilemma as to whether to sit back and defend their advantage or play more openly.

'Either way will suit us,' he declared – and you got the impression he wasn't necessarily playing mind games with his opposite number.

The return game at the Stadio Renzo Barbera will surely be an epic encounter, but West Ham will have to put into practise all the lessons from the first leg if they are to emerge victorious.

Kirk now says: West Ham's return to European competition might have ended in a disappointing defeat, but it did not deter fans from making their way to Sicily for the second leg.

NICE HOLIDAY, SHAME ABOUT THE RESULT (5 October 2006)

There were plenty of 'Cockney Boys On Tour' T-shirts to be seen in the bars overlooking Mondello's sunbaked beach in Sicily last week – but sadly that's where West Ham's latest European adventure came to an abrupt end.

Less a tour and just a trip, as events panned out.

It is fair to say that nothing went right for the Hammers in their two UEFA Cup clashes against Palermo.

The initial target had been to qualify for the competition's group stage that would have guaranteed another four games and two more journeys abroad for the supporters.

Yet with West Ham having been non-seeded, they were always going to face stiff opposition in the first round and Palermo – who topped Serie A following three wins on the spin – proved to be just that.

The first leg at Upton Park saw the visitors sneak a 1-0 win with a goal that was scored after the ball had appeared to run out of play.

Marlon Harewood struck a post late on as West Ham failed to secure the result their performance merited.

By the time the second leg came around, the Hammers had lost three successive games without scoring a goal and were suffering an injury crisis in defence, with right-backs John Pantsil and Tyrone Mears being joined on the sidelines by stand-in Christian Dailly and key centre-half Anton Ferdinand.

To suggest that Alan Pardew's men were up against it at the Stadio Renzo Barbera was an understatement, despite the manager's bold but not entirely convincing pre-match claim that his side's chances of winning through were '50-50'.

The Hammers needed the rub of the green but, after Palermo goalkeeper Alberto Fontana had made a series of superb saves to deny Harewood, Carlos Tevez, Carlton Cole and James Collins in the opening period, those of a claret and blue persuasion began to suspect it might not be their night.

The key moment came in the 35th minute when the hosts were awarded a free kick despite Paul Konchesky appearing to win the ball.

Greek referee Georgios Kasnaferis allowed Palermo to have a second bite of the cherry after they had lost possession with a quickly-taken effort and, with Fabio Henrique Simplicio's shot seemingly taking a deflection to find its way into the net, it was obvious that West Ham's luck was well and truly out.

Any lingering doubts about that were dismissed when the impressive Cole was stretchered off in pain having just seen a header strike a post and David Di Michele was allowed to add to Simplicio's second goal despite looking some way offside.

So that was that – West Ham's first involvement in European competition for seven years was over and it's evident that UEFA Cup success this term was simply not meant to be.

'A 4-0 aggregate scoreline flatters Palermo but after a result like that I can't really claim that we were the better team,' admitted Pardew.

The manager is nothing if not philosophical and at least the Hammers can now focus their thoughts on the Premiership – and trying to stay in it may have to be their most realistic priority after the weekend's disaster against Reading saw the club extend their goalless run of defeats to five games for the first time since 1920.

Kirk now says: Apart from a very enjoyable five-day stay in Sicily, there wasn't much else to smile about with things going very badly wrong for the Hammers on the pitch.

PARDS COULD TEACH WENGER A LESSON (9 November 2006)

Alan Pardew has conducted himself at games with dignity this season.

The West Ham boss has had to watch his team lose eight successive matches, crash out of the UEFA Cup on a 4-0 aggregate to Palermo and suffer an embarrassing Carling Cup defeat at League 1 outfit Chesterfield.

On top of those results, it has been suggested he would quickly find himself out of a job should Kia Joorabchian's takeover be completed, with Sven-Goran Eriksson, Luiz Felipe Scolari and Alan Curbishley being mentioned as possible successors.

He will admit to having made mistakes this term, but Pardew has remained strong, kept a brave face and confronted all the key issues as honestly as possible as the media scrutiny began to get ever more intense.

So the contrast between his behaviour after games and the conduct of Arsenal boss Arsene Wenger at Upton Park on Sunday could not have been any greater.

First Wenger objected to Pardew's touchline celebrations after Marlon Harewood's late winner for the Hammers by inducing a shoving match with his counterpart and exchanging some colourful language.

He not only refused to shake hands with Pardew at the final whistle but also failed to speak to the media following his side's 1-0 defeat, a result that extended the Gunners' winless run to three games.

With young midfielder Cesc Fabregas and volatile goalkeeper Jens Lehmann also throwing their toys out of their prams by provoking confrontations as the players left the field, the overwhelming message was that Arsenal make for dreadful losers.

When things don't go their way, they wave their arms about and stomp up and down in a display of childish petulance. The only thing missing was the tears.

Gunners fans may defend their team's behaviour by dressing it up as a display of passion. 'At least it proves they care,' they'll argue.

But wasn't it a show of passion by Pardew that Wenger seemed to have a problem with?

The Hammers boss did nothing wrong, simply celebrating Harewood's goal in a manner that anybody would have done given the circumstances.

It is not as if Pardew consciously approached Wenger and gave it the big one right in front of his face.

Yes, Wenger may have felt aggrieved that his men had been denied a penalty when Alexander Hleb appeared to be tripped by Jonathan Spector, who did indeed get a slight touch on the ball.

But if managers behaved like the Frenchman did every time they feel a sense of injustice, there would be anarchy every weekend.

Wenger is an intelligent man who commands respect, but he clearly struggles to deal with frustration when events go against him.

Pardew has had to cope with much disappointment himself this term, but has proved he can handle the pressure and criticism.

And in terms of his conduct on Sunday, he certainly has nothing to apologise for.

Kirk now says: The word 'dignity' was often used to describe the conduct of the hapless Glenn Roeder – and we all know what happened next.

EVOLUTION INSTEAD OF REVOLUTION (23 November 2006)

When the initial, highly sensationalistic stories of West Ham being involved in takeover talks emerged back in September, supporters were bowled over by amazing images of a Chelsea-style revolution.

From simply hoping the Hammers could build on the successes of the previous 18 months – promotion, a top-half Premiership finish, an FA Cup Final place and UEFA Cup qualification – fans were suddenly wrestling with the idea of a huge cash injection potentially launching the club into football's upper stratosphere.

The concept divided supporters, some of whom loved the thought of West Ham chasing championships whatever the methods, while others (who dismiss Chelsea's achievements as meaningless given their unlimited wealth) loathed the notion of simply buying success.

Then a fear began to grow as to what kind of dubious hands the club could fall into, with all sorts of mysterious Iranians, Israelis, Russians and Georgians being linked with the funding of a takeover.

Supporters were understandably concerned about these businessmen's possible motives and whether they could ever really have West Ham's long-term interests at heart.

Then an Icelandic former biscuit baron by the name of Eggert Magnusson entered the picture and, although his initial offer was thought to have amounted to, er, just crumbs, it became apparent last week that a much-improved deal was nearing completion.

Throughout the last few months, Alan Pardew has been trying to lift his side out of a dreadful slump while knowing he could be axed regardless of results should new owners want to bring in a new face.

And after the 1-0 defeat at Chelsea on Saturday, Pardew confessed, 'The quicker the situation is resolved, the better it will be in terms of everyone feeling comfortable in their positions at the club.'

Thankfully, with Magnusson's purchase of West Ham being confirmed on Tuesday morning, much of the uncertainty that has engulfed the club over the last few months has been removed.

And Pardew has been assured that his job is safe. But fans will still naturally wonder what the future really holds for their club.

Many will be delighted to finally see the end of chairman Terence Brown, who made some big mistakes prior to relegation in 2003 before pulling the club back from the brink of disaster by restoring them to the top flight.

Others, meanwhile, will say there's little point in seeing West Ham's ownership transferred unless it results in substantially greater funds being made available for team investment in order to move the club on to the next level.

Pardew has insisted that Hammers fans would be impressed by the plans that Magnusson has for the club.

But visions of a massive revolution have somewhat dissipated over the last few weeks.

And fans will ask if Brown has entertained ideas of a takeover simply because of an instinctive desire to cash-in his chips or with the genuine belief that Magnusson is in a much better position to seriously advance the club.

We must now hope that this week's decisions prove to be made in the best interests of West Ham United – as opposed to those of individual parties.

Because that's the only thing that fans can ultimately ask for.

Kirk now says: Fans quickly became comfortable with the £85m takeover, believing that Eggert Magnusson, who was the president of the Icelandic FA and held a seat on UEFA's executive committee, and Bjorgolfur Gudmundsson, the man who provided most of the funds, had the right credentials as well as ambitious and sensible plans to improve West Ham's fortunes. After all, what could possibly go wrong?

PARDS SACKING A STATEMENT OF INTENT (14 December 2006)

The ashen look on Alan Pardew's face as he confronted the media after West Ham's 4-0 drubbing at Bolton on Saturday suggested he feared his number was up.

He had just seen his team crash to their 13th defeat in 16 outings and the naked truth is that few bosses get to survive such a dreadful statistic.

The gleeful Bolton fans taunted Pardew with the chant 'you're getting sacked in the morning' as their team condemned the Hammers to a humiliating loss that proved the last straw for the club's new Icelandic owners.

The axe on Pardew's three-year reign at Upton Park finally fell on Monday morning, prompting various reactions from punters and pundits.

League Managers' Association chief John Barnwell predictably slammed West Ham's 'haste' in sacking a man who had guided the club to promotion back to the Premiership and into Europe via an FA Cup Final appearance.

John Madejski, Pardew's former chairman at Reading, even described the culling as 'brutal'. But the poor results this season really tell their own story, suggesting that the manager's influence on his under-achieving players was diminishing.

Pardew certainly has many qualities, being hard working, diligent and progressive in his approach to management.

He overhauled the training structure at West Ham in a modern way and his achievements at the club will always be fondly remembered.

But he wasn't immune to making mistakes and his judgement this season has been called into question on several occasions.

His failure to successfully integrate two world-class players in Argentina internationals Carlos Tevez and Javier Mascherano did not reflect well on his ability as a manager.

He remained too loyal to certain players who had clearly stopped playing for him, failed to address the woeful lack of creativity in midfield and rotated his strikers with increasing desperation.

Unpublicised issues behind the scenes must also have served to distract his focus in recent months.

Pardew's position had been considered under threat during Kia Joorabchian's attempted takeover of the club.

He certainly looked happy and relieved when Eggert Magnusson and financial backer Bjorgolfur Gudmundsson finally won their battle for ownership last month.

New chairman Magnusson initially stated his support for Pardew but it's clear that the new hierarchy – who splashed some £85m to acquire West Ham – mean serious business.

And for that the club's supporters should be grateful.

The Hammers suffered relegation four seasons ago as a result of chairman Terry Brown sitting on his hands and allowing manager Glenn Roeder to remain in place when the outcome seemed inevitable.

But the new owners are made of bolder stuff and, if the supporters will have demanded anything from Magnusson and Gudmundsson, it's strong leadership and ambition.

One can feel a degree of sympathy for Pardew, who will know he has lost a golden opportunity to lead the club into a bright new era – and that will tear into his soul.

But the new men at the top have made a major statement of intent and, for the time being at least, their judgement should be trusted.

Kirk now says: This columnist later interviewed Magnusson who, on Pardew's sacking, intriguingly said, 'There were reasons why I had to do it … and I will keep those to myself.'

MEDIOCRE FROM REO-COKER (21 December 2006)

Nobody could miss the irony of Nigel Reo-Coker scoring the winner against Manchester United on Sunday.

The West Ham skipper's miserable form this term has been highlighted as one of the reasons why Alan Pardew lost his job as manager last week.

The 22-year-old's name was also booed by a section of the Hammers support prior to kick-off against the Premiership leaders.

It was therefore perhaps inevitable that he would end up ramming those taunts back down the fans' throats by having the final say.

Reo-Coker's surly-faced goal celebration certainly seemed to display a hint of antagonism towards the supporters as he cynically cupped a hand to his right ear as opposed to naturally sharing in their joy.

Nobody likes criticism but players must accept that it comes as part of the package.

And if Reo-Coker had displayed a bit more humility by admitting his form has dipped this season rather than worrying about his bruised ego, then his relationship with the fans would be far healthier.

Which brings us closer to the real reasons as to why West Ham have under-achieved so much this term.

There is no doubt that many players felt they had a point to prove last season after claiming a place in the Premiership.

As new boss Alan Curbishley acknowledged on his arrival at the club, the team had previously displayed a 'newly promoted hunger' that has been missing this time around.

That desire saw the Hammers remain in the top half of the table for the whole of last season and go within a few minutes of a sensational FA Cup Final victory against Liverpool.

But success can easily go to people's heads and it's clear that several players – especially Reo-Coker – and former boss Pardew have suffered from believing their own publicity.

Much has been made of Reo-Coker's head being turned by interest from Arsenal and Manchester United – and many fans obviously believe his heart has not been in it this season.

But the real problem is that the midfielder is just not as good as he thinks he is – and that's always a dangerous situation.

Pardew was certainly not immune to self-appreciation and that's evidenced in the fact he has complained about his sacking, seemingly forgetting that he had lost 13 of his last 16 games.

We can at least be reassured that Curbishley does not suffer from such a trait, preferring to keep his feet planted firmly on the ground.

And if there were any doubts about that, we only have to look at the modest way in which the 49-year-old greeted the shock triumph against United in his first game in charge.

No endless celebrations, just relief that he had got a vital victory under his belt before setting sights on the next game at Fulham this weekend.

If he can instil the same humble attitude into some of his players, he'll have won a major battle as he aims to lift the Hammers up the Premiership table.

Kirk now says: Reo-Coker's relationship with the fans never recovered from this incident and they were glad to see the back of him when he joined Aston Villa in a vastly inflated £8.5m deal the following summer. The fact he then went to Bolton, Ipswich and Vancouver Whitecaps as his career headed in a downward spiral says it all.

CURBS GETS IT ALL WRONG (11 January 2007)

Alan Curbishley never scored an own goal as a player for West Ham but he can be accused of quickly doing so after returning as manager.

The Hammers have taken some flak in recent times – and deservedly so after crashing 6-0 at Reading on New Year's Day.

But with his side bouncing back with a 3-0 victory against Brighton in the FA Cup, Curbishley had the perfect opportunity to shift media attention towards some positives.

He could have praised new signing Luis Boa Morte for a promising debut, highlighted the growing influence of Carlos Tevez and welcomed youngster Mark Noble's first senior goal for the club.

He could also have thanked the supporters for continuing to back the team following a run of three consecutive defeats.

Instead, Curbishley unwisely decided to thrust Nigel Reo-Coker's name back into the spotlight by telling a room full of journalists that he was 'outraged' by recent criticism of his young skipper and then storming off without discussing the game.

If this was an effort to keep Reo-Coker's name out of the papers, it was certainly a funny way of going about it.

But Curbishley's feathers had clearly been ruffled and the word in the press room was that Reo-Coker – dropped for the game and therefore not cup-tied – had expressed a wish to quit the Hammers.

The midfielder has spent much of the season nursing his damaged ego following criticism of his below-par displays and would no doubt have used the negative coverage as an excuse for wanting to move on.

Hence an agitated Curbishley took full advantage of his first opportunity to slam the media for distressing his poor victimised player. Certain key points are being overlooked here, however.

For a start, the fans are the first people to recognise when a player isn't pulling his weight – and they have long realised that Reo-Coker's heart has not been in his performances after his head was turned by Arsenal's interest last summer.

Secondly, it was the player himself who needlessly whinged that 'everyone' was blaming him for Alan Pardew's sacking last month – a massive over-reaction following some fairly obvious complaints that West Ham's under-achieving players had done little to keep their boss in a job.

Curbishley's latest words will simply have helped fuel Reo-Coker's persecution complex.

If we have learned anything this season it's that the midfielder is far too young to have been handed the West Ham captaincy, because his recent behaviour has been sadly lacking in maturity.

And we should perhaps not be surprised that several newspapers have now accused Curbishley of displaying little of that particular commodity following his post-match rant at the weekend.

Teams failing on the field rarely get a positive press – that's obvious.

So what the management and players need to do is spend less time worrying about what's being written in the tabloids and concentrate on what really matters – trying to win football matches.

Kirk now says: The funniest thing about Curbishley's display after the Brighton game was the way veteran journalist Brian Glanville shouted 'pathetic' as the manager stormed past him out of the press room.

CHAMPIONSHIP, HERE WE COME ... (15 February 2007)

Will it be sunny in Scunny? Will we hold 'em in Oldham? We'll soon find out because West Ham will be playing Championship football next season – as will Scunthorpe and the Latics if the current league tables are anything to go by.

Alan Curbishley declared Saturday's visit of Watford, the Premiership's bottom club, as a 'must win' game.

So the 1-0 defeat must surely bang a huge nail into his side's coffin, with the Hammers still five points adrift of fourth-bottom Wigan who have a game in hand.

Yet Curbishley insists he remains 'confident' that West Ham can still secure survival, despite all the evidence pointing to the contrary.

Alan is a decent, hard-working bloke who did a fine job in consolidating Charlton as a Premiership outfit during the later part of his 15 years there.

But he was clearly not the right choice to save West Ham from relegation – not because he's not a good manager but because he's more of a long-term strategist than a short-term saviour.

The dreadful displays since his appointment in December really tell their own story.

As the new boss admits, 'I haven't delivered results.'

Curbishley has guided West Ham to just one league victory – against table-toppers Manchester United a few days after his arrival – in ten attempts.

The last nine Premiership outings have produced just three points and the performance against Watford last Saturday would have embarrassed any manager associated with it.

Of course, Curbishley has experienced plenty of misfortune of late and if it wasn't for bad luck he would have had no luck at all.

Injury problems – not least to new signings Matthew Upson and Lucas Neill – have undermined the team's efforts, while players have suffered moments of madness that the boss simply couldn't legislate for.

Anton Ferdinand's needless tug on Watford's Darius Henderson and Marlon Harewood's careless penalty miss in the same game both fall into that category.

But West Ham were on the back foot from the very first minute against the Hornets, with the players' lack of fight and fervour not reflecting well on the manager's motivational abilities.

Curbishley has frequently referred to the difficulties of 'taking over mid-stream' and being forced to 'learn about players in vital games'.

But the same goes for most managers when they arrive at a new club, not least former Hammers boss Alan Pardew who has been far more successful in collecting eight points from his eight league games at fellow strugglers Charlton.

The overwhelming conclusion is that while Curbishley has impressive credentials in terms of developing a team over a prolonged period of time, there was never anything in his CV to suggest he had the dynamism necessary to make a sudden impact.

One can have sympathy for chairman Eggert Magnusson, who showed courage in dispensing with Pardew's services and backing his new man to the tune of £18m in the January transfer window.

But his decision to go for Curbishley must now be seriously questioned. As a former West Ham player, Curbishley may understand the traditions of the club but he simply hasn't been able to implement his ideas quickly enough. Indeed, some will say the Hammers would have been better off had Pardew been left in charge.

Others, meanwhile, will look at Curbishley and consider him to be the right man at the right club … at the wrong time.

Kirk now says: Assistant boss Mervyn Day later told this columnist that the new management team were 'fire-fighting for the first two months' and that there was 'resistance' to the training methods being introduced. However, there were also rumours of Curbishley keeping his distance from the players, many of which eyed him with suspicion and mistrust, while others, such as Teddy Sheringham, just took a dislike to him.

HEADING FOR A BEHEADING (8 March 2007)

Watch out if you're walking past the Boleyn Ground over the next few months, as there are likely to be so many heads rolling at West Ham that Green Street will resemble a tenpin bowling lane.

Chairman Eggert Magnusson does not appear to suffer fools easily and, with relegation all but certain, the Icelander is set to resume the role of executioner – and the guillotine will surely be kept well greased.

The Hammers lost nearly 20 squad members after they last suffered the drop four years ago – and another player exodus can be expected this time around.

The big-name players set to be on their way out can basically be placed into three categories: the egotistical under-achievers the fans will shed few tears over (Nigel Reo-Coker and his mates), the recent signings whose stays will be brief (Lucas Neill, Luis Boa Morte, Matthew Upson) and the favourites we'll be sad to see go (Carlos Tevez, Yossi Benayoun, Dean Ashton).

It would be nice to think the club's new owners have the funds to soften the financial implications of relegation, but a player clear-out is inevitable regardless.

Roed to nowhere: Glenn Roeder steered West Ham in the wrong direction

Maverick: Paolo Di Canio was majestic, mercurial and magical … and lots of other words beginning with M…

Say it ain't so, Joe: The jury is out as to whether Joe Cole achieved what his early potential suggested

Def con: Jermain Defoe incurred the wrath of West Ham fans after trying to jump ship after relegation

Moore time wanted: Alan Pardew enjoyed success…then lost his way

Making plans for Nigel: Alan Pardew welcomes Nigel Reo-Coker, whose surname interestingly rhymes with mediocre

Bubbles are flying: West Ham's play-off victory against Preston was financially crucial for the club

United: But West Ham didn't get the win they deserved against Liverpool in the 2006 FA Cup Final when losing on penalties

Wham bam, thank you Zam: Bobby Zamora celebrates his most important goal for the Hammers in the 2005 play-off final

Curb your enthusiasm: Alan Curbishley and Eggert Magnusson both left the club before they planned

The Dean machine: Dean Ashton denies that XL stands for his shirt size

Hammers in his heart: Carlos Tevez enjoys a special relationship with the West Ham fans

Ice-Berg: Icelandic chairman Eggert Magnusson was pleased to sign Freddie Ljungberg but it was an expensive mistake

Zo pleased to be here: Gianfranco Zola's lack of management experience caught up with him in the end

Not a perfect ten: Savio Nsereko proved to be another expensive flop

Upton lark: Fans didn't do themselves any favours when invading the pitch in the Carling Cup game against Millwall in 2009

Time's nearly up: Avram Grant proved to be a disastrous appointment

Park life: The man-of-the-match award was in danger of being renamed the Scott Parker award with the midfielder having little competition

Standing their ground: David Gold, Karren Brady and David Sullivan fought hard to win the rights to the Olympic Stadium and rightly so

Rolling the dyce: Sam Allardyce gambled with West Ham's traditions…and proved a winner

Happy Hammers: West Ham under-achieved in only reaching the play-offs in 2012 but victory against Blackpool made it all worthwhile

I've got the Npower: David Gold deserved success for his investment

Andy Carroll proved hugely influential on loan … when fit

There will also be much speculation about the future of manager Alan Curbishley and, if his performance was judged on the same basis as his predecessor Alan Pardew – axed by Magnusson just four games after his takeover – he would surely be handed his P45.

Curbishley's league record since arriving at Upton Park in December is abysmal (one win, three draws, eight defeats) and, although he proved he could build a team over time at Charlton, he has been way out of his depth when asked to solve problems in the short term at West Ham.

Some fans will want to see a change of manager, others will blame the players for their woeful displays and believe Curbishley should be given time to rebuild the team in the summer.

If the former Hammers midfielder does cling on to his post, he's unlikely to survive until Christmas if West Ham are not serious promotion contenders next season.

Magnusson could also be moving the furniture around in the boardroom if the club fails to win its appeal against the charges brought by the Premier League in respect of the registrations of Javier Mascherano (sold to Liverpool in January) and Carlos Tevez.

The Hammers have been accused of withholding information relating to the exact nature of the third-party ownership of the two Argentina internationals and face a serious threat of points deduction if found guilty.

It has been reported that Magnusson will insist a previous hierarchy was responsible for the transfers, with former chairman Terence Brown and managing director Paul Aldridge no longer at the club.

But other members of the old board remain and, if it is proved they were involved in any impropriety, the new chairman will certainly make sure that any guilty parties pay with their jobs.

A turbulent and traumatic season both on and off the pitch is sure to end in further turmoil.

So watch out for those round objects bouncing out of the Boleyn in the near future, because they're unlikely to be footballs.

Kirk now says: Things were going from bad to worse, with a 4-0 thrashing at Alan Pardew's Charlton followed by Tottenham's last-gasp 4-3 win at Upton Park that made it six consecutive defeats for the Hammers, while confirmation that the Premier League had issued charges over the signings of Tevez and Mascherano, stories of a gambling culture among the players and news that Anton Ferdinand had made a secret trip to America to celebrate his birthday all helped to create a massive black cloud that threatened to engulf the club.

THE GREAT ESCAPE IS ON ... (26 April 2007)

There are three things that are guaranteed in life – death, taxes and West Ham producing a late flurry of hope when battling against relegation.

Just four years ago, the Hammers collected an incredible 22 points from their final 11 games only for defeat at fellow strugglers Bolton late on to ultimately condemn them to the drop.

In 1989, they won five of their last seven games before a 5-1 defeat at title-chasing Liverpool in their final outing sent them down.

They even won two of their last three games – helping to wreck Manchester United's championship hopes in the process – when they finished bottom of the old First Division table in 1992.

There have been some successful recoveries, of course.

One defeat in the final 11 games of the 1994/1995 campaign – including a 3-0 victory against Liverpool and the 1-1 draw that denied Manchester United the title in the final week – saw the Hammers finish well clear of the drop zone.

Two seasons later, the signings of strikers John Hartson and Paul Kitson inspired West Ham to safety with a run that saw just three defeats in the final 13 games.

And a full decade on, we find ourselves wondering if the Hammers can really save their Premiership skins following a sequence of four wins in six games that has lifted them to within three points of Sheffield United and Wigan just above the safety mark.

With Fulham just a point above those two clubs, the scramble to avoid the drop is hugely intriguing with just three games left to play.

One thing is for certain, however – and that is that West Ham can't afford to lose at Wigan on Saturday.

Manager Alan Curbishley has insisted his side needs at least another six points to stand a chance of survival.

And they will probably need to come in the next two games – at the JJB Stadium and at home to Bolton the following weekend – with a trip to current Premiership leaders Manchester United to follow on the season's final day.

The only way the Hammers can seriously contemplate picking up anything at Old Trafford is if the Red Devils have already won the title – not something you would necessarily bet on – and choose to rest their top players for the following weekend's FA Cup Final against Chelsea.

It is possible West Ham could go into that game level on points with Sheffield United and Wigan, who play each other on that very same day. Who is to say those two sides won't play out an uninspired draw, knowing the Hammers will need to beat Manchester United to overtake them because of their superior goal difference?

As recent weeks have proved, all we really know is that results are notoriously difficult to predict at this time of year.

But let's hope West Ham's revival over the last month or so doesn't ultimately prove to be in vain – and leave their fans heartbroken yet again.

Kirk now says: Following unanticipated wins against Blackburn, Middlesbrough, Arsenal and Everton, the Great Escape was very much on, thanks to the goals of Bobby Zamora and, er, some bloke called Carlos Tevez.

WHELAN AND WARNOCK SHOULD STOP WHINGEING
(3 May 2007)

The Premier League inquiry's report into West Ham's signings of Carlos Tevez and Javier Mascherano made for fascinating reading when published last week.

Nobody would be happy to learn of the club's 'dishonesty and deceit' in respect of hiding the influence of the third-party ownership of the two Argentina internationals when signed last summer.

But fans can at least breathe a huge sigh of relief that the Premier League decided to hit the Hammers with a massive £5.5m fine rather than deduct the points that would surely have condemned the club to relegation. Predictably, the parties that stood to benefit from any points deduction – namely relegation rivals such as Wigan and Sheffield United – were quick to complain about the verdicts.

Wigan boss Paul Jewell – having just seen Tevez inspire West Ham to a 3-0 win against his dismal outfit on Saturday – complained, 'I guess if it had been Wigan or Watford, or West Ham had already been down, they would have taken points off them.'

His chairman Dave Whelan, who had lobbied hard for a points penalty according to reports, shared his manager's sense of paranoia when moaning, 'If it had been Wigan that had broken rules like that, we would have been deducted ten points.'

Sheffield United boss Neil Warnock – never slow to complain about penalties of one description or another – added, 'If it was us, Wigan or Watford, there would have been points deducted and I think everyone knows that.'

You would fully expect these people to be disappointed by the outcome – especially if the Hammers succeed in escaping the drop – but to insist their clubs would have been punished differently suggests they have huge chips on their shoulders.

There is nothing in the report to indicate that West Ham have received any kind of favouritism – although there's no denying that the Premiership is a far more appealing product when they are in it.

The reality is that had a points deduction been imposed, the Hammers would have instantly appealed against the decision and created a situation whereby none of their rivals near the bottom of the table would know whether they were safe or not until the summer.

More importantly, the Premier League has admitted that, with relegation for West Ham an inevitable consequence, 'We have come to the view that a deduction of points would not be proportionate punishment.' This opens up a huge debate, of course.

Some will argue that if a crime merits, say, a six-point deduction, it should be applied to all clubs whether they are Manchester United at the top of the table or West Ham United near the bottom.

Others, meanwhile, will insist that the consequences of such a penalty must be taken into account – otherwise the punishment, as the report says, can become disproportionate.

West Ham were fined in excess of £5m – as any other club would have been – but that would have effectively become a £40m fine in the club's present circumstances and few, outside Wigan and Sheffield that is, would agree that's fair.

Manager Alan Curbishley, who didn't exactly support the club's case last week by admitting he would have called for points to be docked had he been a rival boss, at least used the lifeline to motivate his troops to the vital win at Wigan.

He must do the same when Bolton visit Upton Park on Saturday, otherwise the whole debate becomes redundant.

Kirk now says: West Ham did indeed secure a 3-1 success against Bolton – thanks to two goals from Tevez, who won the Hammer of the Year award – to move out of the bottom three and set up a final-day game at champions Manchester United in the knowledge that a point would guarantee safety.

OKAY, LET'S TALK ABOUT JUSTICE ... (17 May 2007)

Plenty of people in football have been complaining about so-called 'injustice' in recent times, but Alan Curbishley is entitled to have his own grievances this week.

The West Ham manager has just guided his team to one of the great escape acts in modern history – yet his achievements have been totally overshadowed by events off the field.

When the Hammers crashed to a devastating 4-3 home defeat by Tottenham two months ago, they were all but relegated.

At that time ten points adrift of Premiership safety and 11 league games without a win, there was little hope for a side that must surely have suffered one blow too many in a painful season of hard knocks.

But Curbishley must be given immense credit for having the courage and belief to guide his men to an incredible seven victories in nine games to win their fight for survival.

The Hammers boss points to the Spurs game as being the one where his players started to suggest what they were capable of despite the final result. Other observers will see the following game at Blackburn as the one where fortunes stopped hiding, with a slice of luck involved in the surprise 2-1 success.

From that day on everything seemed to fall in West Ham's favour, with the players and management finally reaping the rewards for their growing spirit and endeavour.

The 3-0 defeat at Sheffield United looked to have negated the shock 1-0 victory at Arsenal a week earlier, but wins against Everton, Wigan and Bolton ensured the Hammers needed just one point at Manchester United last weekend to stay up.

They grabbed all three, of course, with Carlos Tevez claiming the only goal to secure West Ham's first league double over the Red Devils since 1977 and spark delirious celebrations among the travelling support.

Curbishley may have struggled following his arrival at the club just before Christmas but even his fiercest critics would have to admire the way he has turned things around.

Sadly, the week's headlines have been dominated by the threats of legal action by clubs unhappy that the Premier League failed to deduct points from West Ham for rule breaches in respect of the signings of Tevez and fellow Argentine Javier Mascherano.

Relegated Sheffield United chairman Kevin McCabe has demanded that the disciplinary decision be overturned – in a desperate bid to save his side's sorry skins – while Dave Whelan, his whingeing Wigan counterpart, has complained about the 'injustice' of it all.

Indeed, if you believe many of the punters and pundits sounding off on the subject, the vast majority of football folk feel the dissenting clubs are justified in taking some kind of action.

Such views are rooted in ignorance and naivety, however, with very few people – either on the street or in certain club boardrooms – enjoying a true understanding of the case.

West Ham were penalised not for fielding ineligible players – as some would have us believe – but for entering into a contract with a third party that potentially allowed for a 'material influence'.

Side contracts, that were never legally enforceable anyway, have been torn up and the Premier League has subsequently approved the registration of Tevez at Upton Park.

That is not good enough for some parties but, while there's a lot of hot air being spouted, the reality is that any legal threats are likely to come to nothing. Yet unless the media focus quickly shifts, it's unlikely that Curbishley will be afforded the acclaim he deserves.

And for many Hammers fans, that certainly will be an 'injustice'.

Kirk now says: It has since been written into the history books that Tevez scored the goal at Old Trafford that kept West Ham in the Premier League, when the reality is that a goalless draw would have been enough. As for the challenges of Sheffield United, as time would unfortunately prove, they just wouldn't let it lie.

REFLECTING ON SEASON 2006/07

Best signing: Carlos Tevez (Corinthians), undisclosed

Worst signing: Nigel Quashie (West Brom), £1.2m

Best result: Winning 1-0 at Arsenal in April

Worst result: Losing 6-0 at Reading in January

Final position: 15th in Premier League, 41 points

Manager and rating: Alan Pardew 4/10, Alan Curbishley 6/10

Best thing about season: Carlos Tevez inspiring the Great Escape

Worst thing about season: Seeing Tevez and Javier Mascherano being frozen out of action

SEASON 2007/08

'West Ham have a boos problem'

AS expected, Sheffield United continued to whine about their relegation and West Ham's Premier League survival, with all sorts of characters tossing their unwanted thoughts into the ring.

First FIFA president Sepp Blatter entered the row by claiming he had the power to overturn the Premier League's decision not to deduct points over the signings of Carlos Tevez and Javier Mascherano.

Then actor and Blades fan Sean Bean (we'll think of him more as Mr Bean now) announced that he planned to lead a delegation to Parliament to campaign about the affair, while Michael Palin, of Monty Python fame, also pledged his support. Perhaps that was appropriate as their 'Campaign for Fairness' did have a rather comic look about it, being based on ignorance and misunderstanding.

It was considered inevitable that Tevez would leave West Ham during the close season but the circumstances of his departure were always going to be under heavy scrutiny, with various onlookers keen to establish what monies would be paid by whom to which party.

Following a long-running saga that lasted throughout the summer and looked to be heading for the courts, the striker eventually joined Manchester United after the Hammers accepted a £2m settlement from MSI to release his registration.

Hammers chairman Eggert Magnusson immediately declared that £500,000 – the balance after the deduction of legal fees – would be donated for the building of football pitches in east London.

West Ham's initial target to replace Tevez was Charlton striker Darren Bent, who rejected the chance to play again under Alan Curbishley and ended up making a £16.5m switch to Spurs instead.

Magnusson said, 'Feedback from our supporters suggests they are less disappointed that I thought they might be.'

But with the chairman eager to splash some cash – or at least that belonging to owner Bjorgolfur Gudmundsson – some £29.5m was spent on recruiting Scott Parker, Craig Bellamy, Julien Faubert, Freddie Ljungberg, Kieron Dyer and Nolberto Solano.

A Google search on Ljungberg at that time revealed a man posing in his pants, with the former Arsenal midfielder undertaking advertising work for Calvin Klein.

Curbishley had always liked model professionals but now it seemed he was signing a professional model and the Sweden international was restricted by injury to just 22 league starts before being paid a reported £6m to rip up his deal the following year.

Faubert was immediately ruled out for six months with an Achilles tendon injury while Dyer suffered a broken leg just three games into his Hammers career.

Nigel Reo-Coker finally got the big-money move that he was looking for when he joined Aston Villa, which allowed Lucas Neill to replace him as West Ham captain (and do the job properly), while Marlon Harewood also went to Villa Park for a £4m fee.

Yossi Benayoun made a £5m move to Liverpool while Paul Konchesky joined Fulham for £2m and Tyrone Mears went to Derby for £1m as the Hammers recouped a large chunk of their summer outlay.

DON'T EXPECT TOO MANY FIREWORKS (9 August 2007)

All appeared to be quiet on the Hammers horizon this time last year.

There was no sign of two Argentina superstars being recruited in mysterious circumstances, no hint of a season-long relegation battle, no suggestion of a prolonged club takeover and no reason to suspect that manager Alan Pardew might be replaced by Alan Curbishley.

West Ham's unbelievable campaign wasn't confined to those dramas, however, with a Premier League inquiry causing continued controversy into the summer as relegated Sheffield United contested the club's top-flight survival.

The name of Carlos Tevez has dominated headlines for the last four months and, while fans will be disappointed to see the magical maverick leave Upton Park, his long-disputed departure to Manchester United at least draws a line under recent events as West Ham look towards a new era.

Given the Hammers spent most of last season in the relegation zone and appeared doomed going into the final ten games, the majority of fans would no doubt be satisfied with a comfortable, stress-free mid-table finish this time around.

Whether that would be enough for ambitious chairman Eggert Magnusson, who has promised to invest heavily in making West Ham regular contenders for European competition, is a matter of debate.

The club has made some exciting signings in the form of Craig Bellamy, Freddie Ljungberg, Scott Parker and the sadly injured Julien Faubert, yet much depends on how many games they prove fit enough to play. But with most of the £23.5m spent so far having been recouped through the sales of Nigel Reo-Coker, Yossi Benayoun,

Marlon Harewood, Paul Konchesky, Tyrone Mears and, of course, that man Tevez, it's clear the funds are still there for a lot more business to be done before the transfer window closes at the end of the month.

That means it's difficult to predict at this stage exactly what West Ham's prospects for the new season are really like.

If you take any notice of the bookmakers' odds, a finish of anywhere between eighth and 14th is on the cards.

There are a number of clubs such as the Hammers likely to make a big improvement this season, with Newcastle and Saturday's opponents Manchester City also expected to be moving onwards and upwards.

But of the other outfits that finished above West Ham last term, fans would like to think that Middlesbrough, Bolton, Portsmouth and Reading can be overtaken with Aston Villa, Blackburn and possibly Everton also in the team's sights.

Curbishley should feel far more comfortable this time around having been able to implement his ideas during the pre-season period.

He also has the likes of the fit-again Dean Ashton, Matthew Upson and Danny Gabbidon available and they will feel like new signings.

So the Hammers should logically be in a position to look ahead to a stable campaign.

Although as supporters discovered last year, perhaps it might be wiser simply to expect the unexpected.

It wouldn't be West Ham otherwise.

Kirk now says: The Hammers did indeed secure a 'comfortable, stress-free mid-table finish' but perhaps you should be careful of what you wish for, with the campaign – in stark contrast to the previous season – turning out to be one of the most sleep-inducing the club has ever experienced.

SAME OLD SAM AND BRUCE THE EXCUSE (23 August 2007)

They say that leopards never change their spots and West Ham fans have already seen evidence of that from a couple of managers this season.

First we had Newcastle boss Sam Allardyce – a man who has never had much time for the Hammers – accusing West Ham of 'undervaluing' Kieron Dyer before the England midfielder completed his move to Upton Park last week.

It was a preposterous claim, given that Newcastle had accepted the Hammers' original £6m offer before changing their minds and demanding a higher fee.

But we're all used to the former Bolton boss speaking of West Ham with derision.

This was the man who complained that Yossi Benayoun had made a 'stupid' decision and 'a big mistake' after the Israeli midfielder snubbed Bolton to sign for West Ham in 2005.

'If Benayoun didn't want to come to a great club like ours then he went to West Ham for more money,' he claimed.

Benayoun said what everyone else was thinking when he insisted that Allardyce was 'talking nonsense'.

The same could also have been said of Birmingham boss Steve Bruce as he complained about the penalty award that earned West Ham their first win of the season on Saturday.

Bruce questioned whether his goalkeeper Colin Doyle had made contact with Craig Bellamy and insisted that no advantage had been gained even if he had because 'the ball was in the stand'.

When he described the referee's decision as 'a howler' and moaned that 'smaller clubs' rarely get the breaks, it was difficult to avoid breaking into laughter.

You would have thought that somebody who has been in football for 30 years as a player and manager would know the rules by now.

If a goalkeeper takes out a player, it doesn't matter where the ball is – it's a penalty.

Bellamy may have played for the spot-kick but that doesn't mean it wasn't one.

And had the incident taken place at the other end of the pitch, Bruce would have insisted it was a certain penalty in his side's favour.

As for Birmingham being a small club, it leaves you wondering how you would describe Blackburn, Portsmouth, Fulham, Reading and Wigan who all attracted fewer supporters to their Premiership games at the weekend. Bruce visibly contested many of the officials' decisions during West Ham's 1-0 win at St Andrew's and was virtually orchestrating the reactions of the home crowd from the touchline.

Maybe with his post-match comments he's attempting to create a situation whereby referees take a more sympathetic view towards his team in future weeks – a bit like his old boss Sir Alex Ferguson.

On the evidence of the display against West Ham, he's going to need all the help he can get if his sorry outfit are to avoid an instant return to the Championship.

Kirk now says: The stuff about Sam Allardyce offers a certain amount of amusement, given that he would later take charge of West Ham, while Birmingham did indeed suffer relegation.

BELL STARS FOR HAMMERS (6 September 2007)

Fans called for the Hammer of the Year poll to be scrapped last season before the magic of Carlos Tevez finally emerged to help preserve the club's Premiership status. Yet just five games into the new campaign, we already have an outstanding contender for next year's award in the shape of striker Craig Bellamy.

The 28-year-old, signed from Liverpool for a club record fee of £7.5m during the summer, has scored three times in his last two games and quickly become the talisman of the West Ham team.

Many critics questioned the wisdom of signing the fiery Wales international given his history of controversy.

Let us face it – Bellamy is certainly not shy of expressing his opinion.

But the striker has a tremendous will to win and his desire and determination has been there for all to see since his arrival at Upton Park.

Many players might have cried off when a groin strain jeopardised his selection for the Carling Cup game at Bristol Rovers last week.

But Bellamy was desperate to play and his eagerness was rewarded with his first two goals for the Hammers in the 2-1 victory at the Memorial Ground.

He was on target again in the 3-0 win at Reading on Saturday as West Ham chalked up their third away win of the season and their fifth in succession if we include the tail end of last term.

In fact it's not too early to claim that a pattern is already beginning to emerge, with the Hammers enjoying no shortage of success on the road as a result of their ability to hit teams on the break.

This initially became evident in the second half of the victory at Birmingham last month, with both Bellamy and fellow former Newcastle team-mate Kieron Dyer terrorising the home side with their electric pace.

Dyer's loss with a broken leg represents a serious blow to West Ham's ambitions but it was reassuring to see that the team could still spring from defence to attack with lightning speed at Reading.

Left-winger Matthew Etherington, who scored twice in the win at the Madejski Stadium, suggested he could play a key role this season if he can reproduce that kind of form on a consistent basis.

But it's Bellamy who has given fans most cause to believe that West Ham can threaten the top half of the Premiership table this season.

And if he can stay fit for the lion's share of the campaign, there should be little doubt that he'll be lifting at least one trophy next May if the supporters have anything to say about it.

Kirk now says: Sadly, injury restricted Bellamy to just 12 appearances and six goals in what amounted to his only full season at Upton Park (allowing goalkeeper Rob Green to win the Hammer of the Year award), while Dyer (no stranger to nursing wounds) wouldn't play again until the early part of 2009.

HAMMERS RAM THEIR POINT HOME (15 November 2007)

Does a team win a game or do their opponents lose it? On the evidence of the reaction to West Ham's 5-0 thumping of Derby on Saturday, it would appear to be the latter.

The Hammers chalked up their biggest away win since September 1962 (a 6-1 success at ten-man Manchester City), yet the headlines were dominated by the home side's continuing inability to cut it at Premier League level since their promotion last term.

One newspaper typified the reaction by declaring, 'Rams to the slaughter – Billy's boys look like worst side in Prem history.'

And *Match Of The Day* pundits Alan Shearer and Mark Lawrenson concentrated their focus very much on Derby's defensive deficiencies.

But that hardly does justice to West Ham's performance, especially given the injury problems that Alan Curbishley's squad has had to face in recent times.

The Hammers went into the game without some £35m worth of attacking talent in the shape of Dean Ashton, Craig Bellamy, Bobby Zamora, Scott Parker, Kieron Dyer and Julien Faubert.

Hayden Mullins joined fellow midfielder Mark Noble on the casualty list before the trip to Derby.

George McCartney then suffered an ankle injury early in the first half that saw right-back Lucas Neill having to switch to the left.

And it was later revealed that two-goal hero Lee Bowyer had been playing with a groin problem that required surgery.

West Ham would therefore have had plenty of excuses had they become the fourth team this season to return from Pride Park with less than maximum points.

But they produced a fabulous display to tear Derby to pieces, scoring five goals, hitting the woodwork twice and having a penalty claim turned down.

Admittedly, the outcome could have been different had Kenny Miller not wasted Derby's best opportunity when heading wide early in the second period with the score at 1-0.

Within ten minutes the Hammers had stretched their advantage to four goals as they ruthlessly went for the jugular.

'I'm not sure whether it's an excellent performance by West Ham or a really poor display by Derby,' admitted match analyst Gordon McQueen before deciding, 'I think it's probably a bit of both.'

Credit should certainly go to the likes of Carlton Cole, Jonathan Spector and John Pantsil – three players who would see little first-team action in normal circumstances.

And we should thank the midfielders – Bowyer, Matt Etherington and Nobby Solano – who weighed in with most of the goals.

Everybody appears to be pulling together to pull the club through the current injury crisis – and that's what people should really be talking about.

Kirk now says: Such big wins for West Ham away from home are rarer than talking dogs with a degree in philosophy, so it was disappointing that with Derby heading for a record low of 11 points for the entire campaign, the visitors got little credit for their brilliant performance.

WAS EGGY ALL HE WAS CRACKED UP TO BE?
(20 December 2007)

Eggert Magnusson was a popular chairman with the West Ham fans.

Some might say that, as the successor to the often-criticised Terry Brown, it would have been very hard not to be.

But the Icelander, who was the public face of the club's takeover 13 months ago, seemed to be genuinely liked by supporters who appreciated his enthusiasm and commitment to the cause.

So many will have been disappointed – and some a little bemused – to see Magnusson's association with the Hammers brought to an end last week.

In truth, the writing had been on the wall since he lost much of his power and was demoted to non-executive chairman in September.

Bjorgolfur Gudmundsson, the man who provided most of the funds to buy West Ham and has purchased Magnusson's five per cent shareholding, has praised the role played by his compatriot.

The past year has been a traumatic period for the club, given the dramatic battle against the drop and the appeals of relegated Sheffield United for the Hammers to be deducted points for the controversial signings of Carlos Tevez and Javier Mascherano.

But you don't fix something that's not broken and many supporters will suspect that certain elements behind the scenes were not exactly to Gudmundsson's liking.

Magnusson was seen to be the football brains behind the controlling partnership, with the 60-year-old having run the Icelandic FA and held a seat on the UEFA committee.

His successor Gudmundsson, however, is viewed as the calculating businessman after achieving billionaire status as the chairman of Landsbanki.

It is generally believed that he was behind the sacking of former manager Alan Pardew last year and is certainly not the kind of man to tolerate failure.

Current boss Alan Curbishley was very much Magnusson's choice and it's logical to assume his position has been weakened by the latter's departure.

The league and cup home defeats by Everton last week won't have helped his cause as he tries to impress his new chairman.

Curbishley has done well to keep the Hammers in a mid-table position this season after losing so many key players to injury.

Gudmundsson will surely realise the problems his manager has faced. But he will demand success in the long term – and is likely to accept few excuses.

Kirk now says: Little did we know there were dark storm clouds on the horizon for both Curbishley and Gudmundsson, who would both leave Upton Park in circumstances they could not have predicted.

LONG WEIGHT FOR ASHTON (17 January 2008)

Dean Ashton's impressive display against Fulham had one Sunday paper calling for the West Ham striker to receive an England call-up.

Given that the Hammers hitman suffers an injury every time he makes the squad, we might be better off if new boss Fabio Capello decides to ignore him for next month's friendly against Switzerland.

It was certainly pleasing to see Ashton put the frighteners on Fulham, scoring West Ham's leveller in the 2-1 win and only being denied a second goal by two great saves from Antti Niemi.

His improvement was much needed following a poor performance in the goalless FA Cup outing against Manchester City the previous weekend. With a backside bigger than former heavyweight Hammer John Hartson, Ashton looked lardy and lead-footed as strike partner Carlton Cole made the running on that occasion.

Indeed, there were signs that the West Ham fans were beginning to lose patience with the striker as he seeks full fitness following injury.

But will Ashton ever be the player he was – or could have been in the future – after missing the whole of last season with a broken ankle?

There is no doubt that he'll always know where the back of the net is – as his goal against Fulham proved.

But unless he can get back into shape and rediscover his full mobility, the fear is that he'll struggle to fulfil his true potential.

If there's one Hammer who should have caught Capello's eye by now then it's Matthew Upson.

The defender has been outstanding this season and a model of consistency, despite having several partners because of injuries.

Upson has also proved a threat at set-pieces and scored the winner against Manchester United recently.

If Capello is starting with a blank piece of paper – rather than purely using the previous squad as a template – then Upson must surely win the call-up his form deserves.

Goalkeeper Robert Green should also be in with a shout, especially with Paul Robinson having been dropped by Tottenham recently.

As for Ashton, let's hope the idea of England recognition proves a tempting carrot to chase, as the more running he does the better.

Kirk now says: Matthew Upson would indeed start against Switzerland, but Dean Ashton would have to wait until June of that year to win his one and only England cap.

IS ASH WORTH MORE CASH? (31 January 2008)

'C-Ash Storm!' was the headline in one Sunday tabloid at the weekend when it was claimed that Dean Ashton was seeking to double his West Ham salary in order to achieve parity with the club's top earners.

This kind of story is becoming all too frequent in the Premier League, with players' noses quickly being forced out of joint if they hear that one team-mate or another is being paid more than they are.

Needless to say, the man in the street has little sympathy for footballers grumbling about their wages, given the top stars generally earn more in a week than the long-suffering supporters do in a year.

Can we really empathise with Ashton for feeling aggrieved with only picking up around £23,000 a week, particularly when he was quite happy to accept such terms when signing his present contract?

At that point, however, the striker could not have anticipated the changes that have taken place at Upton Park over the past 18 months.

And there's no doubt that he has fallen behind in the pay stakes with the likes of Craig Bellamy, Scott Parker, Kieron Dyer and Freddie Ljungberg arriving last summer on generous contracts.

It is fair to say that none of us would relish the idea of our mates at work earning twice as much for doing the same job.

Not that money has ever been Ashton's god, if stories that the former Norwich hitman waived £150,000 in payments to seal his then club-record £7.25m move to West Ham in 2006 are anything to go by.

But Ashton would appear to have two problems at the moment.

One is that he needs to prove he can still be the player he promised to be before suffering the ankle injury that forced him to miss the whole of last season – a period in which he was paid handsomely, it should be remembered.

The other is that new Hammers chairman Bjorgolfur Gudmundsson is said to be reluctant to make the kind of pay-outs that his predecessor Eggert Magnusson did during his year-long reign.

On the other hand, West Ham will need to extend Ashton's contract if they want to preserve his value in the transfer market.

If an agreement cannot be reached, we shouldn't be too surprised if Ashton finds himself leaving Upton Park for pastures new.

Kirk now says: With 11 goals in 35 outings under his belt that season, Ashton would eventually sign a bumper new five-year contract, said to be worth £50,000 a week or, to put it another way, a total of £13m.

A FAT LOT OF FUN THAT WAS (14 February 2008)

West Ham have a boos problem – and not just because two vital points dropped out of their pocket as they staggered to a 1-1 draw at home to Birmingham on Saturday. The Upton Park crowd's reaction at the final whistle made it clear they didn't like what they had seen.

And it's likely that England boss Fabio Capello would not have been too impressed either on his first visit to Green Street.

The Italian would have heard much about the Hammers' famous tradition of playing stylish, attacking football, with entertainment very much a priority. The disappointing encounter with Birmingham must have left him feeling as if he had taken a wrong turn and arrived at a different ground.

West Ham have done extremely well to spend most of the season in the top half of the table despite losing so many players to injury.

But it's becoming obvious that fans are growing increasingly frustrated with Alan Curbishley's tactics and have virtually lost patience with struggling striker Dean Ashton.

Curbishley is seen to be cautious and conservative – and some would even say negative – in his approach to games.

Fans will accept a 4-5-1 formation taking shape when the likes of Liverpool are visiting Upton Park.

But that's not the case when the opposition is a bottom-three outfit in the shape of Birmingham.

Curbishley spoke of having to sacrifice a striker during the second half because he felt the team was losing its grip in midfield.

But that's two home games in succession when that has happened – and Birmingham weren't even playing five in the middle.

What made it worse was that it was the hard-working Carlton Cole who was hauled off for winger Julien Faubert just past the hour mark – rather than the totally ineffective Ashton.

The decision to take off Cole was jeered while the crowd cheered in approval when Ashton was finally subbed in the closing minutes.

Ashton's recent displays for the Hammers have been nothing short of woeful.

He looks nothing like the player he was before missing the whole of last season with a serious ankle injury. And his lack of movement is evidence that he either can't or won't run – and neither is acceptable.

Ashton's lazy body language suggests he doesn't want to be at West Ham and many fans are clearly turning against him.

The problem needs to be addressed, sooner rather than later.

Kirk now says: Needless to say, patience with Ashton's lack of form was running thinner than his disappearing hair at this point in time.

FRANK'S A LOT ... FOR THE EARLY BATH (6 March 2008)

Suffice to say that the West Ham boo-boys experienced mixed emotions during Chelsea's visit to Upton Park on Saturday.

It is considered part of football's traditions that supporters will voice their dissent against players – generally on the opposing team – who they feel have stepped out of line.

Hammers fans are probably no different to any others when it comes to needing players they love to hate – just ask Paul Ince and Jermain Defoe.

Some say such behaviour is not big and not clever – but many will consider it part of football's banter.

So nobody was too unhappy to see Frank Lampard named in Chelsea's starting line-up despite speculation he could be axed following the Carling Cup Final defeat by Spurs.

The England midfielder, in stark contrast to former Hammers team-mates Rio Ferdinand and Joe Cole, is fiercely reviled for the way he left Upton Park six years ago.

And for many fans, the chance to give him some stick would at least offer some consolation if, as feared, the Hammers fell to a seventh successive defeat against the Blues.

Few anticipated the events that unfolded with Lampard one of several Chelsea players who were booed – including both Joe and Ashley Cole.

Lampard was the first to seek retribution for the abuse, firing home the penalty that put the Blues ahead before showing the home fans exactly what he thought of them.

It was a surprise – and something of a disappointment – that former hero Joe was also subjected to a few jeers.

The midfielder duly responded by doubling Chelsea's advantage, although it says much about his sense of dignity that he did little to celebrate the strike.

The same could not be said of namesake Ashley, who shot down chants of 'there's only one Cheryl Tweedy' by wrapping up the scoring and winging his way down the touchline as if he had just won the European Cup.

By that time, of course, Hammers fans had produced the biggest cheer of the day when Lampard, who had helped set up his side's third goal for Michael Ballack, was sent off ten minutes before half-time for pushing Luis Boa Morte to the ground – a season highlight for many.

A 4-0 home defeat will always leave a bad taste in the mouth – but some fans will at least have one memory to treasure from the game, if nothing else.

Kirk now says: It comes to something when the best you can say about a game is that one of your old players was sent off; but after such a heavy drubbing, there's not going to be much else to celebrate.

SEARS SENDS US POTTY OVER COTTEE (20 March 2008)

A pint-sized teenage striker scores with a header on his debut for West Ham.

For the last 25 years, those words have conjured up images of a certain Tony Cottee helping the Hammers to a famous 3-0 victory against Tottenham.

The 2-1 win against Blackburn last weekend may not live too long in the memory as a game. But the sight of Freddie Sears nodding the winner on his first outing as a substitute surely will do.

The 18-year-old has been causing something of a stir at youth and reserve-team level this season.

And many fans had been hoping the striker would be handed his first-team debut before the campaign expires.

But it was still a surprise – and some would say gamble – when Alan Curbishley threw Sears on against Blackburn on Saturday.

The Hammers desperately needed a morale-boosting win against Rovers following three 4-0 defeats (against Chelsea, Liverpool and Spurs).

And with the game delicately poised at 1-1, some managers may not have thrown a youngster in unless it was absolutely necessary.

So credit must be given to Curbishley for having the courage to give Sears his opportunity.

And the Boleyn boy came up trumps, showing no fear as he grabbed the first chance that came his way to open his first-team account.

It is fair to say the celebrations tore the roof off the Upton Park stands.

Because we all love a homegrown Hammer, somebody who bleeds claret and blue blood in the way the rest of the support does.

The question everybody will now be asking is how far Sears can go in the game.

The popular view is that he can achieve what he wants – as long as he keeps his feet on the ground.

There shouldn't be any doubts about that as the Hammers have a great track record for producing youngsters and establishing them as Premier League stars.

Sadly, they also have a habit of failing to hang on to their best young players, although Mark Noble and Anton Ferdinand seem to have pretty firm roots at Upton Park at the moment.

Curbishley has likened Sears to fellow Hammers striker Craig Bellamy.

But if he can continue to emulate the achievements of Tony Cottee, nobody will be complaining.

Kirk now says: Sears would score just four goals in his next 106 outings for West Ham, Crystal Palace, Coventry, Scunthorpe and Colchester before joining the latter outfit on a free transfer in the summer of 2012.

CURB YOUR ENTHUSIASM (17 April 2008)

West Ham famously won seven of their last nine games to save their Premier League skins last season.

They are now in danger of establishing a similar kind of record in terms of defeats as the current campaign nears its end.

The Hammers have been beaten in six of their last eight games and now it's looking increasingly likely that Spurs will soon overtake them and push them into the bottom half of the table.

Saturday's 1-0 defeat at struggling Bolton – who had dropped into the relegation zone after failing to win in ten games – was sadly entirely predictable.

West Ham are generally the ideal fodder when another team is desperate for a rare victory.

Yet again, the injury curse struck with Lucas Neill and Nobby Solano being ruled out and Anton Ferdinand immediately forced off with a hamstring problem.

The lack of bodies saw teenager Jack Collison being handed his first start in midfield.

Nobody is pretending the present situation is easy for manager Alan Curbishley.

But his insistence on 'matching up' in terms of formation – as he admitted he tried to do at the Reebok – suggests he is spending far too much time worrying about the opposition.

That may have been the right philosophy for Curbishley when he was managing Charlton.

But fans will argue it's not the way things should be done at West Ham. They don't want to see a five-man midfield helping to suffocate the game and one lone striker toiling away up front.

West Ham fans want to see their teams adhering to the club's traditional philosophy of playing attacking football with style and flair.

It comes to something when they start making their own entertainment at games – as one did by turning up at Bolton in a claret and blue Batman outfit.

Curbishley will claim that with Luis Boa Morte and Bobby Zamora supporting Dean Ashton, the formation was more 4-3-3 than 4-5-1.

But they didn't play as three forwards, with Boa Morte and Zamora stuck out on the flanks and Ashton being left isolated.

Striker Carlton Cole was then brought off the bench to play on the left wing before later being switched to the right.

None of these unlikely ideas ever looked like working and it was only when Freddie Sears was brought on to partner Ashton in attack that the Hammers produced a late flurry.

Victory against relegated Derby is now an absolute must – or Curbishley will face calls for his head.

Kirk now says: This, of course, was the season when West Ham spent most of the time in tenth position – something fans would dream of in the years to follow – but the safety first nature of the football was in danger of sending people into a coma. Zzzzzzzzzzzz.

HAMMERS ARE YAWN AGAIN (24 April 2008)

West Ham fans were accused by the media of being fickle for booing the 2-1 win against Derby on Saturday.

If anything, their reaction to the narrow victory over the Premier League's bottom outfit proved the very opposite.

Fickle fans cheer success and jeer failure, whereas the Upton Park faithful tend to judge the football itself.

And the team's inability to provide the entertainment demanded of them this season is the root cause of the supporters' dissent.

This point seems to have passed over the head of manager Alan Curbishley, who complained that fans needed to be more realistic about the problems faced this term.

'When they are not happy they let you know,' he said, without acknowledging what the supporters were actually unhappy about.

It is not just the lack of league goals (20) and wins (seven) at Upton Park this season that has frustrated them but the complete absence of style.

The Hammers are famous for adhering to certain football philosophies but many fans are worried that these have become sacrificed under the current management.

Supporters know West Ham are unlikely to challenge for league honours but will happily accept inconsistent results as long as the team is trying to play attractive football.

They have seen little evidence of that this season.

Curbishley would undoubtedly point to the club's lengthy injury list, which has deprived the squad of key players such as Craig Bellamy and Kieron Dyer.

The early wins at Birmingham and Reading suggested there would be some exciting times on the road, with those two players posing so much danger when hitting teams on the break.

But there is also a suspicion that Curbishley is relying far too heavily on the more cautious methods he employed at Charlton.

Too often we have heard him speak of 'matching up' in terms of formation, suggesting he's more concerned with nullifying the opposition than playing to West Ham's strengths.

That is acceptable when you're playing Liverpool or Manchester United, but considerably less so when taking on Bolton or Birmingham.

Hammers fans don't want five-man midfields, long-ball tactics or strikers left isolated on their own.

They want to see an attractive passing game that produces chances and goals. Only then will the jeers turn to cheers.

Kirk now says: The worst thing was that Alan Curbishley came through the West Ham ranks as a player, so was best placed to understand the playing philosophies of the club, whereas at least Sam Allardyce – who would suffer similar criticism further down the line – could just feign ignorance.

TAKING A PASTING ... IN MORE THAN ONE SENSE (8 May 2008)

West Ham got slaughtered on the pitch and off it when going down 4-1 at Manchester United on Saturday.

It was bad enough that they held out for just two minutes, were 3-0 down before the half-hour mark and then conceded a fourth goal after the league leaders had been reduced to ten men.

But the Hammers were then accused of willingly laying down to gift Sir Alex Ferguson's side three vital points – purely as a result of Alan Curbishley supposedly claiming it would be an 'injustice' if Manchester United failed to win the Premier League trophy.

One Sunday paper referred to West Ham's 'bizarre unwillingness to close opponents down' while describing their defending as 'rancid' and their attitude as 'disinterested'.

It was as if the players decided not to shake a leg just because their manager believed Manchester United to be worthy winners of a second consecutive title.

Or maybe it was payback time after a below-par United allowed the Hammers to claim a final-day win at Old Trafford last term to stay in the Premier League.

Both theories are ridiculous, but that won't stop the media from creating a story out of nothing when they're looking to spice things up around a big game.

Some have questioned the wisdom of Curbishley offering his opinions on the title race when his team was involved in one of the potentially decisive fixtures.

Yet it wasn't as if he said he wanted United to lift the trophy – just that they deserved to, which isn't quite the same thing.

Where the West Ham boss did score an own goal, however, was in passing up an opportunity to put the record straight by failing to attend the post-match press conference.

Instead, assistant boss Mervyn Day was left to fend off the flak by suggesting that Curbishley's words had been misrepresented.

The reality, of course, is that it was always going to be difficult for West Ham to hold out at Old Trafford without any of their first-choice centre-halves, with full-back Lucas Neill partnering the inexperienced James Tomkins in the middle of defence.

Sadly, that fact hardly got a mention – yet it was far more significant to the result than anything Curbishley might have said.

Kirk now says: In retrospect it was three points happily lost, with Manchester United just pipping Chelsea to the title and the Hammers finishing tenth regardless.

AT LEAST WE FINISHED ABOVE SPURS (15 May 2008)

The 2007/08 campaign will be remembered as the season that's difficult to remember for West Ham fans.

Last year the Hammers were celebrating Premier League survival, the year before that an FA Cup Final appearance.

Before that it was promotion back to the top flight after two turbulent seasons in the Championship.

So it's been a while since West Ham supporters have had little to get too excited about.

That said, it was highly satisfying to see the team seal a top-half placing and finish above rivals Tottenham.

If that had been offered at the start of the season, most Hammers fans would have taken it – certainly if they had known of the huge number of injury problems the club would face.

Nearly 20 players have missed games at one stage or another and the long-term absence of Craig Bellamy and Kieron Dyer – who looked so exciting in their early outings – certainly didn't help the cause.

There were some enjoyable moments, however, with the 2-1 home victory against Manchester United and injury-time penalty winner against Liverpool being the obvious ones that spring to mind.

The 3-0 win at Reading and the 5-0 thrashing of Derby were the most emphatic successes on the road.

Freddie Sears scored a memorable debut goal against Blackburn, while Robert Green saved a last-minute penalty from former Hammer Jermain Defoe to deny Spurs an Upton Park victory.

James Tomkins and Jack Collison have also tasted first-team action for the first time while Matt Upson and Dean Ashton have won England call-ups for their club displays.

The disappointments include the Carling Cup quarter-final exit to Everton and the three consecutive 4-0 league defeats in early March.

There have also been big grumbles about the cautious style of football played in many of the games.

So what kind of activity can we expect at Upton Park this summer?

Alan Curbishley has played down suggestions that he is under pressure to reduce the club's wage bill.

But there will inevitably be outgoings and it will be interesting to see what players, if any, new technical director Gianluca Nani brings to West Ham.

Curbishley will need to freshen things up because any team trying to stand still in the Premier League will inevitably find themselves slipping backwards.

Fans will therefore want to see signs of ambition from new chairman Bjorgolfur Gudmundsson if they are to believe that West Ham can seriously push for a European place next term.

Kirk now says: Fans needn't have worried about a season of stupefying stability, because normal service in terms of 'it could only happen to West Ham' would soon be resumed.

REFLECTING ON SEASON 2007/08

Best signing: Scott Parker (Newcastle), £7m

Worst signing: Kieron Dyer (Newcastle), £6m

Best result: Winning 2-1 at home to Manchester United in December

Worst result: Losing 4-0 at Tottenham in March

Final position: 10th in Premier League, 49 points

Manager and rating: Alan Curbishley 7/10

Best thing about season: Enjoying a comfortable mid-table position despite injuries

Worst thing about season: Safety-first football that was dull to watch

SEASON 2008/2009

'Seen your shares crash in value?'

S TOP for just a moment and listen. Can you hear that sound? You mean, to quote the words of Simon & Garfunkel, the sound of silence?

Well, welcome to the summer of 2008, with the close season following the trend of the most recent campaign for the Hammers in terms of being relatively uneventful.

Indeed, not much was happening all round – including a European Championship tournament that was taking place without the involvement of England thanks to the miserable efforts of former boss Steve McClaren.

And to think that West Ham once wanted him as their manager.

Striker Bobby Zamora and the versatile John Pantsil (whose Paintsil family couldn't even spell his name properly) joined Fulham for a combined fee of £6.3m while tattooed Swiss midfielder Valon Behrami signed in a £5m move from Lazio and Herita Ilunga arrived on loan from Toulouse in September.

To bolster the attack, David Di Michele was a belated free transfer signing from Torino while another forward seemingly well past his sell-by date, Spaniard Diego Tristan, would follow in October.

But following the activity of recent years, it was generally fairly quiet on the eastern front, although, in retrospect, this period can now be viewed as the calm before the storm.

ALL SO HUMDRUM AT THE HAMMERS (14 August 2008)

It is a sad thing to admit before a ball has been seriously kicked, but West Ham fans are bored.

Bored with the lack of transfer activity, bored with the team's style of football and bored with manager Alan Curbishley complaining about injuries to his fragile players.

The start of a new season should bring about a sense of expectancy and anticipation, especially following a campaign where a top-half finish was secured.

There should be genuine belief that West Ham can seriously challenge for a European place this time around.

But the reality is somewhat different, with many supporters predicting another campaign of mid-table mediocrity.

Indeed, it seems that little has changed since last season.

Craig Bellamy and Kieron Dyer are injured, five men are being strung across midfield (as was seen against Villarreal on Saturday) and Curbishley has already started grumbling about negative press coverage.

The expensive release of Freddie Ljungberg was one of the worst kept secrets of the summer, while former Wimbledon hardman Ben Thatcher's arrival on trial was greeted with the derision it deserved.

Maggie Thatcher would have got a better reception from the Upton Park crowd.

The bookies are hardly thrilled by the Hammers' prospects, listing them as 1000/1 to win the Premier League title – compared to the 66/1 on offer for Tottenham who finished below them last term – and making Curbishley one of the most likely top-flight bosses to leave his post.

What is certain is that West Ham must get off to a flying start if speculation about the manager's position is not to grow.

It is fair to expect the Hammers to win seven of their first eight games, such has been the kindness of the early fixtures.

Anything less than maximum points from the home games against Wigan, Blackburn, Newcastle and Bolton will be considered a disappointment.

And aside from the trip to Manchester City, the visits to West Brom, Fulham and Hull are hardly daunting.

West Ham then come up against Arsenal and Manchester United at the end of October, with Liverpool, Spurs and Chelsea also on the horizon, so it's imperative to get points on the board as early as possible.

If they fail to do so – and it's a big if because they really shouldn't have any problems – then a campaign of struggle would inevitably follow.

Now that really would liven things up a bit.

Kirk now says: For the record, the Hammers would win only four of their opening eight league games (while losing the other four).

U-TURNS ARE CAUSING A COMMOTION (28 August 2008)

It is no wonder the traffic in Green Street is so bad nowadays given the number of U-turns being performed at West Ham.

First it's insisted that Freddie Ljungberg is staying at the club – then the Swedish midfielder is being paid off to rip up his contract.

Next we have Anton Ferdinand claiming he's 'happy' at West Ham, only for the defender to later reject the club's offer of a new contract.

Finally, Alan Curbishley insists he will 'always have the final word on who comes in and out' of the club.

Yet just a few days later, the manager finds himself admitting that the decision to accept Sunderland's £8m offer for Ferdinand was 'taken out of my hands'.

It is getting to the point where pretty much everything being said has to be taken with a large pinch of salt.

Back in the days of John Lyall and Harry Redknapp, you knew who was making all the decisions at Upton Park. Now fans are not so sure.

Supporters will certainly not be happy about the acceptance of Sunderland's bid for Ferdinand.

Of course, clubs are placed in difficult positions when players refuse new deals.

The last thing anybody wants to see is a valuable asset running down his contract and then freely walking away.

But you also don't want to sell the best components of your squad – particularly not to a team you would be looking to finish above if you're hoping to enjoy a decent season.

And while clubs shouldn't be held to ransom by greedy players, it is indeed worrying that a new agreement could not be reached with Ferdinand.

At the time of writing, the defender is considering Sunderland's approach.

But it will be a major blow if he becomes the latest in a long line of homegrown Hammers – such as Joe Cole, Frank Lampard, Michael Carrick and older brother Rio, of course – to leave Upton Park ahead of schedule.

And if so he must be replaced, as too many of the club's remaining centre-halves cannot be relied upon to avoid injury or simply don't have the necessary experience or quality.

The timing of the Ferdinand issue could hardly be any worse, with the transfer window set to close on Monday.

It is therefore fair to say that the decisions made this week will say much about the club's ambition – or lack of it.

Kirk now says: The Ferdinand issue would spark a disturbing sequence of events that would certainly make things anything but dull at Upton Park over the next few months.

DON'T BELIEVE A WORD (4 September 2008)

West Ham fans shed few tears when former chairman Terence Brown sold the club towards the end of 2006.

But they might now be wondering if they were better off with the devil they knew given recent events at Upton Park.

Because they will have been left utterly dismayed by the sales of Anton Ferdinand and George McCartney to Sunderland without the club signing any replacements.

Ferdinand was West Ham's second best central defender – as his £8m fee would suggest – while McCartney was the only recognised left-back in the first-team squad.

It is claimed that Ferdinand had refused to sign a new deal – yet the player has reportedly suggested the club's latest offer was withdrawn as soon as Sunderland made their interest known.

Meanwhile, West Ham's website insists McCartney was sold because his family were unable to settle in London.

If that's the case, it needs to be asked why the Northern Ireland international signed a new five-year deal earlier in the summer and said, 'I have enjoyed my time at West Ham and have no desire to leave.'

Fans must surely realise by now they should pay no attention to what anyone says.

The club's claim that only 'fringe players' would be sold has been proved to be untrue, with Bobby Zamora and Freddie Ljungberg also being offloaded this summer.

Alan Curbishley also insisted there would be no last-minute sales, which suggests the decision to cash-in on McCartney was made over his head. You can't help feeling that the manager has little or no influence on the decisions being made by the club.

Curbishley had also claimed he was looking to strengthen in 'all three areas of the team'.

Yet links with Stephen Appiah, Paulo Ferreira and Gael Givet have come to nothing.

So West Ham have been left with no left-back, are hugely vulnerable in the middle of defence and have fewer options up front.

Fans have every reason to fear for the club's Premier League status, because the squad has clearly gone backwards.

All the bold talk of challenging for European football has been proved to be nothing but empty words.

And all the reports of the Hammers looking to embark on a cost-cutting exercise have been proved to be totally true.

It is as if the club suspects that Sheffield United will win their claim for compensation following relegation in the wake of the Carlos Tevez affair – and needs every penny it can get.

Kirk now says: Decisions were indeed made over Curbishley's head, while Sheffield United would also win their compensation claim.

CATCHPHRASE CATCHES UP WITH CURBS (11 September 2008)

West Ham fans have complained about life at Upton Park being somewhat dull during the first eight months of the year.

But the events of the last few weeks or so have been anything but.

It says a lot that supporters unimpressed with Alan Curbishley's reign found themselves feeling a great deal of sympathy for the former manager.

The conservative Curbishley might not have produced the stylish football that West Ham fans demanded.

But he can be commended for sticking to his principles and resigning after players such as Anton Ferdinand and George McCartney were apparently sold above his head. And rather than leaving by 'mutual consent' and being gagged by a lucrative pay-off, he swiftly went public as to why he considered his position untenable.

In the end, the man whose latest catchphrase was 'we've just got to get on with it' decided that's exactly what he couldn't do.

So West Ham began the week by narrowing their search for only their 12th manager, with Italians Gianfranco Zola and Roberto Donadoni considered the favourites.

Croatia boss Slaven Bilic, undoubtedly the fans' top choice, appears committed to his country's cause, while former Hammer Paolo Di Canio never had the coaching experience to be seriously entertained.

While it's reassuring that West Ham have sought out big names for the job, the hope is that the final decision is based on coaching credentials as opposed to an outstanding playing career.

You would also like to think that the process of drawing up a shortlist and talking to people – rather than instantly choosing a target and going for him – will result in the right man being appointed rather than the one who simply interviewed well.

Finally, West Ham need to clarify the role of technical director Gianluca Nani and how much influence he will have over the buying and selling of players.

A continental-style, multi-tiered management system won't work unless a proper structure is put in place – which doesn't appear to be the case at the moment.

One thing is for sure – few fans are likely to complain that Upton Park life is uneventful in the coming months.

Kirk now says: West Ham were forced to pay Alan Curbishley a reported £2.2m in compensation after he won his claim for constructive dismissal, with it being found that the club was in breach of the manager's contract by selling players against his wishes. 'I am looking forward to getting back into management,' he said in February 2010.

ZOLA HAS HIS WORK CUT OUT (18 September 2008)

Gianfranco Zola and Gianluca Nani were seen in deep conversation during West Ham's 3-2 defeat at West Brom.

Assuming the two Italians were speaking in their native tongue, it's likely that Zola said to his technical director, 'Chi è la scintilla luminosa che ha pensato era una buona idea vendere Ferdinand e McCartney?'

Which roughly translates as, 'Who's the bright spark who thought it was a good idea to sell Ferdinand and McCartney?'

While it was always going to be a good time for any team to play the Hammers, with Kevin Keen filling in as caretaker boss ahead of Zola's official start, the display at the Hawthorns proved the folly of the club cashing in on two of their best defenders in January.

The facts are that Calum Davenport is not as reliable as Anton Ferdinand and neither Herita Ilunga or Walter Lopez are likely to be as good as George McCartney.

So in order to raise money – admittedly £14m of it – West Ham have left themselves woefully under-strength at the back.

For the record, the Hammers have not kept a clean sheet in their last 17 games.

Already this season they have conceded nine goals, including six in just two away outings.

That is particularly disturbing when it's considered that the opposition was made up of Wigan, Blackburn, West Brom, Manchester City and League 2 strugglers Macclesfield.

Just think what kind of a thumping they might get when they come up against the really big boys such as Manchester United and Chelsea.

So Steve Clarke, who recently quit the latter outfit with a view to joining Zola as his assistant, will certainly have his work cut out when he gets his feet under the table.

Zola is expected to bring back some much-needed flair to the Hammers, while Clarke is believed to be an ideal coaching partner because of his strengths as a defensive organiser.

But it won't be easy to stop the leaks at the back because no team can sell half of its first-choice defence and expect to see an improvement.

West Ham's 38 league fixtures under conservative boss Alan Curbishley last term produced an average of 2.4 goals per game.

With 16 goals witnessed in four league outings so far this season, that figure has seen a stark increase.

That is just as well, because West Ham are going to have to grab a lot of goals to outscore the opposition if recent evidence is anything to go by.

Kirk now says: To be fair to Zola, he did impose his style of football on the team pretty quickly and, although clean sheets were a rarity, there was a gradual improvement in their defensive displays.

PANEL DECISION IS A JOKE (25 September 2008)

The independent tribunal panel that ruled in favour of Sheffield United's claim for compensation against West Ham appears to have been totally hoodwinked.

That is the only rational conclusion that can be reached following news that the Hammers could be forced to cough up almost £30m to the Blades, who complained that their relegation from the Premier League came as a direct result of an 'ineligible' player in Carlos Tevez.

Such an erroneous claim is typical of Sheffield United's campaign of misinformation as they refused to accept any responsibility for dropping into the Championship.

It suited the Blades to believe that Tevez was 'ineligible' to play for West Ham – as a result of third-party owners MSI having a potential influence on the club's policies – because they could then refer to precedents that saw clubs hit with points penalties.

And although a Premier League spokesman confirmed that 'this has never been a case of West Ham fielding an ineligible player', it seems an arbitration panel has acted as if it was the very opposite.

The central plank of Sheffield United's argument was that West Ham had admitted to breaching Premier League rules.

For them to win their case, however, they would have needed to prove that breach directly resulted in their relegation.

That is impossible to do – especially as the Blades had survival in their own hands going into their final game which they lost – yet the three-man panel has arbitrarily decided that 'over the final two games of the season West Ham would have achieved at least three points less without Mr Tevez'.

How can these non-football people possibly know this?

And even if it was true, the Premier League gave West Ham permission to continue playing Tevez, so he was entitled to help them win as many points as possible.

What fans now have to worry about is the potential impact of this decision on West Ham's future.

The club has already sold Anton Ferdinand and George McCartney to Sunderland for £14m, seemingly in the knowledge of what was to come. Losing sponsors XL hardly helps their cause.

Is new boss Gianfranco Zola likely to be deprived of funds to build the team he wants?

And what action can chairman Bjorgolfur Gudmundsson take against the people who were behind the signings of Tevez and Javier Mascherano prior to his purchase of the club?

Somebody, somewhere, should certainly carry the can for the whole debacle.

Kirk now says: The most annoying thing about the whole Tevez affair is that so many people believed that West Ham committed a terrible crime without knowing half the facts of the case – outlined in a 25-page report issued by the Premier League that few bothered to read. QPR were later found guilty of breaching third-party ownership rules in respect of Alejandro Faurlin after winning promotion to the Premier League but were fined a mere £875,000, with nobody making any fuss about it all.

MARK OF WHAT MATTERS (16 October 2008)

A group of West Ham supporters convened in the social club in Castle Street on Friday to lament the passing of one of their own.

Mark was in many ways a typical Hammers fan; he was loyal – not just to the club, but to his friends and family – and could always see the funny side of things.

Inevitably, the conversation turned to West Ham and the latest news relating to the club.

'It's typical,' said one mourner, staring into his pint, as he attempted to lighten the mood.

'West Ham get taken over by a billionaire – and it turns out that he's skint!'

The news of chairman Bjorgolfur Gudmundsson's financial woes in his native Iceland, following the collapse of his Landsbanki empire, has predictably stirred up all sorts of speculation about how it might impact on the Hammers.

It is bad enough that vice-chairman Asgeir Fridgeirsson has admitted there will be no spare cash to spend on players in January.

But to read that the club could go into administration if a buyer isn't found within a month is deeply alarming – whether it's true or not.

With the credit crunch dominating people's thoughts, the media wasted no time in suggesting the Hammers could become one of its first major victims.

Club chief executive Scott Duxbury last week insisted that Landsbanki's crash had 'absolutely no effect on West Ham and Mr Gudmundsson's ownership'.

But that doesn't mean the chairman, who bought the club two years ago, might not decide his investment would be better placed elsewhere.

After all, the Hammers are hardly going to be challenging for Champions League football unless a lot more money is thrown at them.

West Ham fans, of course, are more than used to false dawns by now.

What other club would sign two world-class Argentina internationals – and find it facing a potential £30m bill for another outfit being relegated?

And while foreign ownership usually signals a return to the good times, the Hammers head into the next transfer window knowing players are likely to be sold.

So nobody will be too surprised – or disappointed – if the club does indeed change hands again in the near future.

West Ham's future is a big concern, but death puts everything into perspective.

So those close to Mark probably won't spend too much time worrying about the club's immediate prospects.

Kirk now says: You really couldn't make this up – Landsbanki chairman Bjorgolfur Gudmundsson arrives at West Ham as the 799th-richest man in the world and eventually ends up being declared bankrupt following the collapse of his Icelandic banking empire. Duxbury's claim that it would have 'absolutely no effect on West Ham and Mr Gudmundsson's ownership' was laughable, as time would sadly tell.

LIKE TAKING CANDY FROM A BABY (23 October 2008)

Seen your shares crash in value as a result of the global financial crisis?

Worried about the fall in property prices and the security of your investments?

Want to know a way of making your money work for you that will guarantee handsome returns?

The solution is simply to stick your entire life's savings on West Ham to lose away from home – it's like printing dollar bills.

The Hammers have already lost on four of their five away trips this season. Such a statistic for most clubs would suggest visits to the likes of Chelsea, Arsenal, Liverpool and Manchester United.

Yet West Ham have been beaten at places such as West Brom and Hull – two newly-promoted clubs – and injury-hit Championship side Watford.

Sunday's 1-0 defeat at Hull was entirely predictable.

The home side were buoyed by victories at Arsenal and Tottenham, whereas the Hammers had previously lost at home to Bolton.

And even though Gianfranco Zola's side retained the ball for long periods in the first half at the KC Stadium, they struggled to respond once Hull started to impose their more direct game.

Which is a major cause for concern given that only one of Hull's players – Brazilian playmaker Geovanni – would realistically make it into West Ham's team.

Zola insists his men deserved more for their efforts, blaming the result on a failure to convert chances.

But for all their possession, the Hammers are simply not creating enough of them.

Indeed, there's evidence that the team is beginning to reflect the manager's personality in looking nice but not being nasty enough.

You can't help feeling that while the short-passing game is all well and good in principle, you need far better players than West Ham have to make it successful.

You also need to quicken the pace at times, while the Hammers appeared to be stuck in one gear at the weekend.

Needless to say, it's unlikely that West Ham will pick up anything in their next away game at Manchester United.

In fact, it's fair to say you can bet on it.

Kirk now says: So many teams score goals simply by forcing the opposition into errors, but at this point the Hammers were spending far too much time trying to unlock defences with intricate passes rather than simply getting the ball into the box and letting somebody make a mistake.

ZOLA'S SMILE IS BEGINNING TO FADE (13 November 2008)

What a miserable, horrible, depressing season it's turning out to be for West Ham.

They sold half their first-choice defence in the summer, manager Alan Curbishley walked out in disgust and successor Gianfranco Zola, while imposing a more attractive style of play, has struggled to win games.

The Hammers have collected just one point from the last 18, have not kept a clean sheet in 26 outings, share the worst defensive record in the top flight and are just two points off the foot of the table.

To add to their woes, injured striker Dean Ashton is set to miss the rest of the season, the club is struggling to fend off a £30m compensation claim from Sheffield United, chairman Bjorgolfur Gudmundsson has lost his fortune with the collapse of his Landsbanki empire, sponsors XL have gone bust and former boss Curbishley is claiming damages on the grounds of constructive dismissal.

So the last thing West Ham need right now is a relegation battle – but that's what they're currently faced with.

The 3-1 home defeat by Everton means that Zola has tasted success in just two of his nine games since taking over in September.

The Italian's familiar smile has long since faded and, on the evidence of his post-match comments at the weekend, he appears to be at a loss to explain what's going wrong.

He spoke of trying to find 'solutions' but failed to really convince anybody that he knew how to turn things around.

Zola's philosophy has been that the results will ultimately come if the team continues to play good football.

But while everybody wants to see West Ham playing with a sense of style, it's extremely difficult to see them winning many games at the moment.

If you're lightweight up front and leaky at the back, a lot of fancy football in the middle of the park is not going to get you very far.

Needless to say, the visit of Portsmouth on Saturday is a must-win game if the Hammers want to give themselves hope.

They then travel to Sunderland and Liverpool before entertaining Tottenham and heading across town to Chelsea. Few will fancy them to collect more than a point or two from that batch of fixtures.

As the old cliche goes, it's likely to be a long, cold winter.

And when it rains for West Ham, it always pours.

Kirk now says: The Hammers could only muster a goalless draw against Pompey but won 1-0 at Sunderland and drew 0-0 at Liverpool, so they were clearly improving defensively, which was some consolation given that everything else seemed to be going wrong.

BLADES THREAT WILL CUT DEEP (4 December 2008)

Gianfranco Zola has insisted his players are not concerned by Sheffield United's compensation claim against West Ham.

But that doesn't mean that fans shouldn't be extremely worried about a situation that has now reached farcical proportions.

Just in case you had lost track of events relating to the Carlos Tevez affair – and try not to laugh when reading this – the Hammers are appealing against Sheffield's appeal against West Ham's appeal.

The Hammers are contesting an FA-endorsed arbitration panel's decision that the Blades should be awarded damages for their relegation in 2007.

Despite a Premier League tribunal earlier deciding that a £5.5m fine was sufficient penalty, West Ham have been told to compensate the Blades for their losses because it has now been deemed that Tevez was ineligible to play due to the controversial nature of his third-party ownership. It was also decided that West Ham would have been relegated had the striker not exerted his influence on games.

The Hammers reportedly agreed to abide by the second arbitration panel's verdict in order to avoid being taken to court – a highly questionable decision the club must surely regret.

They are now seeking to take the matter to the Court of Arbitration in Lausanne, even though Sheffield United are refusing to participate as one of two parties in dispute.

Indeed, the CAS themselves are having to hold a preliminary hearing to establish whether they can accept the case – especially as Sheffield United have succeeded in winning a temporary High Court injunction against West Ham's approach to the CAS.

Another trial is due to take place next year, by which time the amount that Sheffield are due to be paid will be properly calculated – by another arbitration panel. West Ham are trying to bring down the figure potentially owed by insisting that Sheffield United's costs would have increased had they remained in the Premier League and that those savings must be offset against the losses.

And to top it all off, the FA have claimed they won't recognise any decision made by the CAS even if the matter does go that far.

So the suspicion is that West Ham could be forced to cough up a figure that could be anywhere between £20m and £50m.

That is going to have a big impact on the spending power of the club and seriously hamper any chances of a big-money takeover.

Needless to say, fans have every reason to fear for the future.

Kirk now says: By this stage, everybody not associated with either West Ham or Sheffield United had stopped paying attention, bored by the legal wrangling and tangling between the two clubs, whether Tevez was eligible to play or not and what the intricacies of his third-party ownership really meant. For the Hammers, of course, another drain on their limited finances was the last thing they needed following the chairman's financial collapse and their sponsors going bust.

AT LEAST THE VOICE IS IN FINE FORM (25 December 2008)

There is a bloke dubbed 'The Voice' who sits in the upper tier of the West Stand at Upton Park.

Everybody knows when he's not happy, because you can hear him shouting from miles away when things are going wrong.

Needless to say, 'The Voice' has been in full flow during a run that has seen West Ham collect just a solitary point from six home games.

Carlton Cole was one of his main targets for abuse in the 1-0 defeat by Aston Villa.

'Get him off!' he boomed after the hapless striker fluffed a decent opportunity to put the Hammers ahead.

Cole is West Ham's top scorer this season with a mighty four goals to his name – the last of which came nearly three months ago.

'He has to score more,' said boss Gianfranco Zola after Saturday's defeat.

But it's not just Cole who is struggling to find the net. West Ham have scored just four times in their last 11 outings.

No team is going to win games and avoid the threat of relegation with such a miserable statistic.

The goalscoring problem has been evident ever since Zola took charge back in September.

You would have thought that somebody who scored more than 200 goals in their club career – including 80 for Chelsea – would have an idea about how to stick the ball in the back of the net.

Yet West Ham's attack is about as dangerous as a small child coming at you with a soggy Farley's rusk.

The Hammers deserved at least a point against Villa, but it wasn't as if they squandered a hatful of chances.

And that has been the case throughout the last few months.

West Ham's play has been attractive to watch, but woefully ineffective in terms of carving teams open.

And prospects do not look like improving, with veterans David Di Michele and Diego Tristan well past their best and young Freddie Sears still searching for his second goal since scoring on his debut last season.

A big responsibility falls on the shoulders of Craig Bellamy, but the Welshman seems to spend as much time trying to create chances for others as he does getting in the box and converting them himself.

And as for goals from midfield, forget it.

Scott Parker, Hayden Mullins, Mark Noble, Matty Etherington, Luis Boa Morte, Julien Faubert, Jack Collison and Lee Bowyer scored just 11 goals between them last season – little more than one each.

At this rate, Zola might as well dig his old boots out and have a go himself.

Kirk now says: First it was too many goals being leaked; next it's the lack of goals being scored. But Zola's 'project', as he annoyingly liked to refer to it, was a work in progress and a revival was seen in the shape of six wins in the next seven league and cup games.

BELLAMY GOES FROM HERO TO VILLAIN (22 January 2009)

The Upton Park faithful love their Hammers heroes. They also love to hate the club's villains.

And who would have believed that strikers Craig Bellamy and Carlton Cole would swap positions in the hearts of West Ham fans?

Bellamy was expected to be a top contender for the next Hammer of the Year award after returning from the injury that restricted him to just seven league starts last term.

Assuming he could stay fit, he would surely begin to justify the £7.5m fee paid to Liverpool for his services two years ago.

He broke a run of 11 goalless games with a fine double that helped West Ham romp to a 4-1 win at Portsmouth on Boxing Day.

But then came media speculation that he could be sacrificed to help improve the club's financial position.

The Hammers insisted they had no intention of allowing their top stars to leave Upton Park this month – and stayed true to their word as they rejected several offers for players.

But that resolve was always going to be tested if, as feared, a player expressed the desire to move on – as Bellamy did last week.

The crowd chants against Bellamy, who was excluded from the 3-1 win against Fulham last Sunday, proved there was no way back for the Wales international and it was a relief when it was confirmed that a fee with Manchester City had been agreed.

He therefore now joins the likes of Paul Ince, Frank Lampard and Jermain Defoe as players the West Ham fans will think of with nothing but disdain.

Meanwhile Cole, who had scored just nine goals in his first two seasons at Upton Park, was dismissed by many as only a stand-in for the injured Dean Ashton and was never fancied to be prolific enough to become first choice.

He had a stinker against Aston Villa before Christmas, yet boss Gianfranco Zola pledged to teach the striker how to score goals.

Lo and behold, Cole has since netted in five consecutive games to take his tally to nine for the season – and become a firm fans' favourite.

It is clear that Zola, who scored 80 goals for Chelsea, has used his experience and coaching skills to make Cole a better player.

West Ham fans will show how much they value the striker next time out – and the same goes for Bellamy if he plays for City at Upton Park on 1 March.

Kirk now says: In reality, the fact that Bellamy wanted to quit the Hammers was never seriously held against him, proving you have to go some if you want to join the likes of Ince, Lampard and Defoe in becoming a target for the Boleyn boo-boys. Also on their way during the January window were Matthew Etherington (to Stoke) and Hayden Mullins (to Portsmouth).

IT COULD HAVE BEEN A HELL OF A LOT WORSE (19 March 2009)

When your team scores an injury-time equaliser, fans go home celebrating as if it's a victory. It feels like a triumph, even though you haven't won.

West Ham fans might have similar emotions after it was confirmed the club had successfully agreed an out-of-court settlement with Sheffield United.

With the Blades reportedly claiming around £45m in compensation over the Carlos Tevez affair, there was a very real fear that the Hammers' Premier League future could be in serious jeopardy had a tribunal panel been sympathetic to their demands.

Thankfully, with a figure of around £15m in staged payments reportedly settled on, West Ham can hopefully focus on their future without being forced to sell their best players.

So there is reason for supporters to cheer – even though the club can think of several better things to do with £15m than hand it over to Sheffield United. That is not to suggest that fans feel the Blades were entitled to blame West Ham for their relegation two years ago.

The Hammers were heavily fined for rule breaches relating to the third-party ownership of Tevez in 2007, so why should they have to carry the can for Sheffield United's failings?

The Yorkshire outfit waged a campaign of misinformation, complaining about ineligibility and of non-existent precedents, as they refused to accept that they dropped out of the Premier League because they weren't good enough.

Remember, it wasn't the third-party ownership of Tevez that was illegal; it was the clause in the contract that allowed him to be moved on irrespective of West Ham's wishes – hardly the most serious of crimes, most would think. You would like to imagine that the recent agreement has brought an end to the whole sorry affair.

Sadly, the alleged findings of an arbitration tribunal, which sided with Sheffield United over their complaints, have prompted the FA to investigate West Ham's conduct after being told to destroy their agreements with Tevez's owners.

That means West Ham's fight goes on and some fans will worry that the club's payment to the Blades will somehow negatively influence the next verdict that's due. The last thing the Hammers want to be faced with is a points deduction next season.

At least one hurdle has been overcome and if that smooths the way for a possible club takeover – as has been suggested – then fans can try to look ahead with optimism.

Kirk now says: Of course, the figure turned out to be closer to £20m, but at least there was the consolation that the money didn't help Sheffield United very much because they ended up getting relegated again to League 1 in 2011, the only surprise being that they didn't blame that one on West Ham as well.

SAVIO SIGNING COULD PROVE COSTLY (16 April 2009)

When West Ham fail to qualify for Europe – as seems probable given the problems they're facing – there is unlikely to be a major inquest.

After all, a relegation battle looked more likely when Gianfranco Zola struggled in the early part of his management reign this season.

And the fact they're challenging for a top-seven finish at all is remarkable given the number of key players recently lost to injury.

So if the Hammers just miss out, the club is likely to simply shrug its shoulders and hope for better luck next season.

Yet with West Ham currently occupying seventh spot with just six games remaining, they might not get a better opportunity to qualify for the Europa League – as the UEFA Cup has been re-branded.

The problem, however, is that they might have already blown their chances this term.

When West Ham sold Craig Bellamy to Manchester City for £14m in January, it was imperative they replaced him with another top-class striker – one that could immediately step into his boots and make a valuable contribution.

Instead, they splashed a potential club record fee on Savio Nsereko – a raw 19-year-old who looks neither a natural goalscorer nor ready for regular Premier League action.

The Uganda-born Germany Under-20 international has made just one start for the Hammers and eight substitute appearances so far – mostly on the flanks.

It says everything that he can't even get into a side that has lost its entire midfield and strike force in recent weeks.

Of course, he is an exciting talent and could well be a superstar in three or four years' time.

But can West Ham afford to invest so heavily in the distant future when their financial resources are severely limited and must also be used to preserve their present position?

It is not as if the club is short of youth academy products they will have to patiently groom and nurture over the coming years.

Fans will therefore be tempted to question the influence of technical director Gianluca Nani, who must surely have played a key role in deciding how a large chunk of the Bellamy money was spent.

And maybe they would have more confidence in the signing of Savio if he was found via an expansive scouting network rather than simply plucked from Nani's former club Brescia.

West Ham might have a bright future – but a place in Europe next term would have made it seem even brighter.

Kirk now says: After going five games without a win, West Ham found some form again to enjoy a five-game unbeaten run to give themselves an unlikely chance of qualifying for Europe, despite losing Craig Bellamy to Manchester City and replacing him with a little boy lost who was clearly out of his depth. Future vice-chairman Karren Brady would confirm in November 2012 that she was investigating the Savio deal.

OFF-FIELD PROBLEMS ARE BUILDING UP (23 April 2009)

In the words of Cockney crooner Ian Dury, West Ham fans will either have 'Reasons To Be Cheerful' come the end of the season or be thinking 'What A Waste'.

It all depends on whether the Hammers cling on to their seventh place in the table and qualify for Europe next term, of course.

Yet it's still a funny time for the club's supporters given everything that's going on at the moment.

In terms of the football, most things are going swimmingly.

The team is challenging for Europe and boss Gianfranco Zola and assistant Steve Clarke are set to sign new long-term deals.

A mass of injury problems have undermined the team's efforts, but some consolation can be taken from the valuable experience that youngsters such as Junior Stanislas and James Tomkins will benefit from in the long term.

It is all looking rosy, then.

Away from the pitch, however, it's a different story. It has been reported that West Ham could be passed into the hands of new owners – Icelandic banking outfit Straumur.

This would be due to the financial problems experienced by Hansa, West Ham's holding company.

Fans won't worry too much over chairman Bjorgolfur Gudmundsson's possible exit because he is no longer in a position to invest in the club. But Straumur would also be unlikely to spend money on the Hammers, meaning the club would have to raise its own funds for new players.

The state of the club's finances will only come to light when the 2007/08 figures are eventually published in the summer – after much delay.

It also remains to be seen if any new board has the necessary knowledge to run a football club and make it successful.

Meanwhile, the joint FA/Premier League investigation into West Ham's conduct over the Carlos Tevez affair is ongoing, despite the near £20m compensation figure recently agreed with Sheffield United.

The potential remains for a points deduction next season, but it's hoped the whole inquiry will simply fizzle out.

And just to compound the problems, former boss Alan Curbishley continues to contest the nature of his departure from the club last September by seeking compensation.

The club's lawyers must be working overtime, poor things.

So there's a lot to be resolved over the coming months before West Ham can seriously focus their thoughts on the future.

But things are rarely quiet down Green Street way, are they?

Kirk now says: The full consequences of Gudmundsson's disaster for West Ham were beginning to become known, with it being obvious that Straumur – themselves in financial difficulty – was never a viable long-term solution to the club's problems after big debts were built up under the chairman's reign.

NOT SUCH A GUD STORY AFTER ALL (3 June 2009)

When Bjorgolfur Gudmundsson bids farewell to Upton Park, how will West Ham fans remember him?

Will the Icelandic businessman be thanked for helping to establish the Hammers as a Premier League club in the two-and-a-half years since his takeover?

Or will he be viewed as the man who promised big things – including European football – and ultimately failed (or couldn't afford) to deliver?

There have been some dramatic events during Gudmundsson's ownership of West Ham.

The first task of early chairman Eggert Magnusson – the football brains as opposed to the financier – was to sack manager Alan Pardew and replace him with Alan Curbishley.

The Hammers were dead certs for relegation in 2007 until a certain Carlos Tevez came to the rescue.

The furore over the nature of the Argentina striker's registration – under the previous administration – caused a dark cloud to hover over Upton Park during the best part of Gudmundsson's reign and resulted in a hefty compensation payment to Sheffield United.

The signings of Scott Parker, Kieron Dyer, Freddie Ljungberg, Julien Faubert and Craig Bellamy vastly increased the wage bill while adding character and controversy to the squad.

But fans were in danger of falling into a coma last term as cautious Curbishley's injury-hit side produced mediocre football and remained stuck in tenth place.

The sales of defenders Anton Ferdinand and George McCartney to Sunderland over the manager's head resulted in Curbishley walking out and complaining that his position had become untenable.

Successor Gianfranco Zola and assistant Steve Clarke quickly introduced the flair that had been missing, but points were thin on the ground until they taught Carlton Cole how to score goals.

And the upturn was so impressive that the team managed to overcome a series of injuries to key players to challenge for a European place until the penultimate game of the season.

That was enough for Zola and Clarke to be rewarded with new four-year contracts recently.

Off the pitch, however, Gudmundsson was fighting for his financial life as his Icelandic banking empire collapsed as a result of the global cash crisis, with reports claiming he was £300m in debt.

Without a buyer for West Ham, the club would find itself in the hands of creditors who would assume its ownership with a view to cashing in on its true value when the economic climate improves.

So fans are entitled to look ahead with a sense of uncertainty, with it looking likely that West Ham will have to be self-sufficient for the time being.

Now, where are those accounts?

Kirk now says: West Ham's accounts for the year ending 2008 were eventually published in September 2009 and revealed that the club had lost £37.4m to push their debts and liabilities towards the £100m mark, with finance director Nick Igoe admitting that the business strategy was 'fundamentally flawed'. The debts would be even higher by the time that David Gold and David Sullivan bought a controlling interest in the club in 2010.

REFLECTING ON SEASON 2008/09

Best signing: Valon Behrami (Lazio), £5m

Worst signing: Savio Nsereko (Brescia), up to £9m

Best result: Winning 4-1 at Portsmouth in December

Worst result: Losing 3-0 at home to Liverpool in May

Final position: 9th in Premier League, 51 points

Manager and rating: Gianfranco Zola 7/10

Best thing about season: Making a surprise late push for Europe

Worst thing about season: The collapse of chairman Bjorgolfur Gudmundsson's financial empire

SEASON 2009/10

'Zola's position has become untenable'

THE big development in the summer of 2009 was that the ownership of West Ham United was indeed transferred to Straumur Investment Bank as part of the debt owed by Bjorgulfur Gudmundsson. However, Straumur themselves were under the control of the Financial Supervisory Authority of Iceland and their problems were such that they were forced to seek a number of reprieves from creditors to avoid going into liquidation, which naturally prompted serious concerns about the future of the Hammers.

It was against this backdrop of huge financial uncertainty that Gianfranco Zola and Steve Clarke, with new contracts in their back pockets, set about trying to improve the squad.

With David Di Michele and Diego Tristan failing to convince anybody they were worthy of new deals, Freddie Sears being loaned to Crystal Palace and Dean Ashton still under the care of the bloke who built the Six Million Dollar Man, the Hammers looked particularly lightweight in attack – even after signing teenager Frank Nouble from Chelsea and recruiting free agent Guillermo Franco in September.

Midfielder Luis Jimenez arrived on loan from Inter Milan while defender Manuel Da Costa was signed as part of the deal that saw the hapless Savio Nsereko offloaded to Fiorentina. And good riddance too … Meanwhile, the loans of left-back Herita Ilunga (from Toulouse) and Radoslav Kovac (from Spartak Moscow) were turned into permanent deals. At the same time the Hammers said goodbye to Lucas Neill, who eventually joined Everton as a free agent after winding down his contract, Lee Bowyer, who went to Birmingham, and James Collins made a £5m deadline-day move to Aston Villa.

Zola and Clarke clearly had their hands tied in terms of funds but with the former providing the inspiration and the latter the organisation – or at least that was the theory – the fans still had a certain amount of confidence in them.

As has been said before, however, the real test of a good manager is when things are going wrong and, needless to say, Zola's credentials would be seriously tested over the following campaign.

WOLVES ARE AT THE DOOR (20 August 2009)

It seems that West Ham fans can never sleep too easily in their beds.

Even when things look bright and rosy on the pitch, there's always some kind of storm cloud in the distance to dampen their mood.

Especially for those who believe everything that appears in the national press.

Last weekend was a classic case in point.

Spirits were high after the Hammers outplayed Wolves to earn an impressive 2-0 win at Molineux.

But supporters who buy one particular Sunday paper were quickly brought down to earth when they read that West Ham's owners had allegedly demanded the sales of the club's top players.

Oh – and manager Gianfranco Zola was set to quit in protest.

According to the story, Matthew Upson, Robert Green, Scott Parker, Carlton Cole and Mark Noble were to be offloaded to ease the financial problems of parent company Straumur.

That is enough to make any West Ham fan turn claret and blue in the face.

But stories of the club having to sell players are nothing new.

In January it was repeatedly claimed that a whole host of stars would be sold as then-owner Bjorgolfur Gudmundsson tried to keep his creditors at bay. In the end, only Craig Bellamy was sold for serious money – and that was after the striker pushed hard to secure a lucrative move to Manchester City.

Subsequent signing Savio may have proved to be an inappropriate purchase but at least it saw the Hammers reinvesting in the squad.

It has long been suspected that defender Matthew Upson might be sold this summer if he failed to sign a new contract.

But it has been denied that Straumur's problems would force him out of the door, with the club issuing a statement last week.

Non-executive chairman Andrew Bernhardt said, 'The club is on a sound financial footing and Straumur creditor meetings have no bearing on the operations of West Ham United. This remains unchanged.'

But disturbing reports continue to emerge and it means fans can only truly relax once the transfer window closes on 1 September.

Of course, the £2m signing of Czech midfielder Radoslav Kovac would suggest the club is not about to be asset-stripped.

And Zola has insisted that his intention is to sign two strikers – even though none had arrived prior to the season's kick-off.

Some reports might be rubbish but that doesn't stop fans from worrying about what the future holds.

Kirk now says: A source at West Ham insisted to this columnist that this story had absolutely no substance – and thankfully that turned out to be the case, with all the top players remaining on board for at least another two seasons. As for the signing of Radoslav Kovac being a sign of the club's ambition, hmmm.

FOCUS ON THE TRUE VILLAINS (3 September 2009)

It is a surprise the residents of Blackburn didn't board up their windows and lock themselves indoors when West Ham visited Ewood Park on Saturday (or maybe some did).

After all, the headlines relating to 'Hammers hooliganism' at the Carling Cup game against Millwall last week did little to preserve the reputation of the club's genuine, law-abiding fans.

Sadly, it was convenient for the media to blur the distinction between the crowd disturbances inside the Boleyn Ground – which included three pointless pitch invasions – and the serious violence outside it. Those not present at the game were left with the impression that there had been fierce fighting between rival sets of fans inside the stadium – which wasn't the case, of course.

There was heavy use of a photograph showing a blood-covered fan being dragged by police up the touchline – but nobody stopped to question how he sustained his injuries (you probably don't need three guesses).

And while certain papers were only too keen to shine a spotlight on the faces of idiots who ran on to the pitch, surely the true villains were those fighting each other and clashing with police in Green Street.

Some critics might suggest it's irrelevant where the trouble took place if it involved those wearing claret and blue shirts displaying the club's crest. But it's hugely significant because West Ham can only be held directly responsible for what occurs inside the Boleyn Ground.

Or is it to be suggested the club should also carry the can for all crimes committed within a five-mile radius?

As a result of the predictably sensationalistic coverage ('worst violence in 30 years' claimed one headline), there have been hysterical reactions from a variety of distant observers eager to jump aboard the bandwagon in order to serve their own motives and agendas.

Some critics insisted West Ham should be thrown out of the Carling Cup or forced to play behind closed doors.

Former boss Harry Redknapp even suggested that cup draws should be re-taken if they throw the Hammers and Millwall together.

Surely the obvious answer is to simply ban away fans from such powder-keg clashes. Certainly if the police are going to allow nearby pubs to stay open before the game so that mobs can drunkenly congregate around them – as was the case in Green Street last week.

There were warning signs on the day of the friendly against Napoli last month – but did anyone heed them?

Kirk now says: Okay, it's not a clever thing to do – and it's technically illegal – but the pitch invasions were largely celebratory, with girls swinging their handbags and fathers carrying kids on their shoulders rather than seeking violent confrontation with opposing fans (which is the story the media would much rather project, of course). West Ham were fined £115,000 plus £5,000 costs while Millwall escaped any punishment despite seats being thrown on to the pitch.

DIAMANTI COULD BE A DIAMOND (23 September 2009)

Given that this column a year ago was singing the praises of David Di Michele – who apparently had 'something about the Paolo Di Canios about him' – it's probably not a good idea to get too carried away by the first impressions of a new striker.

But there was enough about Alessandro Diamanti's display on his full debut against Liverpool on Saturday to suggest that West Ham could have a new cult figure on their hands.

It is obvious the Italian has the passion, skill and maverick spirit to capture the imagination of fans that are desperate for a new hero to worship.

So it's just as well the recent signing opened his Hammers goal account on Saturday despite clearly slipping before looping his first-half spot-kick over Pepe Reina.

In true Di Canio fashion, however, the player insisted he was 'trying to hit it down the middle anyway'.

So fans could be set for all kinds of fun and games from the man with the tattoos and wild hair that suggests he has just got out of bed.

That is certainly the case if a seven-minute compilation of Diamanti highlights on YouTube is anything to go by.

Never mind the goals he scores, the real spectacle is the former Livorno forward's celebrations after hitting the back of the net.

Against Brescia he's doing a backwards jig up the touchline; against Grosetto he's jumping up and down and flapping his arms like a bird; against Pisa he's sprinting around the 400-metre track while pointing to his fans like a rock star.

It would be nice to think that Diamanti will have plenty of reasons to leap around like a madman at Upton Park this season – and the fact he takes free-kicks and penalties means he should occasionally get on the scoresheet. Whether he succeeds in scoring enough goals from open play, however, remains to be seen.

Gianfranco Zola admitted last Saturday that his preferred option is to play with 'one striker and two small ones behind him'.

Yet the game against Liverpool provided further evidence that the West Ham players have yet to get the best out of the 4-3-3 system, with Carlton Cole again being left too isolated up front.

Diamanti was often seen hugging the right touchline, when fans want to see him hugging his team-mates – after getting on the end of a cross and bursting the net.

Kirk now says: Diamanti quickly won the hearts of the West Ham fans but he was never going to score enough goals in the way he was deployed – as his record of eight in 30 outings suggests.

ZOLA, ARE YOU ROEDER IN DISGUISE? (8 October 2009)

It was just under a year ago when this column described Gianfranco Zola's leadership of West Ham as 'well-intentioned but misguided'.

The Hammers had just drawn 0-0 at home to Portsmouth to claim only their second point during a run of seven games without a win.

And while the team was playing some fancy football, it was totally toothless in attack – as two goals in six games would suggest.

Of course, any criticism of Zola's philosophies seemed laughable later in the campaign as West Ham lifted themselves into the top half of the table to mount a serious challenge for a place in Europe.

Indeed, only terrible luck with injuries towards the end of the season denied them seventh place and Europa League qualification.

So it might seem unfair to start questioning Zola now that the Italian is struggling once again to put the Hammers on a winning path.

But West Ham are in a worrying position, having dropped to second from bottom after failing to win a league game since the opening-day success at Wolves.

Five points from seven games represents their worst start to a season since 2006 when Alan Pardew was sacked as boss.

And the last time the Hammers failed to win any of their first three home league games – under Glenn Roeder's control in 2002 – they ultimately found themselves relegated.

One wag in the press box on Sunday even claimed that Zola is beginning to sound like Roeder with an Italian accent when attempting to explain away another disappointing result.

Ouch! Now that really is below the belt.

Zola has been forced to work in difficult circumstances since his appointment in September 2008, but that doesn't mean he has not made mistakes – as he admitted after the recent 3-1 defeat at Manchester City.

And big questions have to be asked of his determination to persevere with a 4-3-3 formation that has repeatedly failed to produce results this term.

With only one top-class striker in his squad, Zola can argue that the idea of Carlton Cole spearheading the attack makes perfect sense.

But the likes of Zavon Hines, Alessandro Diamanti and Luis Jimenez are not providing sufficient support and Cole has been left fighting a lone battle while too many others act as ineffective playmakers.

Diamanti could well solve the problem, but he must work alongside Cole if the goals are to come and lift West Ham to safety.

Kirk now says: The Hammers were on a miserable 11-game winless run as Zola struggled in his second season at Upton Park.

BARON NEEDS TO BE COURTED (15 October 2009)

It doesn't matter if they're a porn baron, biscuit baron or oil baron.

They can wander the earth in military-style clothing, the finest suits available or long flowing robes.

They can originate from east London, Iceland or the United Arab Emirates – or anywhere else, for that matter.

The only necessity is that somebody out there decides they want to buy West Ham United – because the club's prospects as a competitive outfit could depend on it.

In the past week alone, long-term Birmingham owners David Sullivan and David Gold, as well as former Hammers chairman Eggert Magnusson, have been linked with possible takeovers at Upton Park.

Yet, at the time of writing, it appears that any deal is unlikely, with possible purchasers reportedly put off by West Ham's high level of debt and current owners Straumur seemingly reluctant to sell the club until they can gain its full market value when the economic climate improves. That situation may suit Straumur, who see West Ham as a key asset they can eventually exploit to the full when fending off their own creditors.

But it's doing little for the Hammers, with the failed Icelandic banking concern being in no position to invest funds in the club.

West Ham's latest accounts, for the year up to May 2008, revealed a staggering loss of nearly £40m, so it's difficult to see how the club could suddenly have improved their financial fortunes to the extent they're now operating solely on a self-sufficient basis.

They could try to increase their borrowing, but financial director Nick Igoe's admission that the club had breached 'certain banking covenants' in 2007/08 suggests they have already tested the goodwill of several lending institutions.

The fact that sponsors SBOBET had to advance funds to cover the signing of striker Alessandro Diamanti and members of the club's hierarchy reportedly made financial sacrifices to secure the capture of Mexico international Guillermo Franco this summer really says it all.

It is therefore imperative that new investment is forthcoming and West Ham fans are understandably desperate to see a knight in shining armour appear on the horizon.

Outgoing Birmingham MD Karren Brady admitted in her newspaper column at the weekend that colleagues Sullivan and Gold are 'Hammers bred' but claimed a takeover 'under West Ham's present financial arrangements would be madness'.

At the moment, fans will probably say any rich nutter would do.

Kirk now says: Maybe Karren Brady was playing a game by trying to bring down the asking price or deterring possible rivals, but if so it worked because Gold and Sullivan emerged as the leading candidates to buy a controlling interest in the Hammers, unless genuine 'madness' came into play, of course.

FA MUST COUGH UP ASH CASH (12 November 2009)

Take a look at the 'message wall' on Dean Ashton's official website and you'll see a number of West Ham fans over the last year or so pleading with the striker not to retire.

One joker even asks about Ashton's lack of response to the enquiries, before adding, 'You're not exactly busy, are you?'

But the week began with reports that Ashton was finally set to confirm that injury had forced him to quit football at the age of 25.

And that should come as little surprise to supporters, who might be disappointed but also a little relieved that the Ashton saga is nearing an end.

Because West Ham, in their current financial situation, can ill afford to continue paying wages of around £50,000 a week to somebody whose prospects of playing top-level football again have been looking remote for some time.

It now looks to be a matter for the insurance men, with West Ham reportedly seeking £7m in compensation from the FA after Ashton's ankle problems began when he was injured while on England duty three years ago.

And that could be a messy business if the FA chooses to put up a fight by pointing to the fact that 40 of Ashton's 56 appearances for the Hammers came after he suffered the injury.

Indeed, his 11 goals in 35 games during the 2007/08 season even prompted West Ham to hand the striker a fat new contract.

But the fact is that Ashton has never been the same player since missing the entire 2006/07 campaign – and the Hammers must ensure that the FA accepts responsibility for that.

The player had enjoyed an impressive upward career trajectory before joining West Ham in January 2006, scoring 8, 10, 16, 20 and 27 goals in the previous five seasons.

His two goals in the FA Cup sixth-round game at Manchester City helped put West Ham on course to the Millennium Stadium, where he scored in the epic 3-3 draw with Liverpool in the final.

Comparisons were being made with Alan Shearer and international stardom seemed a formality, before that fateful clash with Shaun Wright-Phillips condemned him to a three-year fight for full fitness.

Gianfranco Zola had expected Ashton to return to full pre-season training in the summer and when that didn't happen the writing was clearly on the wall.

It is, of course, a desperate shame – because the Hammers could certainly have made use of his former talents right now.

Kirk now says: It wasn't until February 2011 that it was announced that the Football Association had agreed an out-of-court settlement with Ashton, after he sued them for compensation, while it was quickly revealed that West Ham were seeking £6.8m from the FA after being forced to settle the player's contract due to his injury not being covered by the club's insurance policy. It appears their claim fell on deaf ears.

ONE YEAR ON, THE SAME THREE WISHES (31 December 2009)

This time 12 months ago, West Ham fans had three New Year wishes for the club.

One was that the Hammers wouldn't sell their best players in the January transfer window.

Another was that boss Gianfranco Zola would recover from a poor autumn period to inspire his team away from the danger of relegation.

And the third was that somebody with deep pockets would buy the club from its cash-strapped Icelandic owners.

So here we are – one year on – and those same supporters will be feeling a sense of déjà vu with West Ham in a very similar position.

The Hammers are once again battling against the drop, speculation continues about top players jumping from a sinking ship, while the need for a club takeover is greater than ever.

That is not to say that nothing of significance took place in 2009.

Indeed, the sale of Craig Bellamy to Manchester City last January is something the West Ham attack has never really recovered from.

To his credit, Zola did indeed turn things around with a run of 13 league games in which his side was beaten just twice as they lifted themselves into contention for a European place.

And the Hammers did experience a change of ownership, with Straumur inheriting majority control of the club from Bjorgolfur Gudmundsson following the collapse of his banking empire.

But with things going backwards, West Ham's prospects look even bleaker than they did a year ago – unless a new takeover is soon completed.

At the time of writing, however, former Birmingham owners David Sullivan and David Gold's approach has yet to be embraced.

Straumur have little funds to invest in the squad, so Zola could be forced to cash-in on one of his key assets if he wants to spend money – and there has been much speculation about the likes of Scott Parker and Matthew Upson moving on in recent weeks.

The idea of sacrificing any of the top players, which also include Robert Green and Carlton Cole, to fund new purchases is a dangerous game – and West Ham are hardly in a position to take such risks.

Upson might be running his contract down and in no mood to sign a new one, but it's pointless exploiting his current value in the transfer market if his absence results in relegation.

Not for the first time then, January is likely to be a nail-biting month.

Kirk now says: Thankfully, West Ham fans wouldn't have to wait long for their two knights in shining armour to appear in the middle of Green Street.

WHAT A WASTE OF MONEY (13 January 2010)

When money is tight, common sense dictates that you restrict your spending to what you really need.

That Iron Maiden DVD box set might seem simply irresistible but you can probably live without it – especially if the fridge is emptier than West Ham's trophy cupboard. So why, when it was obvious the Hammers needed an out-and-out striker in the past year, did they invest what limited funds they did have on Savio Nsereko and Alessandro Diamanti?

The folly of those decisions is being felt this week with Guillermo Franco joining Carlton Cole and Zavon Hines on the injury list to leave Gianfranco Zola desperately searching for striking reinforcements.

Savio was recruited in the wake of Craig Bellamy's sale to Manchester City a year ago and it quickly became apparent that the youngster was not the player West Ham needed, being neither a dedicated striker nor ready for regular Premier League action.

Technical director Gianluca Nani clearly had his reasons for bringing the 19-year-old over from his former club Brescia – and there has been plenty of speculation as to what they might have been.

The fact that Savio made just one start before being traded for a defender, Manuel Da Costa, who struggles to get into West Ham's team, says it all.

Diamanti, meanwhile, has become a fans' favourite at Upton Park after scoring six goals so far, but was his tin labelled correctly?

When West Ham signed the player – having gone to sponsors SBOBET with their begging bowl to fund his purchase – the Hammers claimed the Italian would 'add extra firepower to the attack'.

Yet the player has spent most of the season hugging the touchline in a wide midfield role, with Zola reluctant to deploy him as a striker.

As he confirmed after the recent 2-0 defeat at Tottenham, 'Diamanti cannot play up front. His best quality is setting up balls for others.'

So there you have it, the manager admitting that when he needed a striker, he went and bought yet another playmaker – and the Hammers are hardly short of those.

The under-achieving Luis Jimenez is another summer signing who comes into that category, of flitting around the penalty box but rarely getting on the end of things inside it.

So let's hope West Ham do a better job of signing the striker they desperately need while the transfer window remains open – because they can ill afford to get this one wrong.

Kirk now says: The Hammers eventually recruited not just one striker but three in Blackburn's Benni McCarthy, Egyptian nomad Mido and unknown Brazilian Ilan … and a fat lot of good two of them turned out to be.

TWO DAVIDS APPEAR THE PERFECT FIT (28 January 2010)

It is a sad indictment of modern-day football that if you ask many fans what they would ideally want following a takeover of their club, they'd generally say '£200m to be spent on the world's best players so that we can win lots of trophies'.

Ask true West Ham supporters the same question, however, and they're more likely to talk about wanting owners who have ambition but a sense of realism while showing honesty, an understanding of the club's traditions and an affinity with its fan-base.

Which is exactly what they would appear to have in the shape of David Gold and David Sullivan following their arrival as joint-chairmen last week – since when they have proved they mean business by pursuing new players and targeting a move to the Olympic Stadium.

The pair immediately emphasised that West Ham's financial problems are such that they would never have entertained a takeover had it not been for their long-standing affection for the club.

Indeed, they can already boast their greatest possible achievement in making sure the Hammers remained in business without needing to sell their best players.

Furthermore, they purchased their controlling interest in West Ham with their own money – as opposed to borrowing and saddling the club with more debt – and have spare funds available to help the relegation fight.

The Hammers might have failed to sign former Manchester United striker Ruud van Nistelrooy but it was reassuring to see them chase someone whose name only previously appeared in the same sentence as the club when scoring against them.

And while Sullivan has criticised past owners for allowing the wage bill to spiral out of control, he insists that any big spending at this point in time is a short-term solution rather than a long-term philosophy.

The one thing the club cannot afford is relegation – and it's great to see that Gold and Sullivan are being proactive rather than simply sitting on their hands and hoping for the best.

It is fair to say that, for Gianfranco Zola, the new owners represent not just a breath of fresh air but also a whirlwind of ideas and initiative.

Whether the manager enjoyed being told he needs two new strikers and has too many midfield players remains to be seen, but at least he can't complain that he is not getting some much-needed support.

Sullivan's hands-on approach might ruffle a few feathers, but his determination to succeed should be celebrated.

Kirk now says: And Zola's feathers – and what was left of his hair – were indeed ruffled by Sullivan, West Ham's very own Joe Pesci type of character, over the remaining months of the campaign.

NOT ALL SWEET IN GREEN STREET (18 March 2010)

Karren Brady learned during her time at Birmingham City not to say too much about her own club in her national newspaper column.

So it's safe to assume the West Ham vice-chairman chose her words carefully on Saturday when responding to reports that Gianfranco Zola could be leaving the club in the summer.

'I don't claim to have a crystal ball so I can't say what will happen,' she admitted. 'But I know one thing: the club's out of rehab and recovering after David Sullivan and David Gold's energetic re-direction.

'Few people like change, managers included, but most accept it quickly if it's change for the better and that's what we have brought.'

There was a strong feeling that the message was emphasised as much for Zola's benefit as for the general public.

In other words, the Italian might not feel totally comfortable with certain aspects of life under the club's new owners but he should try to remember that the overall picture is a lot prettier than it used to be.

Casual observers would surely wonder what there is for Zola not to like. West Ham now have financial stability and funds were even provided for three new strikers in January.

Running costs have to be reduced but, assuming that relegation can be avoided, the Hammers can soon start to build for the future in positive mood.

But there are those who suspect that Zola's relationship with the club's hierarchy is not without its tensions.

The manager was quick to express his annoyance with co-chairman Sullivan's suggestion that the players needed to be paid less, feeling that such comments undermined his preparations for the recent Birmingham game.

Indeed, Sullivan's approach might leave Zola feeling as if his new chiefs are breathing just a bit too heavily down his neck.

The Italian admitted to knowing very little about Ilan after the striker scored a debut goal at Burnley last month, so how much influence did the manager have over the new signings?

It is hard to imagine that the recent links with three Birmingham players were his idea.

And was he happy to see chief executive Scott Duxbury and technical director Gianluca Nani pushed out of Upton Park?

Could there be a clash of personalities and philosophies?

Sullivan and Gold will be judging Zola on his actions since they took control – and the suspicion is that the manager will be assessing his bosses likewise.

Kirk now says: The early warning signs about Zola's less than harmonious relationship with his new bosses – in particular David Sullivan – would indeed prove there was no smoke without fire. Interestingly, Gianluca Nani and Scott Duxbury would link up again with Zola at Watford a couple of years later.

SLAV FITS THE BIL (25 March 2010)

Once again, reports emerged at the weekend that West Ham will be saying 'arrivederci' to Gianfranco Zola at the end of the season whether the club stays in the Premier League or not.

It is a highly believable scenario.

If David Gold and David Sullivan judge the Italian purely on his record as manager since their arrival – two wins, two draws and five defeats – they're hardly likely to be overly impressed.

Zola's nose has been put out of joint by the outspoken nature of his new bosses.

And Steve Clarke, his right-hand man, has made it known the time is nearing for him to make a step into management in his own right.

So a parting of the ways for all concerned should not be seen as too much of shock if it does indeed take place in the summer.

According to one Sunday newspaper, the most likely candidate to succeed Zola is Croatia boss Slaven Bilic.

Such an appointment would certainly capture the imagination of West Ham fans, who remember the defender's determined displays over 54 appearances for the club in the mid-1990s much more than his defection to Everton after just 15 months.

His record of 27 wins from 38 games as manager of his country is highly impressive, despite Croatia failing to qualify for this summer's World Cup finals. And when he puts on those shades to play guitar with his band Rawbau, he doesn't half look like rock legend Lou Reed, so what more could anybody want?

However, the chances of landing Bilic appear to be slender, with the 41-year-old declaring on *Match Of The Day 2* that his intention was to guide Croatia through to the 2012 European Championship finals.

Even if he were to become available, big questions would have to be asked as to whether Bilic would consider the Hammers an appropriate platform for him to fulfil his club managerial ambitions.

He might enjoy some kind of emotional attachment to West Ham, but bigger clubs – across the whole of Europe – would surely be seeking his services.

Hammers fans have been supportive of Zola, who they appreciate has suffered a real baptism of fire since taking charge 18 months ago.

But that doesn't mean they won't accept change – if the right man is appointed.

Kirk now says: Bilic would indeed take Croatia through to the Euro 2012 finals before switching to club management with Lokomotiv Moscow (and getting sacked the following year).

BLOOD ON ZOLA'S HANDS (1 April 2010)

Gianfranco Zola had the perfect opportunity to throw West Ham a lifeline this week.

All the Italian had to do was follow his initial instincts after Saturday's 1-0 home defeat by Stoke and admit that his best efforts have not been good enough.

Instead, after hotfooting it back to his homeland in Sardinia to consider his position, the Hammers boss has pledged to stay in charge at Upton Park.

Sadly, that decision is likely to result in West Ham being relegated.

It has become crystal clear during the team's run of six consecutive defeats that Zola has run out of ideas.

Some of his team selections have looked like the shirt numbers were selected by the machine that chucks out the National Lottery balls.

And while Stoke boss Tony Pulis was busy issuing instructions to his players from the touchline, Zola stood there looking simply bemused by his team's abject display.

'Do something – show some passion!' screamed one fan from the West Stand.

Even if you forget recent results, the fact remains that when a manager publicly questions if he is the right man for the job, it's time for him to go.

How can players retain confidence in somebody who needs to take a three-day holiday to become convinced he's got what it takes?

Put simply, Zola's position at West Ham has become untenable and he should have done the honourable thing and resigned.

Of course, he doesn't want to be seen as a quitter, but sometimes a manager has to hold his hands up and admit it's in his club's best interests to step down.

West Ham needed an emergency firefighter to shake things up for the final six games. Now, it's impossible to imagine them securing the three wins they probably need to stay in the Premier League.

What we have witnessed over the past half a dozen games is football's equivalent of a very public suicide.

In losing at home to Bolton, Wolves and Stoke, the Hammers have slit their own throats – and the blood is on Zola's hands.

You don't judge a manager when things are going well, you judge him on his ability to solve problems when things are going wrong.

And on that score he has failed abysmally this season.

Zola might be one of the game's true gentlemen but he's not paid to be nice, he's paid to win football matches.

And that looks beyond him right now.

Kirk now says: Ooh, nasty stuff. The Hammers were staring relegation in the face … and in echoing the type of sentiments expressed when former manager Glenn Roeder was doing his very worst in 2003, this columnist's patience had clearly run out.

WHAT'S WRONG WITH A BIT OF PATHETIC STRAW-CLUTCHING? (7 April 2010)

West Ham have taken a bit of a kicking on and off the pitch in recent weeks.

A suicidal run of six consecutive defeats prior to the morale-boosting draw at Everton last weekend has put the club in serious danger of relegation.

Co-owner David Sullivan has been accused of undermining manager Gianfranco Zola by publicly slating the team (or stating the obvious).

And critics have ridiculed West Ham's decision to complain to the Premier League about Fulham playing a weakened side at Hull the weekend before last.

One respected journalist – a Hammers fan, in fact – described the club's grievance as 'pathetic straw-clutching'.

Fulham owner Mohamed Al-Fayed was predictably unimpressed, claiming he would 'stick two fingers up to West Ham's complaint'.

Well, Hammers fans will no doubt be doing likewise to the Egyptian when they visit Craven Cottage on 1 May.

Sullivan later claimed his complaint to the Premier League could be seen as 'a test case' regarding the E20 rule that states that clubs must 'field a full-strength team'.

But regardless of the Premier League's decision, it has somehow been overlooked that West Ham have already achieved what they set out to – and that was to keep Fulham on their toes when they named their team against Wigan on Sunday.

Having taken the foot off the gas in gifting Hull three points the previous weekend, it was highly possible that Fulham might have adopted a similar strategy with Wigan's visit coming in the middle of two Europa League quarter-final ties against Wolfsburg.

Thankfully, the pressure exerted by Sullivan seemed to work, with Bobby Zamora the only notable absentee as Fulham enjoyed a 2-1 victory that leaves Wigan just three points above the Hammers.

With West Ham collecting a hard-earned point at Goodison Park last weekend, it means their fate is in their own hands with a home game against Wigan still to come.

But while the 2-2 draw at Everton stopped the rot, it's essential that the Hammers build on that by beating Sunderland at Upton Park this weekend – especially with Wigan and Hull facing relatively easy home games next time out against Portsmouth and Burnley respectively.

Some assumed it was a straight battle between West Ham and Hull to avoid the third relegation spot, but Wigan – who still have games against Arsenal and Chelsea to come – are very much in the mix.

So, well done, Fulham ... and thank you, Mr Sullivan.

Kirk now says: The relationship with Fulham wasn't necessarily the best after they helped form the so-called 'Gang of Four' who campaigned against West Ham during the Carlos Tevez affair in 2007 and it was suspected they wouldn't exactly go out of their way to do Zola's side any favours.

DOWIE IS A HULL OF A GUY (15 April 2010)

Iain Dowie has never disguised the fact that he was a West Ham supporter as a boy.

And during his two spells as a player at Upton Park, nobody could ever accuse him of giving less than 100 per cent (no jokes about 100 per cent of nothing being nothing, please).

Sadly, his efforts have not always helped West Ham down the years.

Yes, his four goals in 12 games at the tail end of the 1990/91 season played a key part in the Hammers securing promotion to the top flight under Billy Bonds.

But although Dowie finished as the Hammer of the Year runner-up behind Julian Dicks in 1996, his subsequent run of 40 league games without a goal – spanning an incredible 18 months – was hardly conducive to West Ham being successful.

Nor was the ludicrous own goal in the League Cup defeat at Stockport that – as far as the neutrals are concerned – ranks as one of the most comical moments in the history of football.

But at least he could argue he was doing a great job for his employers when managing Crystal Palace to play-off final success against the Hammers in Cardiff six years ago.

So with friends like Dowie, it's fair to suggest that West Ham hardly need enemies.

Yet it's possible that, after all this time, the former striker has finally done the biggest favour for the Hammers he could ever do.

Since taking charge of Hull last month, Dowie has guided a team that West Ham need to keep losing to three defeats in four games.

They were heading to victory in his first game at Portsmouth until they conceded twice at the death.

They beat a weakened Fulham side but then lost at Stoke and were thrashed 4-1 at home by fellow strugglers Burnley at the weekend.

That last result could prove hugely significant and at this stage it appears that Dowie is doing almost as good a job of helping the Hammers stay in the Premier League as manager Gianfranco Zola is.

West Ham's 1-0 win against Sunderland on Saturday was vital to their survival hopes but it's too early to assume the job has been done.

The fact is that 31 points is unlikely to keep the Hammers up and so it's imperative they keep going and secure at least one more victory.

The home game against Wigan on 24 April is massive.

If West Ham do stay up, however, please remember to reserve a special cheer for a particular old boy if he ever returns.

Kirk now says: Dowie did an excellent job for West Ham that season, collecting just one win in his nine games as Hull City's 'football management consultant' to guide them to relegation with only 30 points.

SCOTT'S HOT BUT ILAN'S THE MAN (29 April 2010)

If Scott Parker walked into the Boleyn Tavern, everybody in the pub would be fighting among themselves to buy him a drink.

If Ilan happened to wander in, the chances are that he would struggle to even get served.

Parker was nailed on to retain his Hammer of the Year award long before he scored the winning goal in the 3-2 victory against Wigan on Saturday.

The midfielder has been the driving force of the West Ham team as they have battled their way out of the relegation mire.

And he can consider himself unfortunate not to be part of the England set-up ahead of the World Cup finals in South Africa.

So it was perhaps fitting that Parker claimed all the plaudits for firing the Hammers to safety with that stunning late shot against Wigan.

But any winner was only possible after Ilan had levelled for West Ham after they had fallen behind early in the game.

It was the Brazilian's fourth goal since arriving at Upton Park on a short-term deal and, more crucially, his third in four games.

Those last three goals have helped the Hammers collect seven points from wins against Sunderland and Wigan plus a draw at Everton – and that's why they are staying up.

It doesn't take a lot for a player to write their name into Hammers history and folklore.

Yet it feels that Ilan might quickly be forgotten if – as seems likely – he moves on again in the summer when his short-term contract expires.

He was considered the least likely of the three strikers signed in January to make a significant impression.

All the hopes were pinned on Benni McCarthy and Mido, who had 194 Premier League games under their belts and 59 goals between them.

But the pair have given West Ham absolutely nothing since their arrival, so it's just as well that Ilan has stepped into the breach.

He will never be mentioned in the same breath as Carlos Tevez or Paolo Di Canio, of course.

But it could be argued that his goals have been no less important than any scored by those two illustrious talents. As for Parker, it's hoped that the midfielder will remain at Upton Park next season.

That can hardly be considered a formality, with there likely to be a big list of clubs looking to lure him away in the summer.

And how will he respond if Gianfranco Zola – with whom he has a close bond – does depart?

Kirk now says: Indeed, Ilan's brief, 11-game contribution to the West Ham cause has disappeared into the archives of the internet and the pages of the history books while, if anyone is interested, he was last seen plying his trade during the 2012/13 season for Bastia in France.

WE NEED A MANAGER, NOT JUST A COACH (13 May 2010)

Gianfranco Zola reflected on West Ham's season of struggle by blaming 'circumstances, mistakes and other things' as to why things did not go according to plan.

Not for the first time, the Italian has been far too vague when it comes to identifying problems and finding the 'solutions' he has been looking for over the past nine months.

In fact, the only thing Zola has been specific about is how 'painful and damaging' the recent criticism from co-owner David Sullivan was in relation to the team's performances.

With Sunday's scorer Luis Boa Morte also suggesting Sullivan should have shown 'more composure' before complaining, any neutral could be deceived into believing that all the troubles stem from the outspoken nature of the new Hammers hierarchy.

Zola and his players certainly had their precious egos damaged – but that's not why they finished 17th in the table.

It was always going to be a worrying campaign once West Ham failed to recruit the two new strikers Zola insisted he needed last summer.

Finances were tight but the club's sponsors advanced the cash that was splashed on Alessandro Diamanti – who the manager later claimed couldn't play up front.

Mexican international Guillermo Franco also arrived – but he was free for a very good reason.

Fingers can be pointed at former technical director Gianluca Nani for signing players who failed to meet West Ham's needs.

Yet Zola must also accept responsibility for the overall shape of the squad – which is all over the place at the moment.

It is all very well saying the Italian preferred to concentrate on the coaching aspects of management.

But West Ham needs proper leadership – not somebody who simply enjoys working with players on the training field.

Needless to say, it's going to be one of the busiest summers of all-time at Upton Park as Sullivan and partner David Gold try to point the club in the right direction again.

There is likely to be a huge turnover of players, with some wanting to move on and many others being forced to.

It will be disappointing to see any of the England internationals leave the club.

But fans can take heart from Sullivan's insistence that West Ham will be 'net spenders' in the transfer market.

And the Hammers will need to be – because 35 points surely won't be enough to save their skins next year.

Kirk now says: Zola was sacked on Tuesday 11 May, and typically responded to media interest by generously taking coffee out to the journalists and camera crews that were camped outside the gates of his home. David Sullivan, portrayed as a villain for condemning West Ham's 3-1 home defeat by Wolves in March as 'pathetic', later insisted, 'Sometimes you have to do things that are for the good of the club rather than popularity.'

REFLECTING ON SEASON 2009/10

Best signing: Ilan (St Etienne), free

Worst signing: Benni McCarthy (Blackburn), £5m

Best result: Winning 3-2 at home to Wigan in April

Worst result: Losing 3-1 at home to Wolves in March

Final position: 17th in the Premier League, 35 points

Manager and rating: Gianfranco Zola 4/10

Best thing about season: David Sullivan and David Gold buying the club

Worst thing about season: The season-long struggle for points

SEASON 2010/11

'Grant appears to be deluding himself'

THE date of 3 June 2010 will go down as a dreadful day in the history of the Hammers. It was, of course, the day that Avram Grant was appointed as West Ham's manager on a four-year contract. 'I'm ready to do my best,' said the Israeli, 55, who had taken Chelsea to the Champions League Final in 2008 and debt-ridden Portsmouth to the FA Cup Final two years later.

'We are certain we have got the right man and am confident he will prove a success,' added co-chairman David Sullivan.

As time would tell, Grant's 'best' was nowhere near good enough, while big questions would be asked of Sullivan and David Gold's judgement as the Hammers went from bad to worse.

Steve Clarke left the club by mutual consent and was replaced by former Yugoslav international Zeljko Petrovic, who lasted just four months before describing the Premier League as 'crap' on his departure. What that said for West Ham given they spent the whole season battling against the drop is anybody's guess.

But nobody was seriously considering relegation in the summer of 2010 as striker Victor Obinna (Inter Milan, loan), midfielder Thomas Hitzlsperger (Lazio, free), winger Pablo Barrera (Pumas UNAM, £4m), striker Frederic Piquionne (Lyon, £1m), defender Winston Reid (Midtjylland, undisclosed), defender Tal Ben-Haim (Portsmouth, loan) and right-back Lars Jacobsen (Blackburn, free) all arrived to bolster the squad.

Out went forwards Ilan, Guillermo Franco and, most notably, Alessandro Diamanti, although the Hammers would spend the next few years chasing Brescia for the £1.8m they owed for the Italy international.

FUTURE IS BRIGHT, IF NOT TAKEN FOR GRANTED (12 August 2010)

It is appropriate that West Ham's new manager is named Avram Grant – because a lot is being taken for 'granted' about the club's prospects this season.

There was a very strong feeling towards the end of last term that if the Hammers could only just force themselves over the finishing line and avoid relegation, then there would be no looking back as a new era got into gear under new owners David Sullivan and David Gold.

Gianfranco Zola fulfilled his commitments by ensuring West Ham remained a Premier League club before he was waved on his merry way.

And now it's assumed the team can only enjoy better fortunes, with worries about the drop a thing of the past and there being a realistic hope that the Hammers can challenge for a top-half finish.

That is certainly how things look and feel at the moment – but football has a funny way of making people regret attitudes that could be described by the critics as representing complacency or arrogance.

So while fans can approach the new season with a sense of comfort and confidence that there will be none of the nail biting that took place last term, it's crucial that those in the camp recognise that the hard work starts here.

For that reason, West Ham could have no better man in charge right now.

Because Grant only needs to draw on last season's experience with debt-ridden Portsmouth to realise that you have to fight to earn the right to enjoy any form of reward or success.

The Israeli boss is unlikely to allow his players to develop a false sense of security just because they went through their pre-season programme unbeaten.

If anything, the home game against Deportivo on Saturday revived memories of the problems facing the Hammers this time last year when Carlton Cole shouldered a huge responsibility to score the side's goals. Watching the striker toil away up front on his own for most of the game, it was like very little had changed over the past 12 months.

It needs to be hoped that new signing Frederic Piquionne can at least match the 11 goals he scored while on loan for Pompey last term.

And the Hammers still need more goals from midfield, so new arrival Thomas Hitzlsperger will be expected to help rectify that problem.

Let us be quietly confident … but take nothing for granted.

Kirk now says: West Ham could have 'no better man' in charge? After watching a relative rookie in Gianfranco Zola, who appeared to see management as simply coaching players, this columnist assumed that Avram Grant would have what it takes to get the club back on track. It just goes to show how wrong you can be.

DISCONCERTING AND DISTURBING (19 August 2010)

There are several words that spring to mind after watching West Ham's 3-0 defeat at Aston Villa on Saturday – most of which cannot be printed in a family newspaper such as this.

But adjectives such as dreadful, disgraceful and depressing pretty much describe a display that was as disconcerting as it was disturbing.

It would be bad enough to witness such a limp, lifeless and lacklustre effort at any stage of the season.

But to have to sit through it on the opening day of the campaign, when a team is supposed to be full of fresh drive and determination, was simply unforgivable.

It was impossible to believe the players were making their first competitive outing under a new boss – and it reflects poorly on Avram Grant that they gave him so little.

All this when Aston Villa were supposedly there for the taking after Martin O'Neill walked out last week to leave them without a manager.

Yet Villa's players were full of desire from the very first minute, while the Hammers never looked at the races.

Oh, apart from a brief period early in the second half when Grant laughably claimed his men 'controlled the game'.

Not that looking slightly less rubbish for 20 minutes before Villa scored their third goal should be described as having control.

Grant has a reputation for motivating players but there was little evidence of this at Villa Park.

The Israeli's team selection and tactics were also left with a huge question mark hanging over them.

Carlton Cole looked isolated as a lone striker until Frederic Piquionne and Pablo Barrera offered some support after the break.

Julien Faubert spent the whole of last season operating as a right-back, so it's pure folly to ask the Frenchman to play an advanced attacking role.

Meanwhile, Winston Reid endured a torrid time on his debut at right-back before Grant admitted the New Zealand international is really a centre-half.

And there was absolutely no creativity from the triumvirate of Scott Parker, Mark Noble and Radoslav Kovac in central midfield.

But at least you could say they did get in the way … of each other.

Sadly, all the optimism generated by a strong pre-season has blown up in smoke already. If anybody was lured into a false sense of security about West Ham's prospects this term, they only need to replay last weekend's disaster to say hello to reality.

Kirk now says: Grant made a complete mess of his first match in charge … and set the tone of the season in one fell swoop. How did the bloke ever convince anybody that he was a good football manager?

HELP! THE HAMMERS ARE IN TROUBLE (2 September 2010)

Did you hear that sickening thud just before 5pm on Saturday?

For most West Ham fans it was simply unavoidable, with their team slumping to the bottom of the Premier League table.

And that was BEFORE the Hammers crashed to a 3-0 defeat at Manchester United that evening.

It means that West Ham and Stoke are the only two clubs in the four English divisions yet to collect a point this season.

And the latter will surely fancy their chances of getting off the mark (if they haven't already done so) when the Hammers visit the Britannia Stadium in an early relegation six-pointer on 18 September.

By that time, West Ham will probably have been embarrassed by Chelsea to set a new club record of starting a season with four successive defeats.

So the Hammers find themselves in a similar predicament as the trapped miners in Chile – they might as well make themselves comfortable because they're likely to be stuck where they are for some time. Indeed, it's anyone's guess as to what will happen first – the workmen being hauled to safety or West Ham picking up their first point.

Those who travelled to Old Trafford last weekend might have convinced themselves the Hammers have already got their first win on the board, with the visiting fans celebrating four imaginary strikes during the final stages of the game.

'Let's pretend we've scored a goal!' they chanted while being forced to make their own entertainment.

Some apologists might try to claim that the 3-0 defeat was nothing to be ashamed of, but former West Ham boss Lou Macari said it all when he described the game as Manchester United's 'easiest win for years'. Nobody should be fooled by the fact that the Hammers held out for half an hour before gifting the hosts a penalty to open the scoring.

With just one man up front, the visitors posed no danger whatsoever and resembled a Championship side trying to hold out for a cup replay.

Meanwhile, a post-match pattern has already emerged, with boss Avram Grant playing the same old record when he faces the media.

First he focuses on the 15-minute spell when the Hammers enjoyed a bit of possession (without scoring) before blaming the officials for the opening goal – as he did after defeats by Aston Villa, Bolton and United.

It makes you wonder whom he is trying to fool – the fans or himself?

Kirk now says: The Hammers did indeed concede another three goals to Chelsea to lose their opening four league games of the season. Comparing them to the trapped miners in Chile might seem inappropriate, if only because West Ham dug themselves into an even bigger hole rather than participating in a brave rescue mission.

VERNON'S LOVE IS A MYSTERY (16 September 2010)

NFL star Vernon Davis was recently interviewed ahead of the San Francisco 49ers' visit to London next month and bizarrely admitted that West Ham was his preferred choice of 'soccer' team.

Tellingly, he began to explain his unlikely love of the Hammers with the words, 'I don't know.'

Following the club's worst ever start to a season with four successive league defeats, Davis is probably not the only West Ham fan wondering why they remain so committed to the claret and blue cause.

After all, it's a painful relationship and one that is guaranteed to produce plenty of tears.

Just in case people are questioning their faith, the club's official programme for the game against Chelsea presented a timely article under the heading, 'Ten Reasons To Love West Ham United'.

Number one of which was 'Bobby Moore'. England's World Cup-winning captain was familiar with the under-achieving Hammers sitting in the bottom half of the table during the 1960s and early 1970s.

But quite what the late defender would make of West Ham's current struggles is anybody's guess.

The incident that saw Chelsea go 2-0 ahead on Saturday just has to be one of the most ridiculous goals ever conceded. The Hammers are currently shipping three goals a game and the ease with which the opposition are being allowed to score is nothing short of embarrassing.

New boss Avram Grant keeps insisting that West Ham are 'not playing like a side that will be relegated'.

Yet the defence is a shambles, the midfield lacks creativity and the attack is powder-puff stuff. The Hammers have scored just two goals from open play in five league and cup games – and both of those have come from midfielder Scott Parker.

Parker might have signed a new five-year contract last week but that will be worth nothing if the club fails to avoid the drop this season.

And that won't happen unless England internationals such as Robert Green and Matthew Upson start proving why they went to the World Cup in the summer.

Goalkeeper Green appears short of confidence after his famous blunder against the USA while defender Upson looks out of sorts after also failing to play in England's recent Euro 2012 qualifiers.

'It's West Ham, baby,' insists Vernon Davis. 'I just love them, they're awesome.'

He has clearly been misquoted, because surely he meant 'awful'.

Kirk now says: It can be assumed that Vernon hadn't seen the Hammers play for some time, otherwise he'd have probably been a bit more discreet about his secret love affair.

FREDDIE PIQS ON SPURS AGAIN (30 September 2010)

When West Ham fans are asked what team they support, there is of course only one answer, 'Whoever's playing Spurs next.'

Frederic Piquionne might just think along similar lines, given that he has kicked Tottenham where it hurts in his last two appearances against them.

First the French striker scored as Portsmouth denied Spurs a place in last season's FA Cup Final – for which he should be knighted.

And now he has earned West Ham their first win of the season after heading home the only goal of the game at Upton Park on Saturday.

The 1-0 victory was the first time the Hammers have beaten Tottenham since 2006 and ended a run of five successive defeats against them.

It was also the first time that former West Ham boss Harry Redknapp had tasted defeat as a returning manager having won on his previous five visits with Portsmouth and Spurs. So to suggest it was a highly satisfying result is one of the understatements of the year.

Never mind taking points off Manchester United, Chelsea, Arsenal and Liverpool, nothing beats the feeling of sending Tottenham home with their tails between their legs as far as most West Ham fans are concerned.

Piquionne got the goal but Robert Green played an equally big part in making sure the Hammers claimed the points.

The goalkeeper made a couple of brilliant saves and it's reassuring to see him returning to the form that fans know he is capable of.

However, while Green insists that mistakes and criticism do not affect him, the evidence points very much to the contrary.

He has looked nervous since his blunder at the World Cup and his misjudged salute of defiance towards the press box at the weekend simply proved that he has allowed things to get under his skin.

It is a disgrace that Green has been booted out of the England squad after one mistake but he needs to stop blaming the media and start taking issue with Fabio Capello, the bloke who dumped him.

Meanwhile, Carlton Cole is another Hammer whose England prospects are not looking too hot at the moment.

The striker failed to make the starting line-up against Spurs after boss Avram Grant elected to stick with Piquionne and Victor Obinna who both scored in the Carling Cup win at Sunderland.

And unless injuries intervene, it could take some time for Cole to find his way back.

Kirk now says: Any victory against Spurs has to be celebrated and this result made it two wins on the spin during a period of mini-revival when the Hammers lost just twice in 11 games (although six of them were sadly draws).

ATMOSPHERE LIKE A FAIRY TALE ... GRIMM (4 November 2010)

If rumours are to be believed, the atmosphere at West Ham's training ground makes your average funeral resemble a Madonna show.

Admittedly, the Hammers haven't got much to sing and dance about at the moment.

They are three points adrift at the bottom of the table, have won just once in ten league games and their prospects of reaching the Carling

Cup semi-finals were hardly enhanced when they were paired with Manchester United.

Taking all that into account, you would hardly expect the players to be doing the Hokey Cokey or jigging to the Macarena.

But the whisper is that the mood and morale within the training camp is not always what it might be, with the sense of camaraderie in certain quarters leaving something to be desired.

In terms of developing a close relationship with the players, former boss Gianfranco Zola was always going to be a tough act to follow.

The Italian certainly had his faults (no time to list them here) but he could never be accused of not trying to keep a smile on his face.

The players respected his past achievements as a footballer and were warmed by his affable and highly personable demeanour.

Zola was happy to get his boots dirty on the training field – the area of management he enjoyed most – and the players' bond with him was probably the vital ingredient that helped edge them to Premier League safety last season.

But things have changed and the more experienced Grant would be the first to admit his management style is very different to that of his predecessor.

Only the West Ham players can tell you if they truly look forward to going into work every morning, but the suspicion is that most of them don't as much as they used to.

It is speculated that certain members of the current backroom team have not been fully embraced by parts of the squad.

And although it's not supposed to be a popularity contest, you do want the players to be inspired to go the extra mile when they need to.

Grant insists there is no shortage of spirit within the group, as you would expect him to.

But the team's lowly position suggests the chemistry is not quite right.

Kirk now says: Without being unkind to Avram Grant, fans would take one look at the Israeli's grim poker face and wonder how on earth players could feel inspired to perform for him, with the answer being that they didn't.

EVEN BAUER HASN'T GOT THE POWER (11 November 2010)

Mention the figure of 24 to people and they will probably assume you're talking about the hit American TV series.

Yet it's a fair bet that even special agent Jack Bauer, a man who specialises in salvaging lost causes in the show, could not rescue West Ham's fortunes on the road after their run of winless away league games extended to that particular number last weekend.

That is right, the Hammers have not won any of their last 24 away matches in the Premier League – a statistic that tells you why they have spent the last 15 months struggling against relegation.

Since kicking off last season with a 2-0 win at Wolves, West Ham have collected a mere nine points on their travels.

The 1-0 defeat at Arsenal the weekend before last and the 2-2 draw at Birmingham might not look too disappointing on paper.

Yet both results left the Hammers feeling as if they had been kicked where it hurts, having conceded in the 88th minute at the Emirates and then seeing a two-goal lead blow up in smoke at St Andrew's.

And it's difficult to imagine the winless run of away games ending in the immediate future – especially with a trip to Liverpool (where West Ham have not won since 1963) coming up next.

They surely won't get many better chances than the one they had at Birmingham, who posed little threat before hitting back in the final 26 minutes.

The turning point came when Victor Obinna – a man who shoots first and thinks later – saw a fierce drive hit the bar.

Without that third goal, the Hammers were always going to be vulnerable because they find it almost impossible to keep a clean sheet (just one in 11 league games this term).

Cameron Jerome's strike duly swung the momentum in Brum's favour and after that – in the words of the West Ham website – it was 'squeaky-bum time' as the visitors conceded again.

Carlton Cole claimed his fellow Hammers had got 'a bit complacent' but how they could do that given their miserable record is simply mystifying.

It meant that West Ham started preparing for this week's two home games against West Brom and Blackpool under intense pressure – probably too much.

Kirk now says: Sadly, this proved to be the case, with the Hammers being held to a 2-2 draw by West Brom and then a goalless encounter with Blackpool as the long wait for another win under the clueless Grant continued.

GRANT RUNNING OUT OF TIME (25 November 2010)

It has been suggested that Avram Grant has just three games to save his job as the manager of West Ham – but the reality is that he has just one. The simple fact is that the Israeli's position will become untenable if the Hammers do not beat Wigan at Upton Park on Saturday.

He might remain in office long enough to oversee the Carling Cup quarter-final tie against Manchester United next week.

But his long-term future at West Ham will effectively be over if the team fails to collect maximum points this weekend.

The fans don't need to analyse statistics to be of the view that Grant is the worst manager the Hammers have ever had.

His record of one win in 14 league games is disgraceful. Eddy or Hugh Grant could surely have not done much worse.

Taking into account cup matches, Grant's win ratio amounts to a dreadful 23.5 per cent – lower than Gianfranco Zola (28.75), who was sacked by the club's current hierarchy, and Glenn Roeder (31.30), who guided the team to relegation in 2003.

If he cannot secure a win against struggling Wigan, following home draws against West Brom and Blackpool, you have to ask just where the points will come from if West Ham are going to avoid relegation.

Grant likes to talk about a positive spirit in the camp but there was none to be seen as the Hammers crashed to a 3-0 defeat at Liverpool that left them bottom of the table and five points adrift of safety.

Battered boxer Audley Harrison put up more of a fight when losing to David Haye recently – at least he threw one serious punch.

West Ham barely had an effort on target as they allowed one of the worst Liverpool sides in modern history to brush them aside with embarrassing ease.

The taunts from the travelling fans suggest that Grant has lost their support.

It is now eight league games without a win for the Hammers and another failure against Wigan would be horrendous.

As vital as the three points are, however, there would be some consolation if West Ham fail to secure the victory they desperately need – because Grant's miserable, ill-fated reign would surely be brought to an end.

Kirk now says: Goals from Valon Behrami, Victor Obinna and Scott Parker saw the Hammers secure a 3-1 victory against Wigan ahead of a 4-0 thrashing of Manchester United in the Carling Cup a few days later. They were great results but in retrospect the club would surely have been better off if the team had lost and Grant shown the door.

GRANT SO O'NEILLY ON HIS WAY (20 January 2011)

There were more photographers than you would expect to see at a royal wedding waiting for Avram Grant on Saturday as it emerged that the game against Arsenal could be his last in charge of West Ham.

Even the BBC, an organisation not known for peddling idle speculation, were reporting that Martin O'Neill was being lined up to become the Hammers' 14th full-time manager.

Predictably, the critics were quick to condemn the club for putting Grant in such an uncomfortable position – particularly when he was forced to face the media after the 3-0 defeat.

But while it was considered undignified behaviour for a club that has had so few managers, it's often forgotten that most of them have suffered a controversial demise.

Gianfranco Zola's sacking last summer was one of the worst kept secrets in history, while his predecessor Alan Curbishley stormed off after seeing players sold over his head and eventually won a hefty compensation claim after West Ham were deemed to be in breach of contract. Alan Pardew was fired with chairman Eggert Magnusson claiming 'there were reasons why I had to do it and I will keep those to myself' while Glenn Roeder was dismissed as soon as he lost his first game after recovering from a brain tumour.

Harry Redknapp accused chairman Terence Brown of a 'disgusting' attack after being sacked and slaughtered for how he spent transfer funds, while Billy Bonds has refused to speak to Redknapp in the belief that he was stitched up by his former friend.

Lou Macari quit after being fined by the FA for his involvement in a betting scandal at former club Swindon, FA Cup-winning boss John Lyall was shown the door after 34 years of loyal service in various capacities while first manager Syd King was suspended for three months for allegedly being drunk and insubordinate during a board meeting and was so depressed by his eventual sacking that he committed suicide by drinking alcohol laced with a corrosive liquid.

Whatever a club does in replacing a manager they are invariably criticised, with the League Managers' Association usually the first to complain that one of their members has been harshly treated.

But if there's no firing there's no hiring and when one person is pushed off the managerial merry-go-round with a big fat pay-off it allows another to step back on it. It is nice work if you can get it.

Kirk now says: Martin O'Neill allegedly lost interest in replacing Avram Grant when it became public knowledge that he might be interested in replacing Avram Grant. So it wasn't the replacing of Avram Grant that was a problem for Martin O'Neill, just the fact that it became public knowledge that Martin O'Neill was interested in replacing Avram Grant. Interesting.

NEW SIGNINGS SHOULD SAVE US (3 February 2011)

When West Ham get busy during the January transfer window, it usually means only one thing – they're in deep trouble.

And so, with a feeling of desperation, the club is generally forced to pay through the nose to lure quality players into a relegation fight or take gambles on a bunch of outcasts who are not wanted elsewhere.

As every manager will tell you, January is never a good time to do business – and it can result in devastating consequences if the deals go wrong. Back in 2007, the Hammers splashed out £17m in transfer fees on five players (including Matthew Upson and Lucas Neill) as new boss Alan Curbishley sought to keep the club in the Premier League.

And despite signing Nigel Quashie and Luis Boa Morte, the club eventually won its nerve-jangling battle against the drop – with some bloke called Carlos Tevez thankfully coming to the rescue.

This time last year, Gianfranco Zola's side was perilously short of firepower and so new owners David Sullivan and David Gold rushed through deals for three strikers in the unlikely shapes of Benni McCarthy, Mido and Ilan.

McCarthy and Mido proved to be a fat lot of good – literally – with neither player scoring a single goal as they failed to prove their fitness. Heavyweight flops, indeed.

Yet Ilan, who initially appeared rather flimsy, struck four times in 11 outings to help the Hammers retain their top-flight status as he emerged as the surprise success.

Yet again, West Ham are in big trouble after spending most of the season at the foot of the table and this column recently insisted that the club needed either a change of manager or a significant influx of new playing talent.

Avram Grant remains as boss after the efforts to replace him with Martin O'Neill came to nothing, but nobody can accuse the club of inactivity in the transfer market.

The recruitment of Robbie Keane, Demba Ba, Wayne Bridge and Gary O'Neil should surely be sufficient to see the Hammers finish out of the bottom three.

If they're fit enough, there can be little doubt that they're good enough.

Indeed, fellow strugglers Wolves, Wigan, Birmingham, West Brom and Fulham have every reason to be afraid after seeing West Ham reinforce their team – particularly in attack – in such an emphatic and determined manner. It means Grant really will have no excuses if the Hammers fail to secure survival now.

Kirk now says: But Grant was full of excuses throughout the entire season, blaming referees, linesmen, injuries, bad luck, the weather, you name it. The Hammers had suffered Carling Cup heartbreak the previous week when losing their semi-final second leg at Birmingham and Grant blamed 'bad defending', as if he had nothing to do with it.

POP OFF THOSE CHAMPAGNE CORKS (17 February 2011)

In what has so far proved to be a season to largely forget for West Ham fans, it's an understatement to suggest that the events of 11/12 February will remain in the memory for some time to come.

One will undoubtedly shape the long-term future of the club while the other could prove to be crucially significant if the Hammers are successful in winning their battle against relegation this year.

Friday's victory over bitter rivals Tottenham in the race to win the rights to the 2012 Olympic Stadium was followed by a dramatic 3-3 draw at West Brom, which saw West Ham sensationally fight back from three goals down for the first time since 1975.

And both results were worthy of champagne corks being popped off in gleeful celebration.

Never mind the concerns about the retention of athletics facilities at the Olympic Stadium, history will prove that it was absolutely vital to the development of West Ham that the club moved away from Upton Park to expand their fan-base.

The Premier League is made up of the haves and have-nots and the Hammers need to try to consolidate their place among the big boys rather than being condemned to constant worries about the drop.

Sceptical fans that mourn the departure from the Boleyn Ground need to consider what the alternative would be like, with Tottenham moving into their manor with a 60,000-capacity stadium.

But while it was great to celebrate a winning double over Spurs (following the 1-0 home triumph last September), it was never really just about West Ham and their north London enemies because the successful bid was in conjunction with Newham Council.

So hats off to the Hammers hierarchy for realising they needed a community-based strategy to win support where it mattered, while Tottenham's arrogant efforts – fuelled purely by self-interest – should never have been allowed to get past first base, let alone delay the decision-making process.

West Ham were swiftly brought down to earth as they fell 3-0 behind at the Hawthorns last Saturday, but the astonishing second-half recovery – with two-goal striker Demba Ba emerging as a new Hammers hero – saw the team rescue a vital point in an identical manner to a 3-3 draw at Leicester 36 years ago.

Avoiding defeat at fellow strugglers West Brom was the absolute priority – and it was mission accomplished in the most unlikely of fashions.

Kirk now says: As is typical when West Ham are involved, nothing can ever be taken for granted and that could certainly be said for the club's efforts to relocate to the Olympic Stadium and retain their Premier League place. Just like the Tevez affair, the stadium business became a protracted legal saga, with Spurs and Leyton Orient doing their utmost to block the move, while the morale-boosting comeback at West Brom inspired a three-game winning run … that would be the last time the Hammers celebrated victory this season.

GRANT THE TOP NAME IN BLAME GAME (21 April 2011)

When the post-mortem is held on West Ham's likely relegation next month, the fingers of accusation will be pointed in several directions.

Most of them will quite rightly be aimed at manager Avram Grant, who has proved to be a disastrous appointment.

For that, co-owners David Sullivan and David Gold must accept their share of responsibility.

They were not alone in believing that Grant would represent an improvement on Gianfranco Zola, who they sacked at the end of last season.

But the chairmen have been far too reluctant to admit they made a mistake with the Israeli and their failure to replace him earlier in the campaign is a decision they will surely regret.

Grant's shortcomings have been well documented in this column.

His communication skills and motivational powers have long been ridiculed, while any strategic and tactical abilities he may have had appear to have deserted him.

Fans will question team selections and formations at any club, but there's no way that Grant's ideas can escape criticism.

Certain players have been deployed out of position; others have been dropped and recalled with little reason, while the promise displayed by new boys Demba Ba and Thomas Hitzlsperger has quickly been stamped out of them.

On top of that, Grant appears to be deluding himself when trying to convince pundits and punters that West Ham are performing much better than they really are.

He really needs to study the statistics if he believes his men matched Aston Villa in the second half on Saturday before succumbing to a calamitous 2-1 defeat.

If Grant has been right about anything, however, it's that the big decisions have repeatedly gone against his side.

Mark Halsey might have warmly embraced Grant after the 3-1 win over Liverpool in February but the referee did his friend few favours against Villa and failed to award the Hammers a clear penalty when they were 1-0 up – not that he got any help from his assistant.

It was a similar story against Manchester United earlier this month and it's beyond belief that West Ham have lost two home games in succession after officials failed to show mandatory red cards.

It seems that fate is conspiring against the club, with injury problems simply making a bad situation even worse.

The Hammers need three wins to survive – or the blame game really will kick off.

Kirk now says: West Ham had lost four of their last five games … and the misery didn't end there.

NOW IT'S PUDDLE TROUBLE (28 April 2011)

There was a well-worn record being played at Stamford Bridge on Saturday.

It wasn't 'Blue Is The Colour', 'I'm Forever Blowing Bubbles' or the song that suggests where Chelsea fans can stick their blue flag (ouch!).

Once again, it was the sound of West Ham boss Avram Grant blaming everybody – and everything – but himself for his team's failings.

It is the same old story every week, with Grant complaining about nothing going his side's way as another disappointing result kicks the Hammers towards the drop.

It is true that West Ham have been on the rough end of some poor decisions from officials this term.

And injuries suffered by midfielders Scott Parker, Gary O'Neil and Mark Noble in recent weeks do suggest that fate is conspiring against the boys in claret and blue.

But not once has Grant held his hands up after a loss and admitted that he was at fault, either in his team selection or tactics.

The Israeli is always looking to deflect responsibility elsewhere.

Last Saturday, however, his excuses plunged to new depths when he pointed an accusing finger at a puddle after West Ham's 3-0 defeat.

'The pitch helped [Fernando] Torres to score the second goal,' moaned Grant after the Spaniard killed off the Hammers late on.

Blaming a pool of water might have been a new one, but everything else Grant said had a familiar ring to it.

'We created chances and played well, but then we conceded a goal,' he said, before adding, 'This is football.'

Yet Grant never explains why his men fail to score goals when they have threatening periods or how the opposition seems to find it so easy to hit the net.

Any goal conceded is dismissed as if it was an act of God.

Furthermore, the manager seems incapable of doing anything to change a situation that fans have been forced to suffer since the start of the season.

Needless to say, Grant claimed that Portsmouth's relegation under his command last year had little to do with him after they were deducted nine points for going into administration.

'Relegation happened in the offices of the Premier League,' he insisted, despite Pompey needing another 17 points to have survived.

It is looking increasingly likely that West Ham will also drop into the Championship – but don't expect Grant to accept much of the blame.

After all, he's only the manager.

Kirk now says: Water joke! Even the puddles are against West Ham. But, hey, this is football, if you believe the line that Grant must have trotted out hundreds of times during his spell as manager.

AV SOME OF THAT, GRANT (19 May 2011)

Football clubs are repeatedly criticised for their hire and fire tendencies, while supporters are accused of being fickle and lacking patience.

West Ham's owners stuck with misguided manager Avram Grant throughout a miserable campaign and the fans avoided unrest for the sake of their team – but what did such misplaced faith and hope achieve?

The Hammers have been relegated, the woeful Grant eventually suffered the axe he long deserved and the new manager faces the daunting task of chasing promotion after the squad has been ripped apart.

So much for keeping your fingers crossed that things will simply turn out for the better.

West Brom took some flak after sacking promotion-winning boss Roberto Di Matteo – and reaped the rewards by securing safety.

When a manager loses games it's his fault. When a club's directors allow that situation to result in relegation the blame game shifts.

And so West Ham's hierarchy must accept responsibility for not ditching Grant when two wins in his first 18 league games provided ample evidence that the Israeli was out of his depth.

As co-chairman David Gold admits, he should have 'done things differently'.

The club's mid-season efforts to recruit former Aston Villa boss Martin O'Neill also backfired when the news broke and the Irishman retreated.

Gold and co-owner David Sullivan rescued West Ham from the financial abyss and their decision to dispense with rookie manager Gianfranco Zola's services last year was fully understandable.

But their appointment of Grant was a serious error of judgement and their reluctance to admit they made a mistake – or pay him off – months ago has proved costly.

West Ham's fans are famously loyal but in the days of old they would have been angrily chanting for the manager's head had they been forced to suffer the ineptitude and tactical incompetence witnessed this season.

Yet Grant escaped major abuse from the Upton Park faithful and enjoyed a relatively comfortable ride given his inability to win games.

Had the Hammers hardcore been more vociferous about the manager's failings and their desire for change, the club would have come under far greater pressure to remove Grant from office.

It is difficult to feel anything but sympathy for the long-suffering supporters, who really deserve so much better, but like Gold and Sullivan they failed to exploit their power and exert enough influence.

Getting rid of Grant was an easy decision. The club now faces much tougher ones ahead.

Kirk now says: It wasn't quite worth getting relegated for, but the black comedy that ensued after the decisive 3-2 defeat at fellow strugglers Wigan – after the Hammers had led 2-0 at half-time – was priceless. David Sullivan waited in the tunnel after the final whistle before dragging his manager into a room and telling him that he was sacked. This columnist was tipped off that Grant was history, so it was something of a shock to see the Israeli fulfil his duties by attending the press conference … and then pretend he was still in a job! The bloke couldn't even admit to being sacked properly.

REFLECTING ON SEASON 2010/11

Best signing: Demba Ba (Hoffenheim), £500,000

Worst signing: Pablo Barrera (Pumas UNAM), £4m

Best result: Winning 4-0 at home to Manchester United (Carling Cup) in November

Worst result: Losing 3-2 at Wigan in May

Final position: 20th in Premier League, 33 points

Manager and rating: Avram Grant 2/10

Best thing about season: Avram Grant's belated sacking

Worst thing about season: The failure to sack Avram Grant when the club was staring relegation in the face

SEASON 2011/12

'Go for Tevez and Torres ... get Vaz Te and Maynard'

KEVIN KEEN took charge of the West Ham team on a caretaker basis for the 3-0 home defeat by Sunderland on the final day of the season and then admitted, 'I don't think it's going to happen.'

He was joking about managing either Barcelona or Real Madrid but he might as well have been talking about the Hammers, as co-chairman David Sullivan had already insisted he had no intention of appointing a 'novice' when asked about the chances of former hitman Paolo Di Canio.

Another former West Ham player, Chris Hughton, was quickly installed as the favourite while Steve McClaren – yes, him again – denied any interest in the position before going to Nottingham Forest.

This columnist insisted that Sam Allardyce would be an 'unpopular choice' but the former Bolton, Newcastle and Blackburn boss soon emerged as the most likely candidate and was officially appointed on 1 June on a two-year contract.

The 56-year-old, hardly associated with stylish football during his reasonably successful managerial career, was immediately interrogated about the 'West Ham way', but insisted he was far more interested in 'winning football matches'. And under Avram Grant, that was something the Hammers had forgotten to do.

At first it seemed as if Big Sam was recruiting for the Hammerettes dance troupe rather than the first team when he signed somebody called Faye and then one of the Nolans.

Defender Abdoulaye Faye became his first acquisition on a free transfer from Stoke while Newcastle skipper Kevin Nolan surprisingly agreed to step down a division in a £3m move that represented something of a coup. The power of money ...

Other new recruits would follow in the shape of Matt Taylor (Bolton, £2.2m), John Carew (Aston Villa, free), Sam Baldock (MK Dons, undisclosed), George McCartney (Leeds, loan), Joey O'Brien (free agent), Papa Bouba Diop (AEK, free), Guy Demel (Hamburg, undisclosed), Henri Lansbury (Arsenal, loan) and David Bentley (Spurs, loan), although the latter quickly broke down.

Heading out of the club were loan signings Robbie Keane, Victor Obinna and Wayne Bridge, while Kieron Dyer, Matthew Upson, Danny Gabbidon, Jonathan Spector, Lars Jacobson, Thomas Hitzlsperger and, thankfully, Luis Boa Morte were all out of contract.

Radoslav Kovac and Manuel Da Costa were sold to Basel and Lokomotiv Moscow respectively while homegrown Hammers Zavon Hines and Junior Stanislas both went to Burnley and Demba Ba activated a relegation release clause to join Newcastle.

As for the remaining England internationals, Scott Parker's departure seemed inevitable as the season began while striker Carlton Cole and goalkeeper Robert Green decided to remain at the club (for what would ultimately appear to be for very different reasons).

FIGURES DON'T ALWAYS ADD UP (11 August 2011)

There was no sign of Bill Murray at Upton Park on Sunday but it was certainly a case of *Groundhog Day* – with West Ham fans being forced to relive the match day horrors of last season as if nothing had changed.

The Hammers lost nine home games when being relegated from the Premier League and the 1-0 defeat by Cardiff – thanks to a 91st-minute goal – saw the new campaign begin the way the last one finished.

It is no wonder that Sam Allardyce looked as glum as former manager Avram Grant did for the whole of last season.

The new boss was possibly a statistician in a former life because he was quick to trot out the numbers in terms of how many chances (14 apparently) West Ham had to wrap up the game long before Kenny Miller's late winner.

And he threw a different figure at one reporter who dared to question why the Hammers had played with just one up front.

'Three!' he insisted, although the identity of the other two players was something of a mystery given the lack of close support that Frederic Piquionne had before being replaced by Carlton Cole late on.

Freddie Sears and Matt Taylor played as providers rather than finishers, while skipper Kevin Nolan was deployed much deeper than expected.

'Cardiff played with two up front and created just three chances, so the equation tells you that our system was better from an attacking point of view than theirs,' said Allardyce.

As the manager admitted, it was just the finishing that let West Ham down on the day.

'We weren't clinical enough to put one in the back of the net,' he said.

Which emphasises the need to study the issue of forwards.

Even if the Hammers did play with three up front, only one of them (Piquionne) was an out-and-out striker.

It might be an old-fashioned concept, but the reason that certain players are deployed in attack is that they're skilled in the special art of putting the ball over the line.

These are people who are better at converting scoring chances when they present themselves than other members of the team.

Play with just one instead of two and the side is naturally less likely to be as clinical when the opportunities come along.

Which was the very problem that Big Sam was complaining about after Cardiff stole three points they failed to deserve.

Kirk now says: This was not the only time that Sam Allardyce refuted this columnist's claim/complaints about West Ham playing with one striker. And he set the pattern of the season by trotting out the number of goalscoring chances – as if every aimless ball into the box counts as such – to emphasise the team's dominance if the result went against them.

PARKER PENS A BAD DEAL (1 September 2011)

Scott Parker was left out of West Ham's impressive 4-1 win at Nottingham Forest at the weekend.

And it was no surprise that manager Sam Allardyce refused to confirm which club was negotiating to buy the England midfielder – even though everybody knew anyway.

Because it's embarrassing that the Hammers were prepared to even talk to Tottenham Hotspur following recent events.

The relationship between the two clubs is at an all-time low, with West Ham so unhappy with the tactics allegedly employed by Spurs to challenge their move to the Olympic Stadium that they have put matters in the hands of their lawyers and the police.

So, as far as the club's fans are concerned, any inquiry from the north London club should have been met with a barrage of expletives before slamming the phone down.

Just last week, the Hammers issued a statement to insist they had no intention of dropping their complaint against Spurs, who have won the right to a judicial review of the Olympic Stadium affair.

West Ham were acting on a point of principle – so why then entertain the idea of doing business with Tottenham over the sale of Parker?

Surely those principles should extend to the point of the Hammers telling Spurs they just don't like the colour of their cash.

Indeed, this column recently suggested that West Ham would almost prefer to give Parker away to another club than allow him to move to White Hart Lane.

Such an idea might be ridiculously fanciful, of course, because there are other realities to consider.

West Ham have admitted their need to sell one of their England stars, while they also probably felt they owed it to Parker – the three-time Hammer of the Year – to consider the move he seemed to prefer.

The Hammers have spent most of the summer assuming the midfielder would be sacrificed to ease their finances following last season's relegation.

And nobody wants to see the player running around with a face like a slapped backside.

His body language in recent games has not been good.

Allardyce revealed that the negotiations last weekend were anything but straightforward and the hope was that West Ham were driving not just a hard bargain but speaking to Tottenham in the kind of language they understand.

In other words, they should use all the leverage possible to ensure that any kind of deal suits the Hammers – in every respect.

Kirk now says: This columnist maintains that West Ham should have refused to do any kind of business with Tottenham at this stage and, if Scott Parker didn't like it, that was just tough. As it was, Spurs paid £5m.

IS BIG SAM REVERTING TO TYPE? (29 September 2011)

Billy Bonds admitted it in the programme for West Ham's home game against Peterborough on Saturday.

'People talk about the West Ham way,' said the Hammers legend of 793 games from 1967–1988 and former manager, 'but that was some time ago. We haven't played like that for a few years now.'

And if further evidence was needed, the 1-0 win against Posh didn't do a bad job. For anybody to complain about the style with which West Ham secure their victories this season seems rather churlish.

Everybody knows the priority is for the Hammers to win promotion back to the Premier League at the first attempt – and nobody should really care how they achieve it.

But the suspicion among some fans is that Sam Allardyce's preference of deploying a lone striker for home games is undermining his side's efforts.

The Hammers have looked imperious on the road, winning three games out of four and scoring nine goals in the process.

But they have huffed and puffed at Upton Park, where defeat by Cardiff and a draw against Leeds was followed up with one-goal victories against Portsmouth and Peterborough.

The less said about the embarrassing home Carling Cup defeat by League Two outfit Aldershot Town the better.

Allardyce has spoken about psychological factors increasing the pressures of playing at home.

But isn't it just as likely that the formation – the fans call it one up front but the manager insists it's 4-3-3 – is far more suited to away games than home ones?

Everybody hoped that Allardyce would name two strikers against Peterborough with new signing Sam Baldock expected to partner Carlton Cole.

But an isolated Cole was forced to battle away on his own before being replaced by John Carew, who simply became the target of long balls down the channels for 35 uninspiring minutes.

The say a leopard cannot change its spots and there's a feeling of Allardyce reverting to type with his team playing a direct style with a big target man up front.

It is not quite like watching Sam's old Bolton side but it seems like the Hammers might be getting there.

Hey, goalkeeper Robert Green can score every goal direct from his boot if such a ploy helps get the club promoted.

But is the concept of playing two strikers – part of the West Ham way – really such a bad idea?

Kirk now says: This became something of a recurring theme during the season, with Allardyce defending his tactics for home games despite failing to get the results that were expected.

TEVEZ LINK IS THE STUFF OF DREAMS (6 October 2011)

When Carlos Tevez left West Ham to join Manchester United in the summer of 2007, there were no circumstances in which it could ever be imagined that the Argentina striker might return to Upton Park.

Quite simply, Tevez was too good to be playing for the Hammers in the first place.

Of course, his third-party ownership at that time helped make that possible and, despite West Ham being fined £5.5m and forced to pay an estimated £20m in compensation to Sheffield United, fans still love the magical player who inspired Premier League survival four years ago. With the Hammers dropping into the Championship this year, it was unlikely he would even visit the Boleyn Ground as an opposing player for some time.

But the concept of Tevez wearing a claret and blue shirt again became a possibility last week when he was suspended by Manchester City and the story broke that West Ham could sign him on loan.

The idea sounded ridiculous, but with transfer rules severely limiting the striker's options were he not to resolve his problems, it was possible that fantasy could indeed become reality. Sam Allardyce admitted in his press conference at Crystal Palace on Saturday that he would be delighted to sign Tevez if he became available.

Yet when speaking to this columnist on the Selhurst Park terraces a few moments later, he denied that a formal request had been made.

'The club has not made an official approach to City,' he insisted.

It was therefore a surprise to later read in West Ham vice-chairman Karren Brady's newspaper column that same day that she had indeed made contact.

'First job today is to ring Man City to ask if we can borrow Carlos Tevez for the rest of the season,' she said in her diary entry for last Wednesday, before adding: 'The answer is unprintable.'

We will write that one off as a breakdown in communication.

Of course, by the time this column is published it's likely that the Tevez situation has become a lot clearer.

City were never going to ship him out last week while they were initiating an investigation into the player's conduct.

As Allardyce admitted, 'It's a case of waiting to see what the situation is.

'If his club feels a loan situation is the right idea, we would love to be in the frame.'

You have got to admire his ambition.

Kirk now says: Well, it was a nice idea while it lasted, but Tevez spent the next few months seemingly playing golf in his homeland of Argentina before eventually being brought in from the cold (or rather the heat) to return to first-team action in March 2012 as City went on to win the Premier League title.

SAM'S EFFORTS COUNTER-PRODUCTIVE (13 October 2011)

Blackpool boss Ian Holloway is rarely shy of expressing his point of view after games.

So it's safe to assume that Sam Allardyce will be taking note of what he says following his side's visit to Upton Park on Saturday.

Because it appears the West Ham manager is in defensive mood when it comes to comments about his team's style of play.

When you're angry about what somebody has said and perceive it as a criticism, there are two things you don't really want to do.

One is to bring further attention to their opinions by broadcasting them from the rooftops.

The other is to prove the opposition have ruffled your feathers and got under your skin.

So why did Allardyce do both of the above last week after learning of Crystal Palace boss Dougie Freedman's post-match comments?

Freedman referred to the Hammers as 'a very physical, powerful team that hit a lot of long balls' following the 2-2 draw at Selhurst Park last time out – and got right up Big Sam's nose in the process.

So West Ham responded by attempting to set the record straight on their website with a story that highlighted the fact their team had '366 passes in play compared to the home side's 224'.

The club continued to stir up a blizzard of stats to support their argument that the Hammers produced most of the football, with Allardyce concluding, 'We outplayed the home side so it disappoints me to hear a young manager talking in the way he did about my team.'

Whether Freedman's description of West Ham hit the nail on the head or was miles off target is a matter of debate.

Yet Sam's reaction can only be considered as counter-productive.

The reality is that few people aside from Palace fans – and there aren't many of those – were even aware of Freedman's comments before Allardyce focused the media's spotlight on them.

And in doing so, the West Ham boss promoted the idea that he really does worry about what other people think after all – despite looking like the kind of bloke who couldn't care less.

The long-ball tag attached to Sam's sides might annoy him, but the best way of rising above such remarks is to ignore them and concentrate on winning games – as he did at Bolton.

Nevertheless, Blackpool boss Holloway might be best advised to tread carefully when speaking on Saturday.

Kirk now says: It just goes to prove that Sam Allardyce is far more sensitive than he pretends, although you would have thought that he would have got used to this kind of criticism by now. Whatever, he scored something of an own goal as he tried to offer his defence.

DIOUF WILL ALWAYS BE ON TRIAL (27 October 2011)

When it was revealed last weekend that El Hadji Diouf was on trial, the obvious question to ask was, 'What's he been accused of now?'

The bloke is no stranger to controversy.

And West Ham fans need no reminding about the time it was alleged that he had spat towards them during his spell at Liverpool.

Indeed, the Reds were even forced to retract a statement in which they denied the incident took place before admitting that 'Mr Diouf did spit on the ground' during the match at Anfield in November 2002.

So it was inevitable that Sam Allardyce would be questioned as to how Hammers fans would react to the signing of the Senegalese international if he proved himself worthy of a contract after undertaking a trial with the club.

'They'll love him,' said Allardyce. 'Dioufy is a quality player who West Ham fans will appreciate if they see him.'

The West Ham boss was either oblivious to what had taken place at Anfield nine years ago – or chose to pretend it hadn't happened.

It is difficult to imagine he isn't fully aware of the player's history, given that he has signed him twice – for Bolton and Blackburn.

So it has to be assumed he chose to brush past events under the carpet when singing Diouf's praises.

What it all proves is that Allardyce is prepared to go to any lengths to try and secure promotion for the Hammers this season.

Some fans won't care what he does if West Ham secure themselves an instant return to the Premier League.

Others will question the manager's methods – especially if things go wrong. It is not easy for Hammers fans at the moment.

They have been brought up to support the club because of its traditions for playing football with style and doing things the right way.

Yet many admit it might be necessary to sacrifice certain principles to escape the Championship at the first attempt.

There is little point in playing fancy football if West Ham fail to win at least a play-off place next spring.

Indeed, the Hammers should be winning the division in style given the players they have at their disposal.

Whether Diouf is one of those might be known by the time this column is published.

And the reaction of the supporters will speak volumes.

The forward was not without a club, having been released from his contract at Blackburn, without good reason.

Kirk now says: Thankfully, Allardyce decided against signing Diouf claiming his 'conditioning wasn't good', although David Sullivan later insisted it was because 'the supporters indicated he'd not be acceptable'.

SPOT-KICKS HAVE MARK OF TERMINATOR (26 January 2012)

There was a distinguished guest in the press box at Upton Park on Saturday.

He is a shaven-headed bloke, with big eyes and who was prone to fits of temper during his playing days.

He answers to the name of Julian Dicks – and he's a West Ham legend, of course.

His tackles were heavier than a stack of Iron Maiden albums.

And his penalty kicks were harder than the burgers they sell in Green Street long after games have finished.

So when the referee pointed to the spot – not once but twice – against Nottingham Forest, nobody would have complained if the man dubbed the 'Terminator' had declared 'I'm back' before stripping off his civvies to smash those two penalties into the net.

Thankfully, in a month when Thierry Henry and Paul Scholes have made comebacks for Arsenal and Manchester United respectively, there was little need for a former Hammer to return from the mists of the past. That is because West Ham have Mark Noble in their team. He is not as scary as Dicksy, rarely gets sent off and doesn't exactly hold cult status among the Hammers faithful.

But he's looking equally as mean from the penalty spot – as he proved with his two goals against Forest that lifted West Ham to the top of the Championship table on Saturday evening.

With the exception of the time when Dicksy once missed a penalty against Arsenal when virtually unconscious, he could generally be relied upon to do the business from 12 yards.

And Noble, the man currently entrusted with the spot-kick duties, is certainly letting nobody down at the moment, having scored all six of his penalties this season – including three in the last two games.

After he had converted his first against Forest, there were doubts that Noble would beat Lee Camp for a second time because there is always extra pressure when trying to repeat the trick.

QPR's Heidar Helguson wasted a second spot-kick against Wigan on Saturday, while Fulham's Danny Murphy, after scoring once, allowed Bobby Zamora to bang in a second penalty against Newcastle.

Noble might not smash them into the net in the way that Dicks or fellow Hammers legend Ray Stewart used to, but he mixes them up and knows how to put the round white thing over the long white thing.

And at the end of the day – one of Dicksy's most-used phrases – that's all that really matters.

Kirk now says: At a time when everybody keeps referring to Ashley Cole as the 'best left-back in the world', it's worth mentioning that few West Ham fans – if any – would choose him over Julian Dicks in his prime.

BIG ERNIE DESERVES SHOW OF RESPECT (2 February 2012)

Ernie Gregory deserves a minute's silence on Saturday – but he's not expected to get one.

The former West Ham goalkeeper, who made 406 appearances between 1946 and 1959 and spent an incredible 51 years at the club as a player or coach, sadly passed away at the age of 90 on 21 January.

And under normal circumstances, such a legend would hopefully be commemorated in the form of a well-respected minute's silence before his team's next home outing.

Unfortunately, that game just happens to be against bitter rivals Millwall, whose fans, it would be an understatement to say, don't generally hold the traditions of West Ham United in high regard.

So the Hammers' hierarchy have been put in a very difficult position.

They know that a minute's silence on Saturday would be the most appropriate way of remembering Ernie Gregory.

But the club is also acutely aware that it only takes one dissenting voice to ruin such an occasion – and so a minute's applause would be a much safer option, if indeed they even go for that.

Anybody attending West Ham's visit to Coventry City last November will recall the embarrassing scenario when the minute's 'silence' – to commemorate Remembrance Day – degenerated into farce.

A voice was heard in the away end, a home supporter shouted 'shut up' and the sound of silence became a wall of noise as hundreds of fans told each other to put a sock in it (or words to that effect).

So it doesn't necessarily matter who the opposition is, because anything can happen in those situations.

However, the fact that West Ham's next opponents are Millwall could not be ignored, given the history of hostility between the two sets of fans.

A visiting supporter was stabbed in the streets when the Lions came to Upton Park for a Carling Cup game in August 2009 and many home fans were pursued by the authorities for running on to the pitch at various times. It goes without saying that there will be a high police presence around the Boleyn Ground on Saturday.

Many Millwall fans might feel they're unfairly victimised, yet the irony is that the game at Upton Park could actually provide them with an opportunity to win some accolades.

It might seem implausible to some, but should the visiting supporters show full respect for Ernie Gregory – whatever the club decides to do – then maybe broken bridges could start to be repaired.

It was just a thought.

Kirk now says: Sadly, Ernie's passing was acknowledged only in the form of West Ham's players wearing black armbands and a brief round of applause when his face appeared on the two screens, which was disappointing considering his lengthy service with the club. Still, at least the Hammers collected three points in a 2-1 win despite having skipper Kevin Nolan sent off after just nine minutes.

ENGLAND TIMING ALL WRONG FOR SAM (16 February 2012)

It may have escaped many but there was a strong claret and blue thread running through recent events regarding the England manager's job.

Former West Ham boss Harry Redknapp was quickly installed as the bookies' hot favourite to succeed Italian Fabio Capello.

Alan Pardew, who managed the Hammers from 2006–2008, was also listed as a possible candidate following his success with Newcastle, but thankfully ruled himself out.

Current West Ham chief Sam Allardyce was even quoted on his interest in the England job, having previously been linked with the post. Former Hammers defender Stuart Pearce, who played under Redknapp at Upton Park, has been put in charge for the friendly with Holland later this month. As has been well documented, Capello bid arrivederci to England after the FA stripped John Terry (who we'll forget trained with West Ham as a youngster before signing for Chelsea) of the national captaincy.

Terry's position was considered untenable following a charge that he racially abused former Hammers defender Anton Ferdinand.

And one of the men responsible for selecting the next permanent England boss, the FA's director of football development, is none other than West Ham legend Sir Trevor Brooking.

Allardyce was interviewed by the FA in 2006 yet has distanced himself from the role this time, insisting he is fully focused on guiding the Hammers to promotion.

It was as recently as last September that Big Sam admitted he would walk over hot coals to become manager of England.

At that time, however, it was believed that Capello would remain in place until after Euro 2012, by which time Allardyce would hopefully be a Premier League boss again.

His stock would be high, his mission at Upton Park will have been accomplished and he could throw his hat into the ring with gusto.

So the timing of Capello's departure would not have best pleased Sam, who knows he has a job to finish at West Ham before he can consider advancing his career elsewhere.

Redknapp, meanwhile, is considered a certainty for the England job, but it would be interesting to know what Brooking's thoughts are.

Old Hammers defender Kevin Lock once told this columnist about how former manager Billy Bonds regrets not taking Brooking's advice when recruiting Redknapp as his right-hand man in the early 1990s.

However, Trevor is far too professional to allow personal feelings to intervene – and too nice, of course.

Kirk now says: With Harry Redknapp arguably carrying too much baggage, the FA decided to go for the uninspiring Roy Hodgson (no West Ham connection there), who fully bought into the concept of the St George's Park national centre, suggesting they wanted an office manager just as much as a football manager. Brooking insisted his relationship with Redknapp didn't influence the decision, while Harry later perhaps had a little dig at Trevor after the England Under-21s crashed out of Euro 2013 by saying, 'Brooking has been with the FA for ten years now and I don't see that too much has changed.'

SULLIVAN MAKES A STRIKING ADMISSION (23 February 2012)

Some would say that's typical of West Ham – they go for Tevez and Torres and end up with Vaz Te and Maynard.

In other words, they try to sign international stars from Manchester City and Chelsea, but eventually raid Barnsley and Bristol City.

On the face of it, the club would appear to have been forced to lower their sights somewhat.

The reality, however, is that the Hammers have bought very well in January given their current circumstances.

And Ricardo Vaz Te and Nicky Maynard, who bagged 20 goals between them this season before moving to Upton Park, should do enough to help West Ham win promotion to the Premier League.

Having said that, you have got to admire co-chairman David Sullivan's audacious efforts to land Carlos Tevez and Fernando Torres on loan – as confirmed in an interview this week.

Either player would have represented a massive coup for the Hammers, but the chances of signing them were always minimal at best. Tevez had been linked with a loan return to West Ham ever since he spectacularly fell out with Manchester City last September.

And Sullivan revealed that three requests had been made to take the Argentine off their hands – all to no avail.

Tevez still has an emotional attachment to the Hammers and he would have surely preferred to score a few goals in the Championship than play golf and sun himself in his home country – well, maybe not.

The real revelation by Sullivan was that West Ham had made an inquiry about Torres spending a month at Upton Park.

That was never realistic given the Spanish flop – who has scored just two league goals this season – was needed by Chelsea while Didier Drogba was playing at the Africa Cup of Nations.

Indeed, there would have been more chance of signing Brazilian actor Fernando Torres – and he has been dead for four years.

At least it suggests that West Ham are prepared to do whatever it takes to push themselves over the promotion line.

However, Sam Allardyce needs to prove he can get the best out of his strikers – and he has struggled on that front this term.

Summer signing Sam Baldock has scored for fun during his career but has been restricted to five goals and ten league starts for West Ham ahead of this week's trip to Blackpool.

The manager seems to prioritise systems over players – and even Tevez and Torres might have a thing to say about that.

Kirk now says: Ricardo Vaz Te turned out to be the hero over the coming months but his dozen goals still weren't enough to win the Hammers automatic promotion as they dropped vital points during a run of five consecutive draws in March.

HAMMERS IN VITAL PERIOD OF RECOVERY (8 March 2012)

Some interesting things took place in football on Sunday, with Chelsea sacking Andre Villas-Boas, the BBC broadcasting *QPR: The Four-Year Plan* and West Ham winning 2-0 at Cardiff City, among others.

The Chelsea and QPR episodes were deeply embarrassing for the west London clubs, with billionaire owners demanding instant success, trendy foreign managers being hired and fired and the team repeatedly being referred to as 'the project'. Ring any bells?

It wasn't long ago that West Ham were being run on similar lines, until Bjorgolfur Gudmundsson's financial empire collapsed into the Icelandic waters and Gianfranco Zola's inexperience as a manager caught up with him.

Now, of course, the Hammers are playing in the Championship and taking on the likes of Watford and Doncaster Rovers this week.

But at least they are in a period of recovery, with David Sullivan and David Gold steadying the sinking ship from a financial point of view, while Sam Allardyce is building a team on strong foundations.

The victory at Cardiff saw West Ham move to within a point of table-topping Southampton and open up a four-point gap on third-placed Reading ahead of the midweek games. Once the Hammers have entertained Doncaster on Saturday, we should be able to assess the team's automatic promotion chances in a much clearer light.

But the comfortable win at Cardiff was reassuring for the fact that West Ham never really needed to hit top gear to see off a side that also has aspirations of winning a place in the Premier League.

That makes it ten away league victories for the season – the first time the Hammers have reached double figures since winning promotion in 1993. With six away games still to play, you have to fancy their chances of beating the club's record of 11 they established when claiming the Second Division title in 1958.

It was also pleasing to see James Tomkins return to the defence at Cardiff after being asked to play four games in midfield.

Winston Reid's absence through injury made it an easy decision for Allardyce, but fans will always want to see West Ham's best central defender playing in his natural position.

The Hammers belong in the Premier League and the hectic March and April periods will determine if they get there.

The top flight is their natural home – alongside the billionaire owners, trendy foreign managers and all those other 'projects'.

Kirk now says: It's all very well chasing records away from home but it's not much good if you're not doing the business at Upton Park.

SAM CAN FORGET 92-POINT TARGET (15 March 2012)

West Ham's season was supposed to be a work in progress, in which Sam Allardyce's new team got better as the months rolled on.

On the evidence of the last two results, however, they seem to have gone backwards.

Last August, the Hammers asserted their authority to win 1-0 at Doncaster and then turned on the style in a 4-0 victory at Watford.

The Vicarage Road performance suggested that West Ham could combine their traditional free-flowing football with the defensive organisation and set-piece efficiency that Allardyce is associated with.

Yet West Ham have rarely looked as good since and their failure to collect more than two points from the home games against Watford and Doncaster last week proves they have problems.

The Hammers racked up 34 points from their opening 17 games but have amassed just 32 points from their last 18 games.

They would have remained on course to collect two points per game had they beaten Watford and Doncaster at home.

But the two 1-1 draws, which extended West Ham's winless run at home to a disturbing four games, confirmed the view that Allardyce has yet to find the winning formula at Upton Park.

Away from home, where the manager's tactical approach seems to work to perfection, it's a different story.

The Hammers have won ten times on the road and look likely to beat the club record of 11 away league victories set in 1958.

But they have failed to win half of their 18 home league games this term – and if they don't win promotion that will explain why.

Allardyce complains about his side missing chances to score, but the reality is that West Ham's overall performances against Watford and Doncaster weren't good enough.

The simple fact is that the manager is failing to get the best out of his players at Upton Park – something the fans are painfully aware of.

Allardyce set a target of 92 points to guarantee automatic promotion and that demands a minimum of eight wins from 11 games.

That looks an extremely tall order and so the likelihood is that West Ham's final points tally will be somewhere in the high 80s.

With Reading having won 15 of their last 18 games before their midweek visit to Doncaster, it looks like a three-horse race with the Hammers and leaders Southampton.

And the runner in claret and blue appears to be falling behind.

Kirk now says: The sense of pessimism proved not to be premature, with the disappointing results against Watford and Doncaster setting the pattern for the month, as the Hammers were also held by Leeds, Middlesbrough and Burnley to put a massive dent in their hopes of automatic promotion.

CLOCK IS TICKING ON BIG SAM'S REIGN (5 April 2012)

Sam Allardyce admitted earlier in the season that anything less than promotion for West Ham would represent failure.

The Hammers boss therefore has just six games – and potentially nine – to prove he has not been an Upton Park flop.

Indeed, with the lottery of the play-offs looking far more likely than a top-two finish, many believe that Big Sam has already under-achieved.

The indisputable fact is that West Ham have the best squad of players in the Championship and they should be top of the pile.

But the 4-2 home defeat by Reading on Saturday has left the Hammers in third place, four points adrift of the automatic promotion places with just six games of the regular season to play.

West Ham have equalled their club record of 11 away wins and picked up more points on the road than any other team in the division.

So you don't need to be a genius to calculate that it's at Upton Park where things have gone badly wrong.

The Hammers have won just nine home league games – less than mid-table sides such as Peterborough, Derby and Ipswich.

Indeed, they have not won in their last six games at the Boleyn – collecting just five points – and that's relegation form.

West Ham were unfortunate against Reading, with the horrible scoreline failing to reflect the true pattern of the game.

But the fact is that Allardyce has struggled to get the best out of his players at Upton Park since the opening day of the season.

The strategy that has proved so successful away from home just doesn't work at the Boleyn and Sam has failed to find a solution.

Even the singer of the Cockney Rejects, the man formerly known as 'Stinky' Turner – who announced the team line-up on Saturday – was foaming at the mouth at half-time over the manager's preference for naming just one out-and-out striker.

The fans have been extremely patient and have tolerated Big Sam's approach on the basis that the team will win promotion.

But they won't sit there and watch the club's playing principles being sacrificed for no tangible reward.

Allardyce admitted last year that his position as West Ham manager was dependent on getting the club back into the Premier League.

'It's my responsibility to get them there and if I don't I'll be sacked,' he said.

If that's the case, the clock would appear to be ticking.

Kirk now says: It would have been nice to lock 'Stinky' Turner in a room with Sam Allardyce so that the two men could enjoy an exchange of opinions, but you get the feeling that they would have struggled to control their tempers.

ROAD FORM IS MUSIC TO OUR EARS (3 May 2012)

Mike Love, the lead singer of the Beach Boys, once told his colleagues not to 'muck with the formula' – or something that rhymes with that.

Sam Allardyce would be well advised to follow his advice.

West Ham finished third in the Championship thanks to their excellent away form.

A club-record 13 away wins is all the evidence you need to know that the manager has got his tactics right on the road.

So it's vital that the Hammers approach their play-off semi-final first leg at Cardiff in the same way as they have their league games.

There is absolutely no need to deviate from the methods that have worked so well so far.

That might, of course, seem rather obvious. Yet there's a nagging fear that Allardyce could be tempted to think differently because of the two-legged nature of the tie with Cardiff.

The standard practice is for teams to take a defensive, cautious approach in the away leg, with a view to avoiding defeat and then finishing the job at home.

However, it would be dangerous for West Ham to be drawn into such a trap.

For starters, the Hammers beat Cardiff 2-0 away just two months ago and they should be looking to go there and secure a similar result.

Secondly, West Ham's home form has been so unreliable that you just can't depend on them winning the second leg at Upton Park.

For the record, the Hammers won less than half of their home league games this season. Fans will need no reminding that West Ham began their campaign with a home defeat by Cardiff – and it could easily be finished with another one.

You would like to think the manager would keep faith with the philosophies that have worked so well away from home this season.

But he could end up trying to be too clever for his own good. If West Ham play for a draw at Cardiff, they could end up with egg on their faces.

Big Sam seems to think his men have rectified their problems by winning their last two Boleyn battles.

But there are fundamental reasons why they have struggled at home and those should not be ignored.

The Hammers simply must reach the play-off final at Wembley on 19 May.

And to quote those Beach Boys once again, 'God Only Knows' what will happen if they don't.

Kirk now says: Sam Allardyce must have been listening because the Hammers chalked up another 2-0 win in Cardiff before completing the job with a comfortable 3-0 success in the home leg four days later to set up a meeting with Ian Holloway's Blackpool at Wembley.

ARISE SIR SAM, YOU'RE THE MAN (24 May 2012)

Had West Ham lost to Blackpool in the Championship play-off final at Wembley on Saturday, this column would have been calling for Sam Allardyce's head.

Now, following the dramatic 2-1 victory that catapulted the Hammers back into the Premier League, the only sword that should be waved in the manager's direction is the one that taps his shoulders in a knighting ceremony.

'Arise, Sir Sam …'

With the best squad in the division, West Ham under-achieved by finishing third and being forced to pursue promotion via the play-offs.

Had the club been condemned to another year outside the top flight, fans would have been entitled to question if Allardyce deserved a second chance next season. Could he be relied upon to get the best out of his players if he failed at the first attempt?

Now, however, those thoughts are irrelevant because, at the end of the day, Big Sam has achieved his sole objective.

West Ham are back where they belong – and it's a case of mission accomplished and job done. And that's all that matters.

Indeed, many will insist there is no better way of returning to the promised land of the Premier League than to enjoy a winning day at Wembley in a highly anticipated showpiece final.

As Allardyce proudly declared after the fizzle of fireworks and champagne had subsided, 'With the trophy, the medals, the celebrations, this is a memory for life.'

The manager rightly paid tribute to his two goalscorers on the day – Carlton Cole and Ricardo Vaz Te.

Cole showed tremendous loyalty last summer when a move to Stoke City was on the table. And Vaz Te, who struck the late winner, has been a revelation since his £500,000 arrival from Barnsley in January.

As Big Sam rightly stated of the player who scored a dozen times in 18 outings, 'His goals are probably the reason we're back in the Premier League.'

Co-chairmen David Sullivan and David Gold also deserve full credit for providing the financial support that allowed the club to bounce back at the first time of asking.

And so it's goodbye Millwall, hello Manchester United.

We can now enjoy a summer of anticipation, with the Hammers being linked with quality new signings instead of costs being cut.

Typically, there were some heart-stopping moments against Blackpool, but we got there in the end.

Maybe Allardyce does understand the 'West Ham way' after all.

Kirk now says: It was fantastic to see West Ham back at Wembley for the first time since 1981 but it was all about the result and the performance – which wasn't the best – didn't really matter. And just to round off a day of great celebration, Chelsea's victory against Bayern Munich later that evening – witnessed by so many Hammers fans in the bars along Finchley Road – saw bitter rivals Tottenham excluded from the Champions League. As the mighty Lou Reed once sung, 'Oh, such a perfect day…'

REFLECTING ON SEASON 2011/12

Best signing: Ricardo Vaz Te (Barnsley), £500,000

Worst signing: John Carew (Stoke), free

Best result: Winning 2-1 against Blackpool (play-off final) in May

Worst result: Losing 5-1 at Ipswich in January

Final position: 3rd in Championship, 86 points

Manager and rating: Sam Allardyce 7/10

Best thing about season: Winning promotion at Wembley

Worst thing about season: The disappointing home form

SEASON 2012/2013

'One minute it's food poisoning, the next it's sour grapes'

NOBODY really fancies the team that wins promotion via the play-offs to pull up any trees in the Premier League, but the fact that West Ham had been out of the top flight for only one season meant they had far less work to do than Reading and Southampton, who finished above them, in terms of making themselves competitive.

Most of Sam Allardyce's recruits – mainly those with Premier League experience – would prove to be astute acquisitions, despite arriving on loan deals, free transfers or for modest fees.

However, it was the more expensive players – most notably Modibo Maiga and Alou Diarra – who would give little return on the £6.75m invested, while the jury remains out on Matt Jarvis, who became the club's record signing shortly after the campaign began.

It is also the manager's job to decide which players he feels are less equipped to deal with the step up following promotion and so it was a case of bidding farewell to John Carew, Papa Bouba Diop, Abdoulaye Faye, Freddie Sears, Frank Nouble, Pablo Barrera, Sam Baldock and Nicky Maynard at this time. Robert Green always looked set to leave after cynically running down his contract, while Julien Faubert was also released after a five-year spell at Upton Park that saw him fail to live up to his 'Le TGV' express train nickname and run more like 'the DLR' (that's the Docklands Light Railway in case you didn't know).

SAM HAS A PLAN BUT IS HE STILL THE MAN? (16 August 2012)

What with the recent preoccupation with a load of running, jumping and peddling (otherwise known as the Olympic Games), it has been easy to overlook the fact that a new football season is now upon us.

Not that West Ham need reminding, given the club has spent the summer feverishly trying to bolster their squad ahead of their return to the Premier League.

At the time of writing, eight players have been signed on permanent deals – namely Jussi Jaaskelainen, George McCartney, James Collins, Mohamed Diame, Alou Diarra, Modibo Maiga, Stephen Henderson and Raphael Spiegel, while big bids have been made for Matt Jarvis.

With three of the new recruits being goalkeepers, the sceptics would suggest that West Ham might need to play all of them at once if they are to stand a chance of staying up this season.

Yet the transfer window remains open for a further fortnight and even the bookies think the Hammers will probably survive.

Manager Sam Allardyce should have enough strategic acumen to make sure that West Ham's heads remain above the relegation waters.

He under-achieved with a third-place finish in the Championship last term, but the play-offs saw him achieve his objective of securing promotion and the fans got to enjoy a great day out at Wembley.

Indeed, so caught up in the euphoria of the moment, this column even suggested – in tongue-in-cheek fashion – that Allardyce should be rewarded with a knighthood.

West Ham fans took a pragmatic approach when Big Sam was appointed last year, believing the sacrifice of the club's playing traditions was a price worth paying if they returned to the top flight.

Everybody could worry about the style of football once the team was back in the Premier League – and that moment has now arrived.

Allardyce is unlikely to dispense with the methods that have served him so well during his managerial career.

And he admitted after the Wembley success against Blackpool that he was in no rush to extend the remaining year of his contract – giving the impression he wanted to keep his options open.

With that in mind, some might wonder if the club should have been ruthless by thanking Sam for accomplishing his mission, paying him off and doing everything possible to bring former boss Harry Redknapp back to Upton Park once Tottenham put him back on the market.

The critics would naturally be outraged – but would Hammers fans have a very different view?

Kirk now says: It might have seemed a bit harsh suggesting that West Ham should have got rid of Sam Allardyce before a ball had been kicked, but Harry Redknapp was never going to stay out of work for long and he would have surely kept the club up while getting the team playing with the sense of style they're traditionally associated with.

AN ANDY SIGNING BUT BAD LUCK IS TYPICAL
(6 September 2012)

West Ham fans were delighted to hear that Andy Carroll had arrived on loan from Liverpool last week, but the more pessimistic among them headed to the Fulham game on Saturday while muttering things like, 'Knowing our luck, he'll go and get crocked.'

And so it was just typical when the England striker was forced off midway through the second half, clutching his right thigh after suffering a hamstring injury.

It has happened before, of course, with big signings such as David James, Matthew Upson, Kieron Dyer and Julien Faubert all being sidelined within moments of commencing their Hammers careers.

Carroll's injury shouldn't keep him out for an extended period of time, but it still took the gloss off the 3-0 win against Fulham.

What made it worse was the fact that he got hurt in what appeared to be a needless challenge with Brede Hangeland, with neither of the pair likely to reach Guy Demel's punt upfield.

And to rub salt into Carroll's wounds, Sam Allardyce then announced that he was about to substitute the striker anyway, with his job on the day having been completed.

The 23-year-old might not have scored but he frightened the life out of Fulham with his very presence and created so much space for Ricardo Vaz Te, Kevin Nolan and Matt Taylor to exploit.

Carroll will score goals for fun – but let's hope we get more than 30 games out of him.

* * * * *

With the exception of that sneaky 4-3 win for Tottenham five years ago, Martin Jol is generally left grumbling after his visits to Upton Park.

In May 2006 he was blaming a 2-1 defeat – which cost Spurs a Champions League place – on a dodgy lasagne, when the reality turned out to be a virus that affected only a handful of players.

And after his Fulham side's 3-0 defeat on Saturday, the Dutchman was complaining about 'long balls' and 'set-pieces'.

One minute it's food poisoning, the next it's sour grapes.

Kirk now says: Andy Carroll was restricted to just 22 league starts due to hamstring and knee injuries – and then picked up a heel problem in the final game of the season as his bad luck continued.

WE'RE ALL GOING ON A EUROPEAN TOUR (25 October 2012)

At the start of last season, Sam Allardyce set his West Ham side an ambitious target of two points per game in a bid to secure automatic promotion to the Premier League.

Ultimately they fell just short, collecting an average of 1.87 points per match as they finished third in the Championship table before winning the play-offs.

If the Hammers triumph at Wigan on Saturday (admittedly a big if) they will be picking up points at a better rate than they did last term – which would be a stunning achievement considering they're back among the big boys.

Even at the present ratio (after the 4-1 win against Southampton), they are on course to earn 66 points, which in recent years would be good enough to finish in fifth place and qualify for the Europa League.

So fans can boldly claim that West Ham are heading for Europe!

Okay, it's a bit premature to start dusting down those passports and checking out currency exchange rates.

After all, the Hammers have only played eight league games so far. Maintaining their form over the course of an entire campaign is the hard part – as we saw last season.

And as Allardyce has been quick to admit, West Ham have played only one team (Arsenal) that finished in the top eight last term.

That means the games are going to get much tougher – and the likes of Manchester City, Newcastle, Tottenham, Manchester United, Chelsea and Liverpool are queuing up like buses in Green Street.

We will then find out how good the Hammers really are – and the 3-1 home defeat by Arsenal suggests there's much work still to be done.

But the fact they currently have twice as many points (14) as newly promoted Reading and Southampton put together proves that West Ham are back where they belong.

And you can't necessarily say that about the two clubs that finished above them last season.

Kirk now says: Of course, nobody really thought that West Ham would qualify for Europe – including this columnist – but it was worth using the early stats to highlight how strongly they had started the campaign. Predictably, the Hammers lost 2-1 at Wigan, by the way.

SITTING PRETTY AFTER CITY (8 November 2012)

The home crowd is screaming for the final whistle as Carlton Cole runs the ball towards the corner flag to waste away the dying seconds.

Moments later, the referee signals for full-time and a huge cheer of joy and relief erupts at Upton Park.

Faces are beaming as fans happily head to the pubs, where pints are thirstily necked back in celebration.

There is talk about getting home in time to watch the game again on *Match Of The Day*, while others hotly anticipate the end-of-season DVD.

In years to come, those same supporters will be able to tell their young grandchildren about the glory of following West Ham United.

'I was there!' they can proudly boast when they reflect on one of the greatest results of the 2012/13 season.

Yes, the day the Hammers took on mighty Premier League champions Manchester City … and drew 0-0. You would have thought West Ham had just stuffed a team by the way the fans left Upton Park on Saturday evening with a spring in their step.

But they were entitled to be buoyant after the Hammers became the first side to prevent City from scoring in 21 games.

The big-spending visitors – whose match-day squad at the weekend cost £290m in transfer fees opposed to just £28m for West Ham – remain unbeaten in the Premier League this season.

So a draw felt very much like a hugely significant victory as the Hammers consolidate their position back in the top flight.

Of course, some will point to Kevin Nolan's wrongly disallowed goal and suggest that West Ham were denied a possible victory.

The poor decision by the linesman proved that the biggest clubs continue to win the benefit of the doubt.

But maybe it was a blessing in disguise, with the likelihood being that a fourth-minute opener would simply have provoked City into a response that would have proved too hot to handle.

A point was gratefully accepted – and it was clearly one worth toasting (hic!).

Kirk now says: It was also nice to see City striker Carlos Tevez greet the Upton Park faithful with a crossed Hammers salute, proving that there's a tremendous affection on both sides.

NO MORE WHITE HART PAIN, PLEASE (21 November 2012)

When the fixtures were published in the summer, West Ham fans would have made a special note of the coming weekend.

That is because – as if you needed reminding – the Hammers visit Tottenham Hotspur on Sunday.

It is one of the most hotly anticipated fixtures of the season and one that fans yearned for when they were trudging their way towards the likes of Barnsley, Burnley and Bristol City last season.

Going to White Hart Lane – that's what top-flight football is all about for Hammers supporters.

But is the idea of it rather better than the reality? Elvis Costello once suggested that the *concept* of chaotic punk rockers The Damned was far more appealing than actually listening to their music.

And the same can perhaps be said of West Ham's visits to Tottenham – when the theory is rather more enjoyable than the practice.

After winning on two of their first three Premier League visits to White Hart Lane, the Hammers have not experienced victory there since April 1999. They gained a point at Spurs before being relegated two seasons ago, but have not won in their last 11 visits.

So recent history should suggest it's hardly a place that West Ham should enjoy visiting – especially as defeat there is a painful experience.

Yet fans continue to look forward to the fixture with keen excitement – in the knowledge that a surprise win at Tottenham is one of the most satisfying feelings one can get.

To add fuel to the fire, the Hammers' hierarchy will be desperate to enjoy revenge against the people they believe did so much to undermine their efforts to move into the Olympic Stadium.

Spurs boss Andre Villas-Boas insisted he was 'proud' of his players following their 5-2 defeat at Arsenal on Saturday. Let us hope he is 'proud' of his team for similar reasons this weekend.

That is after Tottenham visit Italy on Thursday for an important Europa League game against Lazio.

West Ham's chances might be helped if Spurs try the lasagne.

Kirk now says: Typically, Spurs romped to an easy 3-1 success with former Hammer Jermain Defoe scoring twice. Aaaarrrgghh!

WELL DONE, SAM, LET'S TALK ABOUT CHELSEA (5 December 2012)

It is West Ham's most thrilling result since winning promotion and surely won't be bettered this season.

Yet as Sam Allardyce faced journalists after the 3-1 win against Chelsea, he was being asked about one thing only – the opposition.

Does he sympathise with rival boss Rafa Benitez? Can the Spaniard succeed without the fans' support? What does Benitez need to do to turn things around and get the best out of Fernando Torres, etc etc?

To be fair to Big Sam, he did his best to accommodate the one-dimensional line of questioning and was forthright in his honesty (having never been famous for delivering dull diplomacy).

But he could have been forgiven for exclaiming, 'Gimme a break! We've just embarrassed the European champions and all you wanna do is talk about the other side!'

What with recent events, however, the story was always going to be about Chelsea's trauma rather than West Ham's triumph.

That was inevitable, but the reality is that the context of the game did indeed make the result all that much sweeter for Hammers fans.

When the media spotlight was finally focused on West Ham, Allardyce was rightly congratulated for the success of his half-time substitutions.

The introductions of Mohamed Diame and Matt Taylor did indeed make the difference as the Hammers fought back from 1-0 down.

But without wanting to be too critical, you can't help but think the manager got it wrong in the first place with his cautious selection of defender James Tomkins in midfield and the ineffective Gary O'Neil.

It was also suggested that West Ham got lucky when Carlton Cole was allowed to clamber over Branislav Ivanovic for the equaliser.

After Kevin Nolan's first-half 'goal' was harshly disallowed, it would perhaps be wrong to suggest the referee believed he 'owed us one'.

So let's just say he felt the Hammers deserved the benefit of the doubt.

Kirk now says: It was indeed the highlight of the season for West Ham – with Chelsea's chubby-cheeked interim manager Rafa Benitez never looking more embarrassed than when Modibo Maiga wrapped up the memorable win in the final minute.

IS THE OLYMPIC-SIZED FARCE NEARLY OVER?
(12 December 2012)

West Ham fans could have been forgiven for feeling a sense of déjà vu last week when it was announced that the club had won 'preferred bidder' status to secure the keys for the Olympic Stadium.

After all, we have been here before, with such a title initially bestowed upon the Hammers in February 2011 when their joint bid with Newham Council was given the thumbs-up only for the deal to collapse eight months later following challenges by Tottenham Hotspur and Leyton Orient.

A decision on a tenancy-only agreement was expected in May this year before the bidding deadline was extended to make the process more 'competitive' – prompting the feeling that the goalposts were once again being moved as a political situation became increasingly farcical. Take into account the number of warring factions with conflicting agendas, plus the suspicion that dark forces have been at work (not to mention a police investigation that has put three men in the dock) and it's a wonder that West Ham have retained their patience and dignity to again get the nod.

Not that it's a done deal, with London mayor Boris Johnson warning that 'a lot of negotiation' still has to take place.

Most of it would appear to be about how much cash the Hammers need to hand over in various ways – and the demands seem to be rising.

Of course, the Hammers expressed their pride and gratitude, while Orient chairman Barry Hearn, having seen his own club's bid falter, claimed he was still interested in a potential ground-share.

Given that Hearn has insisted that Orient's future existence would be jeopardised if West Ham reduced the four-mile distance between the two clubs, it has to be asked why he wants to close that gap to nothing.

It is estimated that up to a third of Hammers fans remain unconvinced by the idea of relocating to Stratford, but resistance is likely to fall if the club gets the green light and steps up their public relations initiatives, with close consultations having been promised.

For what it's worth, this columnist firmly believes that West Ham must move to the Olympic Stadium and expand their fan-base if they want to be a serious top flight force.

In 20 years or so, it will surely be considered the best thing the club has ever done – if it's ever allowed to happen, of course.

Kirk now says: This columnist had previously been asked to be careful of upsetting Orient fans who might be reading the paper, but given there are so few of those that was unlikely to be too much of a problem.

WELCOME BACK, JOE (10 January 2013)

He looks older, heavier, slower and balder, but West Ham fans are naturally delighted to see Joe Cole back at Upton Park, where he belongs following nearly ten years at Chelsea and Liverpool.

Given the choice of rejoining his first club or his former boss Harry Redknapp, now at QPR, the 31-year-old thankfully declared his 'love' for the Hammers by returning home.

Whether the playmaker ever reached the anticipated heights after being labelled one of England's most exciting teenage prospects is questionable. But we should all thank manager Sam Allardyce for a belated Christmas present.

Cole's two crosses for James Collins to score twice in the 2-2 draw with Manchester United proved he still has magic in his feet.

And he's got to be better than Gary O'Neil.

Kirk now says: Cole was restricted to just seven league starts due to a hamstring injury, but it was nice to see him back in the claret and blue.

SAM MUST CURE TRAVEL SICKNESS (17 January 2013)

As West Ham visited Sunderland on Saturday, many fans may have headed to the bookmakers with two phrases in mind – 'life's savings' and 'home win'.

Why the pessimism? Well, this time last year the Hammers were on course for a record-breaking 13 away wins in a league season as they secured promotion back to the Premier League via the play-offs.

Following the 3-0 hammering at the Stadium of Light, however, they have already lost two more away league matches than they did in the entire Championship campaign.

They have scored in just four of their ten away league games, during which they have bagged just five goals – the lowest in the entire four divisions. And just as worryingly, they have collected just one point from their last five games on the road and failed to score in their last four – and that's relegation form in anyone's book.

It was always going to be more difficult in the top flight, of course, but it's interesting how the situation has reversed from last season, when Sam Allardyce's biggest problem was winning home games.

Now it's only the form at Upton Park that is keeping the side out of relegation trouble – and that won't remain the case if the Hammers don't pick up points against QPR and Swansea in their next two home games. Injuries haven't helped the situation, but Allardyce needs to question his strategy away from home because it's clearly not working.

Otherwise it could be a worrying end to the season.

The life's savings produced winnings of £11.50, by the way.

Kirk now says: The away form would get worse before it got better.

POTTS NOT ALONE IN FEELING DAZED AND CONFUSED (31 January 2013)

According to Sam Allardyce, it was discovered that West Ham defender Dan Potts had concussion at Arsenal last week when he was 'unable to give the correct answers to the questions he was asked'.

Given the doctor probably asked him what the score was at the time, you would have to have some sympathy for the youngster – as anybody would have lost count by that stage.

For the record, the Hammers were 5-1 down having conceded four goals in a traumatic ten-minute spell at the start of the second half.

'Having lost consciousness for a time, there will be a minimum recovery time of about two weeks,' added Allardyce, although whether he was talking about Potts or his entire team was open to debate.

Everybody wishes the defender well, of course, but how quickly West Ham get back on their feet after nearly being knocked for six remains to be seen.

To be fair to West Ham, they did go ahead at the Emirates and were still level at the break after Lukas Podolski wiped out Jack Collison's opener.

But their early efforts proved in vain and the Hammers crashed to their second 5-1 defeat in 51 weeks (although at least this one wasn't to Ipswich Town).

Kirk now says: If you're going to fall to such a heavy defeat, you might as well allow those fans who backed the Hammers to be losing at both half-time and full-time to console themselves in the form of some winnings. But no, this is West Ham we're talking about.

TIME FOR BOSS TO ADMIT HIS ERRORS (13 February 2013)

West Ham's 2-1 defeat at Aston Villa on Sunday was nothing short of embarrassing.

Okay, the visitors were on top in the second half before Mark Noble brought down Charles N'Zogbia for Christian Benteke's penalty opener. And yes, they could have snatched a point with some better luck late on. But the reality is that Villa were one place off the bottom of the table having not won in eight Premier League games.

And the result was so predictable, with the Hammers having also been beaten by strugglers such as Wigan and Reading this season.

West Ham have lost their last six away games and haven't won on their travels since a 1-0 success at Newcastle back in November.

So manager Sam Allardyce needs to stop making excuses and start examining his team selection and tactical decisions.

The Hammers boss named four strikers in his 18-man squad – but predictably stuck three of them on the bench.

It is the same old story, which sees West Ham go behind before throwing on second-half substitutes to try and salvage something.

You would think the fact that the Hammers have scored the equal lowest number of away goals (eight) in the entire four divisions would tell Allardyce that his methods are not working.

But the manager rarely admits he gets things wrong and would much rather blame players for missing chances than question his strategic approach to games.

West Ham had to wait until midway through the second half before registering their first shot on target.

And when you're playing teams that are there for the taking, that's just not good enough.

Kirk now says: Once again, West Ham proved they have a nasty habit of throwing struggling teams a lifeline when they need it most.

TWO DAVIDS MUST CONSIDER OPTIONS (20 February 2013)

With West Ham fans still pouring out of Wembley Stadium after the play-off final victory against Blackpool last May, this writer suggested to Sam Allardyce that he would quickly be looking to renegotiate his contract, which had just one year remaining.

'Not for me,' said the manager, somewhat surprisingly. 'I'm my own man now,' he added, giving the strong impression that he wanted to keep his options open. Some Hammers fans might have been relieved, believing that Allardyce had accomplished the sole mission he had been recruited for – to win promotion to the Premier League.

Indeed, this column even went so far as to suggest that West Ham could have shown a ruthless streak by thanking Sam for his services, paying him off and bringing Harry Redknapp back to his spiritual home.

After all, do the supporters really want to watch Allardyce's one-dimensional style of football for the rest of their lives? No, thought not.

With the Hammers occupying a comfortable mid-table position for most of the season, however, it was assumed the manager would be rewarded with a new contract around the turn of the year.

Not so, with the club announcing that no discussions about a new deal would take place until their 'Premier League status has been confirmed and not before'.

With the Hammers having won just one of their last eight games – and relegation still a possibility – chairmen David Sullivan and David Gold are absolutely right to tell the manager that survival comes first.

But what's difficult to swallow is the claim that such a decision has been made so that nothing can 'distract attention' from the immediate priority of picking up points.

Because by making an official statement – bizarrely published during the 2-1 defeat at Aston Villa – the club's efforts have proved counter-productive, with the uncertainty simply fuelling speculation about the manager's future and potential replacements.

Indeed, Brighton boss Gus Poyet, legendary former striker Paolo Di Canio and, rather ludicrously, Watford coach Gianfranco Zola (who has already once been sacked by the current Hammers hierarchy) have all recently been linked with the Upton Park post.

What kind of distraction will such stories pose if they continue to appear until the Hammers limp over the line to Premier League safety?

Ultimately, however, fans should be thankful that Sam wanted to keep his options open – because that means that West Ham can now consider theirs.

Kirk now says: Do you get the feeling that this columnist would not have been unhappy to see Sam Allardyce leave Upton Park at the end of the season?

WHAT A HORRIBLE NIGHT! (27 February 2013)

Five complaints to make in the wake of West Ham's gut-wrenching 3-2 home defeat to Tottenham Hotspur on Monday evening:

1) Emanuel Pogatetz: If there's a dodgier defender to pull on a Hammers shirt it's hard to imagine who he might be. His arrival as a 72nd-minute substitute signalled West Ham's demise. Abysmal.

2) Howard Webb: The referee went to show a yellow card to Mousa Dembele in the first half – and changed his mind when realising the Spurs man had already been booked and would have had to be sent off. Oh no, mustn't do that.

3) Sam Allardyce: He picks one striker and then complains about a lack of goals. His cautious tactics don't work. His contract is soon up and it's time to get rid.

4) Gary O'Neil and Matt Taylor: West Ham will never get anywhere with those two. Not good enough.

5) The bookmakers: Why do they only allow this columnist to win bets he would prefer to lose? Enough said already.

* * * * *

West Ham fans rightly loved Paolo Di Canio for the unpredictable entertainment he provided as a striker at Upton Park.

But can you even begin to imagine the chaos and carnage if the Italian ever managed the Hammers?

In his short spell at Swindon, Di Canio had physical and verbal bust-ups with players, publicly complained about his bosses, incurred touchline bans after being sent off three times, was involved in a race row and walked out on the club just days before a takeover.

He also won promotion to League 1 and took the club to a Wembley cup final, so he clearly has managerial qualities.

Di Canio may be a magician but he is also a maverick who is controlled by his emotions.

Appointing him as a successor to Sam Allardyce would be like spraying a grey car the brightest shade of yellow and painting a clown's face on its bonnet.

Di Canio is guaranteed to provide great comedy but staying in the Premier League is a serious business – and that's why Hammers co-chairman David Gold was right to insist there is 'no managerial vacancy for Paolo' (although it would be nice to think other candidates are being considered).

Kirk now says: By the end of the following month, Paolo Di Canio was appointed boss of Sunderland and was immediately engulfed in controversy after being accused of having fascist beliefs, which he staunchly denied. The Italian kept his side up but branded some of his players' behaviour as 'pathetic' following a breach of discipline.

O'S REMAIN QUIET ON STADIUM CASH (13 March 2013)

Barry Hearn has had a lot to say about West Ham's anticipated move to the Olympic Stadium – some would say too much.

The Leyton Orient chairman fought against the original joint bid with Newham Council to take control of the stadium and then missed out when the London Legacy Development Corporation named the Hammers as preferred bidders for a tenancy agreement.

Hearn has insisted that West Ham's relocation to Stratford would threaten his League 1 outfit's future existence because of the reduced distance between the two clubs.

And he has spent the last week or so talking of seeking a judicial review in the hope that Orient can ground-share with the Hammers.

But within all the campaigning and complaining, moaning and groaning, Hearn has forgotten to mention one thing – how much Orient would pay towards the stadium being fit for football.

Since being named as preferred bidders, West Ham have been in deep discussion with the LLDC over how much they will contribute to conversion costs.

It has also been suggested that West Ham co-chairmen David Sullivan and David Gold should give up a share of their profits if the club was ever sold.

One thing is clear – securing the rights to playing in the stadium will not come cheap.

Yet Orient insist they should be allowed to jump into bed with the Hammers.

'Our legal advice is that there is a fundamental flaw in the LLDC's bidding process,' said Hearn.

Of course, if you talk to a lawyer, they will always say you have a case because they want the business.

But the real issue here is that Orient have yet to suggest how they would split the costs with West Ham over stadium conversion.

Would they be prepared to pay the same as the Hammers?

Or would they only want to pay a small percentage on the basis that they currently attract less than 4,000 fans to most home games?

By the way, given that people have questioned how West Ham will fill the 54,000-capacity stadium, can you even begin to imagine what it would be like if Orient played there? The fans would be rattling around like peas in a container truck.

You get the feeling that one club wants to enjoy the benefits of playing in the Olympic Stadium while another stumps up most of the cash.

If we're looking for fundamental flaws, there's one right there.

Kirk now says: Some Orient fans were of the view that Hearn should spend less money on legal fees and more on players to improve the club's League 1 squad.

STRATFORD STIRS UP A BIG DEBATE (27 March 2013)

Harry and Barry are two West Ham fans sharing a few beers in a Green Street pub when the topic of conversation turns towards the club's move to the Olympic Stadium in Stratford in 2016 …

HARRY: 'We might not have played at the weekend but I reckon we got our best result of the season with the Olympic Stadium decision being confirmed in our favour.'

BARRY: 'I'm not so sure, mate. I've always wanted to stay at Upton Park myself.'

HARRY: 'You're having a laugh, aren't you? We need a bigger ground if we want to become a Premier League force. We'd always be a yo-yo club otherwise. And that queue outside Upton Park station after games is a bloody joke.'

BARRY: 'Yeah, but I'm worried about the lack of atmosphere – and it'll cost me a fortune on binoculars if I want a decent view.'

HARRY: 'I think it'll be great – a place to be proud of. I can't wait.'

BARRY: 'We might win a few more games – but we seem to have lost a few friends over this. All I've had are complaints about what it's costing the taxpayer.'

HARRY: 'Shut it! Anyone who criticises the decision either hates West Ham or has got another agenda. What these people fail to realise is that we've actually saved the government money. We're paying £200m in rent for the entire 99-year lease and the taxpayer would have a far bigger bill if they were left with a white elephant. Remember the Dome?'

BARRY: 'And Orient are still complaining and talking of another legal challenge. It could kill them off.'

HARRY: 'That's rubbish. We've got every right to move within our borough. And if Orient wanna share with us, they should stump up half the cash to convert the stadium – and they can't afford it.'

BARRY: 'Even the former sports minister has slagged off the decision.'

HARRY: 'Yeah – and that'll be the government that built an Olympic arena without knowing what they were gonna do with it. Everyone's complaining about the benefits for West Ham – but they should also consider what's best for the stadium and the local community. The government will make money – and so will we.'

BARRY: 'I don't know why Joe Cole and Kevin Nolan were looking so happy outside the new ground. I can't see them still playing for us in three years' time.'

HARRY: 'Er, you might have a point there. More importantly, it's your round.'

Kirk now says: Fictional characters Harry and Barry proved to be a useful device in terms of presenting both sides of an argument without seeming to favour one … or at least doing so in a more subtle way.

ANDY SET TO BE ON HIS WAY (3 April 2013)

It might break the hearts of some West Ham fans – but it seems the club has little intention of signing Andy Carroll on a permanent basis.

The Hammers have the option of securing the striker, who agreed a loan move from Liverpool last summer, for an estimated £17m at the end of the season.

And after watching Carroll score twice in the 3-1 win against West Brom on Saturday, Sam Allardyce insisted he would like to capture the England man on a long-term basis.

But he was also careful in his words, admitting that 'a lot of things need to happen' for the deal to be done.

The BBC were quick to run a 'West Ham hopeful of keeping Carroll' story after the game.

But the biggest clue as to the 24-year-old's future came not in the words of Allardyce but Hammers co-chairman David Sullivan when discussing his plans last week.

'I'm seeing someone on Monday that, if it comes off, will be the biggest signing in our history,' he said. 'We lack goals and have got to sign a top-class striker.'

He clearly wasn't talking about Carroll and West Ham were quickly linked with a £12m move for Vitesse Arnhem forward Wilfried Bony.

If Sullivan is chasing other strikers, it's natural to assume the club has already decided against signing Carroll on a permanent basis – unless circumstances change, of course.

The reality is that the Hammers had fears about extending Carroll's stay when he was restricted by injury to just nine starts and one goal in the five months that followed his arrival in August.

The striker has since boosted his tally to five goals in 17 appearances and he could even make it into double figures.

But you suspect a final flourish might not be enough to salvage a full-time move to Upton Park – and that's assuming Carroll wants to stay. The simple fact is that the club are unlikely to want to invest nearly £20m plus lumpy wages in a player who has struggled with injury.

It is a big shame because Carroll has actually proved a hugely influential figure – when fit – in keeping the Hammers out of the relegation dogfight in their first season back in the Premier League.

The fans recognise his passion and commitment – and that's why he'll be given a standing ovation if he bids farewell in May.

Kirk now says: Despite such doubts, the Hammers negotiated a reduced £15.5m fee with Liverpool before Andy Carroll did indeed agree a permanent move.

LET'S WAVE BYE BYE TO WIGAN (24 April 2013)

Two years ago, West Ham threw away a two-goal half-time lead at Wigan to lose 3-2 and suffer the consequences of immediate relegation.

Following the weekend's 2-0 home victory, it's to be hoped the Hammers have inflicted a similar fate upon the Latics.

Saturday's game was less of a do-or-die situation, of course.

But the win means West Ham are surely safe on 42 points while Wigan remain in the bottom three.

If the Latics do indeed go down – as they should have in 2011 – few Hammers fans will shed any tears.

That is not just for what happened two years ago, but also for Wigan chairman Dave Whelan's role in forming the 'Gang of Four' that fought to see West Ham docked points and relegated – albeit unsuccessfully – over the Carlos Tevez affair in 2007.

The Hammers escaped that penalty but were eventually forced to pay relegated Sheffield United around £20m in compensation.

It had a debilitating effect on the Hammers over the past few years and many feel it was an unjust decision.

To make matters worse, Whelan insisted that West Ham had received preferential treatment in avoiding a points penalty because of being a big London club. Anyone would think the Wigan chairman had a chip on his shoulder.

The Latics may well defy the odds once again and wriggle off the relegation hook.

But if they don't, Hammers fans will be able to reflect on Saturday's victory by knowing their side helped to bang a final nail in Wigan's coffin.

Kirk now says: Hoorah! Wigan eventually returned back to where they belong after eight seasons and the Premier League certainly won't miss them.

TWO-YEAR DEAL POSES QUESTIONS (15 May 2013)

As expected, the West Ham website confirmed that manager Sam Allardyce had signed a new contract at the weekend.

Interestingly, there was no mention as to when the new deal expires, so we have co-chairman David Gold to thank for revealing on his Twitter account that the agreement is for another two years.

The question is: why two and not three?

West Ham are set to move into the Olympic Stadium in 2016, so it was logical to assume that any new deal would extend up to that point in time. Instead, the Hammers are faced with the possibility of a change of management just 12 months before moving into a 54,000-capacity arena – and that can't seem like a good idea.

In one sense it's reassuring that the manager is being kept on his toes without the cosy security of a three or four-year package.

It has worked so far, with Allardyce winning promotion and securing a possible top-half finish within the time-span of his original contract. But one senses that it's more Big Sam's idea to stick to two-year deals than the club's.

Indeed, after the play-off final success against Blackpool last year, he insisted he had no intention of discussing a new contract at that point because he wanted to remain his 'own man'.

That sounds like somebody who wants to keep his options open – or at least one that is eager to remain in control of his destiny.

It is as if he is keeping his eye open for a bigger job – in which case the Hammers will just be seen as a stepping-stone.

That could suit West Ham, of course. Allardyce can consolidate the team's place in the Premier League before moving on. And the Hammers can look to appoint a manager who is more in tune with the club's traditions of playing stylish football.

Or, more likely, he'll be signing another two-year contract in 2015.

Kirk now says: You always got the feeling that Sam Allardyce's relationship with West Ham was a marriage of convenience, but that the divorce papers would ultimately be served one day. It remains to be seen when.

HERE COMES THE (BUSY) SUMMER (22 May 2013)

Sam Allardyce shared a post-match drink with Reading boss Nigel Adkins on Sunday as the two men reflected on their contrasting fortunes this year.

Allardyce could celebrate West Ham's 4-2 win that saw them secure a top-ten finish, while Adkins was entitled to drown his sorrows as his side returns to the Championship after just one season.

The Hammers became the first club to secure a top-half placing immediately after winning promotion to the Premier League via the play-offs since the last time they achieved such a feat in 2006.

It means the club pockets £8.3m in prize money as opposed to the £6.8m they would have been forced to settle with if the team had suffered defeat in their final game.

That extra £1.5m will surely help Allardyce as he looks to improve his squad during the summer.

The Hammers boss said he was hoping to enjoy a 'quieter time in the transfer market' this year but the reality is that he has a lot of work to do if he wants to make the team stronger.

The fact of the matter is that he could find himself needing to replace SIX strikers over the next few months.

Allardyce insisted that securing Andy Carroll on a permanent deal was his 'main priority' and, although a £15.5m fee has been agreed with Liverpool, it remains to be seen if the England man will put pen to paper.

Carlton Cole is leaving the club after holding talks with Big Sam on Monday, while loan signings Marouane Chamakh and Wellington Paulista have proved to be a total waste of time.

Modibo Maiga has been out of favour and is likely to move on, while Ricardo Vaz Te has looked out of his depth in the top flight.

However, the Hammers have been linked with Chelsea striker Romelu Lukaku following his impressive loan spell at West Brom.

The brilliantly named Razvan Rat has already been recruited to fill the left-back slot, but there is sure to be further speculation about the future of midfielder Mo Diame this summer, while Gary O'Neil is in talks about a new contract.

Add in the need for another centre-half and that's ten holes that Allardyce could need to fill before the transfer window closes.

Sam can enjoy a few beers on holiday but his summer is surely to be busier than he would like.

Kirk now says: From a distance, everything looked to be good at West Ham but deeper scrutiny of the squad revealed that the club was going to have to be proactive in the transfer market if they wanted to enjoy a comfortable second season back in the top flight.

REFLECTING ON SEASON 2012/13

Best signing: Andy Carroll (Liverpool), loan

Worst signing: Alou Diarra (Marseille) £2m

Best result: Winning 3-1 at home to Chelsea in December

Worst result: Losing 5-1 at Arsenal in January

Final position: 10th in Premier League, 46 points

Manager and rating: Sam Allardyce 8/10

Best thing about season: Securing a top-half finish

Worst thing about season: The lack of goals away from home

THE SUMMER OF 2013

'Carroll signing a huge statement of intent'

THE good news was that Andy Carroll signed a six-year deal with West Ham in June 2013 after Liverpool accepted a £15.5m fee for the England striker.

The not-so-good news was that the 24-year-old reportedly insisted on a weekly salary of £100,000 before putting pen to paper on a permanent contract.

The media were quick to calculate that the entire agreement would cost the Hammers a minimum of £46.5m over the entire period – and that's before any wage increases they will have to entice Carroll with if they want to preserve his transfer-market value with another deal.

The size of the package prompted criticism in some quarters that the player simply 'wasn't worth it', with some pointing to a season in which he had picked up three significant injuries.

It also resulted in one tabloid paper suggesting that the expenditure on Carroll would force the Hammers into sacrificing other players such as Modibo Maiga, Ricardo Vaz Te, Matt Taylor and Alou Diarra in order to fall in line with the incoming financial fair play rules.

The reality, of course, was that those players – who made only 35 league starts between them during the 2012/13 campaign (with Vaz Te making half of those) –

were always going to be considered as surplus to requirements (although all four of them returned to pre-season training). Carroll will believe his wages reflect the true value of a striker who cost Liverpool a massive £35m when leaving his home city of Newcastle two years earlier.

But another school of thought is that when a player needs to have so much money thrown at him to convince him to sign, it has to be wondered how keen he really is to play for the club. If Carroll really wants to play for West Ham, surely £75,000 a week would be enough.

The other potential problem is that other players at the club could start to resent the idea of the striker's wages dwarfing theirs – especially if they feel they are contributing just as much to the team.

It wouldn't be the first time that dressing-room dynamics have been changed by such events.

Yet for all the negativity, the long-term signing of Carroll represents a huge statement of intent by West Ham ahead of their anticipated move to the Olympic Stadium in 2016.

And that's what this is really all about.

Of course, with the bumper new television deal agreed by the Premier League commencing from the 2013/14 campaign, every club is going to want their slice of the £3bn pie. So it's absolutely imperative that the Hammers remain in the top flight before they collect the keys to their big new ground – and Carroll's signing (whatever the cost) is a major part of that strategy.

And that's great news for the fans because Carroll played a huge role in helping to keep West Ham out of the relegation waters upon their return to the Premier League.

His seven goals in 24 appearances might not have won over the cynics observing the Hammers from a distance, but the fans were fully aware of the job Carroll did and the difference he made.

It is no over-statement to suggest that West Ham could have returned to the Championship without his efforts – and it's absolutely right that the club pushed the boat out to secure his signature.

Having been confirmed as anchor tenants for the Olympic Stadium in March, the club immediately set about gauging the mood of the fans. And an independent poll revealed that 85 per cent supported the move – a much bigger figure than anticipated before the unveiling of the conversion plans, the planning permission for which was granted in May.

Hell, even Portuguese legend Luis Figo backed West Ham's ambitious plans when declaring, 'For the club it is fantastic.'

Of course, West Ham fans can never take too much for granted – as the rollercoaster events of the past dozen years have proved.

But with just a little bit of luck, if everything goes to plan, with the wind blowing in the right direction and everybody keeping their fingers crossed, that little bit of fortune might not always be hiding from the Hammers after all.